The Future of Digital Business Innovation

Vincenzo Morabito

The Future of Digital Business Innovation

Trends and Practices

Springer

Vincenzo Morabito
Department of Management and Technology
Bocconi University
Milan, Italy

ISBN 978-3-319-26873-6 ISBN 978-3-319-26874-3 (eBook)
DOI 10.1007/978-3-319-26874-3

Library of Congress Control Number: 2016933148

Printed on acid-free paper

This Springer imprint is published by Springer Nature
The registered company is Springer International Publishing AG Switzerland

Foreword

The Digital Revolution is one of the *buzzwords* in 2015 among both academics and practitioners. Coping with the Digital Revolution requires members of an organization to adapt to new measures, something individuals do not always find easy. The challenges of innovation in increasingly digitized businesses require a clear understanding about the role of IT in the definition of business models—what are the (possibly new) targets, which resources should be involved, and where should investment be centralized?

A strong understanding of *what's out there* and an intelligent use of appropriate business models are necessary to enable the alignment and convergence among vision, strategy, and resources of any company to then clarify and simplify governance choices, to weigh up the value of resources, and to define the correct policies that complement the organization's operations.

This book identifies the challenges, ideas, and trends to provide a "management toolkit for survival" in the Digital Revolution. The first part deals mostly with the technological trends emerging from the increased use of intelligent computers and advanced IT platforms and discusses topics like wearables, machine-to-machine communication, the emergence of digital currency, and data visualization and security.

The Internet of Things or *smart objects linked to the Internet* and in particular the proliferation of wearables are extremely interesting and insightful to understand seemingly irrational consumer behavior. Machine-to-machine communication complements and, in part, substitutes the human factor in manufacturing and is likely to represent a USD200 billion industry by 2020.[1] The opportunities of this phenomenon seem limitless.

Digital currency destabilizes the concept of money dating back to the beginning of civilization. Virtual currency was defined only 3 years ago—in 2012—by the European Central Bank as "a type of unregulated, digital money, which is issued and usually controlled by its developers, and used and accepted among the members of a specific virtual community" and may soon replace traditional

[1] Source: http://www.statista.com/statistics/295685/m2m-total-industry-size-worldwide/

currencies even without a legal tender. Finally, digital transformation also requires dealing with much more data than ever before but not with more value de facto.

Everybody talks about volume, velocity, variety, and veracity, but few deal with the business relevance of data visualization, which is also discussed in the first part. Finally, Part I closes with the discussion of one of the most challenging and social aspect of digital business: the protection of organizations by malevolent attacks through an improved attention to digital security.

The second part highlights the main managerial trends that effectively address the trends identified previously. It takes the reader on a journey through neuro-information systems, IT ambidexterity, and IT-Business alignment evolution. Recent progresses in cognitive neuroscience are exposing the neural bases of cognitive, emotional, and social processes and give new insights into the complex interplay between IT and information processing and decision making in business-related situations. The importance of ambidexterity and the use of market information to obtain competitive advantage also represent an important tool of successfully dealing with Digital Transformation and can eventually form a new basis for a better development of the IT role in the company.

Finally, the third part of the book discusses, through structured case studies and business evidence, global innovation initiatives in 2015. This last chapter provide a guideline for different possibilities of innovation practices in the digital context.

This book provides a uniform understanding of the challenges and opportunities of trends and practices in digital business innovation, and most importantly, it provides readers with the right stimuli to take a first step towards change.

Ludwig-Maximilians-Universität München Tobias Kretschmer

Preface

In this book, we aim to discuss and present the main challenges and trends for the future of Digital Business Innovation to a composite audience of practitioners and scholars. This volume follows the one published in 2014 for Springer, aiming to fill a similar gap [1]. Indeed, looking at the state of the art, we believe that it is still yet difficult, as actually it was two years ago, to find a unified survey of current scientific and managerial work having an impact on future business, which also considers the diverse perspectives characterizing the Information Systems research (from management to computer science and engineering, among others). Such a summary should be suitable to be used by practitioners in their day-to-day activities or simply as an update on what the state of the art in academia and managerial contributions may offer with regard to future IT strategy as well as business value propositions in different industries. Indeed, it is worth noting that today as in 2014, notwithstanding journals such as MIT Sloan Management Review, IEEE Spectrum, or the Communications of the ACM (CACM) have such a mission of connecting research and industry practices, to the best of the author's knowledge they do not provide a yearly integrated review, encompassing all their respective areas (management, engineering, and computer science).

However, these publications are going to be part of the usual large body of knowledge together with journals, such as Management of Information Systems Quarterly (MISQ), Journal of Association of Information Systems-JAIS, Management of Information Systems Quarterly Executive (MISQE), Information Systems Research, European Journal of Information Systems, Journal of Information Technology, and the Journal of Strategic Information Systems, and conferences, such as International Conferences of Information Systems (ICIS), European Conferences of Information Systems-(ECIS), Americas Conferences of Information Systems (AMCIS), among others (just to mention the Management of Information Systems research sources), which this book aims to consider for identifying the challenges, ideas, and trends, that may represent "food for thought" to practitioners. Accordingly, each topic considered is analyzed in its technical and managerial characteristics, also through the use of case studies and examples.

Outline of the Book

The book's argument is developed along three main axes, following the same macro structure adopted in [1, 2]. In particular, we consider first (Part I) Digital Systems Trends issues related to the growing relevance, on the one hand, of machine intelligence (Chap. 1), wearable technologies (Chap. 2), digital currencies, and distributed ledgers for business (Chap. 3); on the other hand, a specific attention is devoted to data visualization (Chap. 4) and digital security (Chap. 5) trends and challenges for understanding organizations and user behavior, needs, and digital services/products requirements.

Subsequently, Part II considers Digital Management Trends, focusing on the impact of neuroscience for management of information systems, with a focus on the area of Neuro-Information Systems (Chap. 6), the role of IT ambidexterity in managing digital transformation (Chap. 7), and how IT strategy and alignment are reconfigured by digital business (Chap. 8). Finally, Part III of the book presents and reviews cases of Digital Innovation at a global level in a section called Innovation practices. Thus, the book adopts a scientific approach as for methodological rigor; however, it is also concrete and describes problems from the viewpoints of managers, adopting a clear and easy-to-understand style for the flow of the discussion as well as the arguments treated, in order to capture the interests of managers.

In summary, this book and the other former volumes on digital trends and Big Data and analytics [1, 2] are ideally connected as subsequent stages of a journey across digital business innovation; consequently, in line with the former stages' value propositions for the reader, this book also aims to be unique for its intention to synthesize, being a simple yet ready to consult scientific toolbox for both managers and scholars.

Milan, Italy Vincenzo Morabito

References

1. Morabito V (2014) Trends and Challenges in Digital Business Innovation. Springer, Heidelberg doi:bfm:978-3-319-04307-4/2/1
2. Morabito V (2015) Big data and analytics. Springer, Heidelberg

Acknowledgments

This book is the result of the last 2 years of research, where several people are worth to be acknowledged for their support, useful comments, and cooperation. A special mention to Vincenzo Perrone, Professor of Strategic Management and Organization at Bocconi University, Prof. Vallabh Sambamurthy, Eli Broad Professor and Chair of the Department of Accounting and Information Systems at the Eli Broad College of Business at Michigan State University, and Prof. Franco Fontana at LUISS University as main inspiration and mentors.

Moreover, I acknowledge Prof. Giuseppe Soda, Head of the Department of Management and Technology at Bocconi University, and all the other colleagues at the Department, in particular Prof. Arnaldo Camuffo, Prof. Anna Grandori, Prof. Severino Salvemini, and Prof. Giuseppe Airoldi, all formerly at the Institute of Organization and Information Systems at Bocconi University, who have created a rich and rigorous research environment where I am proud to work.

I acknowledge also some colleagues from other universities with whom I've had the pleasure to work, whose conversations, comments, and presentations provided precious insights for this book: among others, Prof. Anindya Ghose at New York University's Leonard N. Stern School of Business, Prof. Vijay Gurbaxani at the University of California Irvine, Prof. Saby Mitra at Georgia Institute of Technology, Prof. Ravi Bapna at University of Minnesota Carlson School of Management, George Westerman at MIT Center for Digital Business, Stephanie Woerner at MIT Center for Information Systems Research, Prof. Ritu Agarwal at Robert H. Smith School of Business, Prof. Lynda Applegate at Harvard Business School, Prof. Omar El Sawy at Marshall School of Business, Prof. Tobias Kretschmer, Head of the Institute for Strategy, Technology and Organization of Ludwig Maximilians University, Prof. Federico Pigni at Grenoble Ecole de Management, Prof. Vincent Mangematin at Grenoble Ecole de Management, Prof. Roman Lopez-Cortijo Garcia at Universidad Carlos III de Madrid, Prof. Antonio de Amescua Seco at Universidad Carlos III de Madrid, Prof. Elisabetta Di Nitto at Politecnico di Milano, Prof. Chiara Francalanci at Politecnico di Milano, Prof. Andrea Montefusco at the Institute of Economics, Pisa S. Anna School, and Senior Researcher at the Center for Research in Organization and Management (CROMA), Bocconi University, Prof. Stefano Denicolai at Università degli studi di Pavia, Damian Tamburri Research Fellow at Politecnico di Milano, Prof. Paolo

Giacomazzi at Politecnico di Milano, Prof. Marco de Marco at Università Cattolica del Sacro Cuore di Milano, Prof. Jan Mendling, Department of Information Systems and Operations at Wirtschafts Universität Wien, Prof. Marinos Themistocleous at the Department of Digital Systems at the University of Piraeus, Wolfgang König at Goethe University, Luca Giustiniano at LUISS University, Prof. Zahir Irani at Brunel Business School, Prof. Sinan Aral at MIT, Prof. Adam Mohamedali Fadlalla at Qatar University, Prof. Nitham Mohammed Hindi at Qatar University, and Prof. Paolo Aversa of Cass Business School.

Furthermore, I want to gratefully acknowledge all the companies that have participated in the research interviews, case studies, and surveys. In particular:

For the Financial Institutions: Agos Ducato, Aldermore Bank, Bayern LB, Banca Carige, Banca Euromobiliare, Banca Fideuram Group, Banca d'Italia, Banca Mediolanum, Banco Popolare, Banca Popolare dell'Emilia Romagna, Banca Popolare di Milano, Banca Popolare di Sondrio, Banca Popolare di Vicenza, Banca Popolare di Bari, Banca Sistema, Barclays, BCC Roma, BBVA, Banco Santander, Bank Austria, BNL-BNP Paribas, Cariparma Credit Agricole, CACEIS Bank Luxemburg, Cassa Depositi e Prestiti, Cassa di Risparmio di Firenze, Cedacri, Che Banca!, Compass, Corner Bank, Commerzbank, BAWAG PSK, Commerz Finanz, Credito Emiliano, Deutsche Bank, Dexia, HypoVereinsbank, ECB—European Central Bank, Erste Group Bank, ICBPI, ING Direct, Intesa Sanpaolo Group, Istituto per le Opere Religiose, Luxemburg Stock Exchange, Landesbank Baden-Wurttemberg, JP Morgan Chase, Mediobanca, MPS Group, Poste Italiane Group, Raiffeisen Bank International, SEC, Société Européene de Banque, Standard Chartered, Royal Bank of Scotland, UBI Banca Group, Unicredit Group, Veneto Banca, WeBank, and Kathrein Privatbank.

For the Insurance Sector: Allianz Group, Assimoco, Aspe Re, Argos, Automobile Club d'Italia, Coface, Ergo Previdenza, Europe Assistance, Generali Group, Groupama, Liberty Seguros, Munich RE, Poste Vita, Reale Mutua, Novae, Quixa, Sara Assicurazioni, UnipolSai, Vittoria Assicurazioni, Reale Mutua Aassicurazione, UNIQA, and Zurich Group.

For the Industrial Sector: ABB, Acea, Aci Informatica, Acqua Minerale S. Benedetto, Adam Opel, Adidas Group, Alpitour, Alliance Boots, Amadori Group, Amazon, Amplifon, Anas, Angelini, ArcelorMittal, Armani, Astaldi, ATAC, ATM, AstraZeneca, Arval, Auchan, Audi Group, Augusta Westland, Autogrill, Autostrade per l'Italia, Avio, Baglioni Hotels, BMW, BASF, Barilla, Benetton, Brembo, Bravo Fly, British Petroleum, BSH, BOSH, Boeing Defence, Cementir, Centrica Energy, Cerved Group, Chiesi Farmaceutici, CNH Industrial, Coca Cola HBC, Coop Italia, Costa Crociere, D'Amico Group, Danone, Daimler, Decathlon, Diesel, Dimar, Dolce and Gabbana, General Electric, Ducati, Elettronica, Edipower, Edison, Emmilibri, Eni, Enel Group, ENRC, ERG, Fastweb, Fincantieri, Ferrari, Ferrovie dello Stato Group, FCA, First Utility, Finmeccanica Group, Gala Coral Group, GlaxosmithKline, GE Capital, Grandi Navi Veloci, G4S, Glencore, Gruppo Hera, Gruppo Coin, Gruppo De Agostini, Gtech, Gucci, H3G, Hupac, Henkel, Hugo Boss, Infineon, Interoll, Il Sole24Ore, IREN, Istituto Poligrafico e Zecca dello Stato, ITV, Kuwait Petroleum, La Perla, Labelux

Group, Lamborghini, Lavazza, Linde, LBBW, Levi's, L'Oreal, Loro Piana, Luxottica Group, Jaguar Land Rover, Lucite International, MAN, Magneti Marelli, Mapei, Marcegaglia, Mediaset, Menarini, Mercedes Benz, Messaggerie Libri, Miroglio, Mondelez International, Mossi and Ghisolfi, Natuzzi, Novartis, Oerlikon Graziano, OSRAM, OTTO Group, Piaggio, Perfetti, Pernod Ricard, Philips, Pirelli, Porsche, ProSiebenSat1, Procter&Gamble, Prysmian, RAI, Rexam, Premier Oil, Rolex, Roche, Retonkil Initial, RWE, Saipem, Sandoz, SEA, Seat PG, Selex, Snam, Sorgenia, SKY Group, Schindler Electroca, Pfizer, Telecom Italia, Tenaris, Terna, Tyco Holding, TuevSued, Telefonica Group, Unilever, Unicoop Firenze, Virgin Atlantic, Volkswagen, Vodafone Wind, OVS, Bravofly Rumbo Group, Ge Oil&Gas—Nuovo Pignone, ING Luxembourg, Maserati, Roberto Cavalli, Salvatore Ferragamo, CEPSA, NH Hotels, Acciona, Red Electrica de España, El Corte Ingles, The Coca Cola Co., Gestamp, Carrefour Group, Endesa, PRISA, Heineken, Grupo VIPS, Sandoz International, ZF Friedrichshafen, Nokia Networks, Sixt, TÜV SÜD, ProSiebenSat.1 Media, RHI—AG, Webasto Group, Syneco Trading, Verbund Services, Bayer Gruppe, Bosch, Carl Zeiss, Celesio AG, Continental, Deutsche Post, Deutsche Telekom, E.ON, Faber Castell, Lufthansa AG, Media-Saturn-Holding, REWE Group, RWE, Thüga, and ThyssenKrupp.

For the Public Sector: Agenzia per l'Italia Digitale, Comune di Milano, and Consip.

I would especially like to acknowledge all the people who have supported me during these years with insights and suggestions. I learned so much from them, and their ideas and competences have inspired my work: Laura Cioli, Alessandro Garofalo, Marcello Guerrini, Giuseppe Capponcelli, Roberto Ferrari, Marco Sesana, Riccardo Delleani, Carlo Cimbri, Salvatore Poloni, Francesco Donatelli, Paolo Fiorentino, Ervino Riccobon, Marco, Jesus Marin, Milo Gusmeroli, Cecchella, Massimo Messina, Vincenzo Tortis, Mario Bocca, Massimo Schiattarella, Paolo Cederle, Pierangelo Mortara, Maurizio Montagnese, Pierluigi Berlucchi, Massimo Basso Ricci, Silvio Fraternali, Dario Scagliotti, Massimo Milanta, Maurizio Pescarini, Giovanni Sordello, Fabio Momola, Jean-Claude Krieger, Edoardo Romeo, Gilberto Ceresa, Riccardo Amidei, Umberto Angelucci, Gloria Gazzano, Diego Donisi, Alfredo Montalbano, Nazzareno Gregori, Nunzio Calì, Pierluigi De Marinis, Carlo Bozzoli, Roberto Tundo, Sandro Tucci, Matteo Attrovio, Giuseppe Dallona, Gian Enrico Paglia, Jeremy Vincent, Nuno Pedras, Prasad Meharunkar, Alberto Ripepi, Stefano Achermann, Carlo Achermann, Ottavio Rigodanza, Luciano Bartoli, Pierpaolo Taliento, Luca Severini, Luciano Romeo, Luciano Dalla Riva, Samuele Sorato, Giovanni Damiani, Marco Fanizzi, Aldo Bisio, Antonella Ambriola, Vittorio Giusti, Maria-Louise Arscott, Nino Lo Bianco, Raffaele De Benedetto, Marco Prampolini, Valerio Momoni, Mauro Viacava, Marco Valioni, Vittorio Boero, Massimo Palmieri, Eike Wahl, Enrico Baldisserri, Paolo Gasparato, Reinhold Grassl, Roberto Burlo, Francesco Germini, Paola Benatti, Francesco Pedrielli, Michele Maria Ungaro, Ivano Bosisio, Alessandro Guidotti, Alessandro Cucchi, Alessandro Bruni, Domenico Solano, Luca Vanetti, Roberto Andreoli, Fabio Gatti, Gianluca Pancaccini, Roberto Conte, Antonio Samaritani, Vittorio Mondo, Alberto Grigoletto, Marino Vignati,

Marco Campi, Stefano Malvicini, Nikos Angelopoulos, Roberto Coretti, Giovanni Bolzan, Andrea Ferrarese, Alberto Ricchiari, Luana Barba, Fabio Troiani, Gianluca Guidotti, Alessio Pomasan, Daniele Panigati, Danilo Augugliaro, Mauro Bernareggi, Alessandro Capitani, Alessandro Ventura, Giulio Giorgini, Piera Fasoli, Stewart Alexander, Federica Dall'ora, Andrea Caligaris, Vincenzo Russi, Federico Gentili, Marco Zaffaroni, Marco Ravasi, Roberto Fonso, Jesús Soto, Marco Bertazzoni, Vincenzo Campana, Giorgio Faietti, Gianbattista Piacentini, Pierantonio Azzalini, Massimo Paltrinieri, Diego Pogliani, Salvatore Stefanelli, Luca Falco, Elvio Sonnino, Ettore Corsi, Luca Paleari, Daniele Rizzo, Guido Albertini, Stefano Gentili, Giovanni Pietrobelli, Silvio Sperzani, Giulio Tonin, Cristina Porzio, Daniele Bianchi, Gabriele Raineri, Bruno Cocchi, Marco Zanussi, Michele La Rosa, Gianni Fasciotti, Mauro Pianezzola, Massimo Pavan, Stefano Levi, Luca Tiepolo, Massimiliano Gerli, Alessandro Campanini, Maurizio Galli, Dario Pagani, Paolo Crovetti, Luca Ghirardi, Marco De Paoli, Davide Carteri, Cristina Boschesi, Giuseppe Michelizzi, Demetrio Migliorati, Matthias Schlapp, Silvia De Fina, Paolo Lissoni, Guido Oppizzi, Marcello Ronco, Christian Altomare, Alessandro Sala, Federico Niero, Andrea Scotti, Elisabetta Nobile, Giuseppe Alibrandi, Maurizio Castelletti, Francesco Bardelli, Massimiliano De Gregorio, Elvira Fabrizio, Antonio Chiappara, Luca Ingrao, Giovanni Rossi, Umberto Stefani, Giorgio Nardi, Gianni Rumi, Leonardo Boccaperta, Angelo Colla, Vanessa Cuniberti, Enrico Ugoletti, Dante Bucelloni, Mauro Frassetto, Marco Gallibariggio, Federico Boni, Pablito Rosa, Tommaso Pellizzari, Fabio Maini, Igor Bailo, Riccardo Riccobene, Dario Tizzanini, Gianlorenzo Magnani, Alessandra Grendele, Luca Terzaghi, Mauro Restelli, Fabio Oggioni, Luigi Zanardi, Andrea Mazzucato, Gianbattista Rosa, Alex Eugenio Sala, Cristina Bianchini, Marco Tempra, Franco Collautti, Riccardo Scattaretico, Alessandra Testa, Enrico Bagnasco, Mario Costantini, Raffaella Mastrofilippo, Laura Wegher, Massimiliano Baga, Walter Facchi, Marco Ternelli, Mario Collari, Stefano Signani, Fabio Degli Esposti, Miriam Imperato, Marcello Cristiano Sala, Pietro Giardina, Sebastiano Cannella, Massimo Alberti, Maurizio Pellicano, Roberto Scaramuzza, Paola Formenti, Riccardo Pagnanelli, Fabrizio Lugoboni, Pierluca Ferrari, Francesco Frau, PierPaolo Tamma, Francesca Gandini, Martin Brannigan, Gianluca Zanutto, Andrea Facchini, Raffaello Infantino, Mario Sostegno, Luca Spagnoli, Roberto Mondonico, Riccardo Sfondrini, Marco Zaccanti, Claudio Tancini, Elisabetta Castro, Mirco Carriglio, Stefano Gandini, Matteo Formenti, Carlo Castiglioni, Paolo Brusegan, Susanna Nardi, Graziano Tosi, Christian Ciceri, Armando Gervasi, Carlo Balestrieri, Carlo Brezigia, Fabrizio Lugli, Davide Barbavara, Beppe De Iaco, Davide Casagrande, Massimo Zara, Andrea Messina, Veronica Chinello, Monica Colleoni, Vincenzo Montanaro, Anna Miseferi, Filippo Brognoli, Luca Martis, Pier Luigi Curcuruto, Fiore Della Rosa, Frediano Lorenzin, Daniele Pagani, Benoit Fagneray, Daniele Cericola, Massimiliano Ciferri, Stefano Firenze, Vahe Ter Nikogosyan, Thomas Pfitzer, Giorgio Voltolini, Maurizio Dellucca, Gian Piero Pepino, Giorgio Coraggioso, Massimo Rama, Fabio Boschiero, Chiara Manzini, Claudio Beveroni, Paolo Beatini, Guido Vetere, Maurizio Romanese, Dario Scagliotti, Gianluigi Farinetti, Ugo Salvi, Alessandro Tintori, Walter Carmagnini,

Giovanni Ferretti, Alberta Gammicchia, Carlo Capalbo, Lorenzo Bianchi, Lucilla Colabucci, Fabrizio Furnò, Franco Balsamo, Marco Poggi, Alessandro Banci, Mauro Minenna, Guido Massimo Mannella, Francesco Barbieri, Elisabetta Marcovaldi, Massimo Salvati, Flavio Ercolani, Luca Lambertucci, Marco Lanza, Fabrizio Frustaci, Vincenzo Pensa, Giuseppe Langer, Arturo Baldo, Sabina Di Giuliomaria, Gianfranco Ardissono, Adolfo Pellegrino, Massimo Romagnoli, Salvatore Impallomeni, Alessandro Galaverna, Pablo Mariano Picabea, Marco Pavonio, Pasquale Tedesco, Paolo Capodanno, Fabrizio Beco, Bernardo Babbini, Giovanni Pepicelli, Luigi Borrelli, Danilo Gismondi, Marco Tognaccini, Gabriele Sirovich, Manuele Marra, Silvia Zanni, Marco Iacomussi, Francesco Mastrandrea, Gianluca Giovannetti, Francesco Del Pizzo, Giovanni Rando Mazzarino, Claudio Colombatto, Anna Pia Sassano, Pietro Pacini, Luca Verducci, Elena Maria Bisogni, Fabrizio Virtuani, Fabio Cestola, Alberto Alberini, Giovanni Paolo Bruno, Marco Franzi, Luciano Albanese, Claudio Contini, Mario Di Mauro, Simone Battiferri, Maurizio Irlando, Carlo Di Lello, Alessandro Cozzio, Carlo Cautillo, Fabrizio Casali, Lorenzo Pizzuti, Nicola Grassi, Fabio De Santis, Matteo Coppari, Pietro Amorusi, Barbara Karuth-Zelle, Heinz Laber, Daniel Leiber, Jochen Werling, Martin Fluch, Florian Forst, Alfred Spill, Adnan Khan, Mauro Di Pietro Paolo, Ralf Schneider, Arne Benzin, Pierantonio Azzalini, Dirk Rodax, Torsten Holst, Jan Spelsiek, Markus Lohmann, Fabio De Ferrari, Elke Knobloch, Eckart Pech, Umberto Costanzini, Isabella Hackel-de Witt, Andrea Weierich, Florian Baumann, Andreas Teischl, Horst Griebaum, Martin Stahljans, Bernhard Kainz, Ulrike Groettrup, Manfred Kibler, Johann Gschwendtner, Silviu Popescu, Pierre-Yves Ily, Joerg Marx, Thomas Pfitzer, Michael Pretz, Andreas Riegg, Michael Gorriz, Jean-Luc Vey, Philipp Marten Natter, Stefan Gaus, Maurizio Daneluzzi, Koenraad De Geest, Jan Michalewicz, Peter Weiss, Mario Breuer, Walter Kirchmann, Thomas Plank, Monika Jurowicz-König, Michael Hesse, Klaudia Seiling, Wolfgang Keichel, Robert Leindl, Andreas Luber, Thomas Steinich, Sandeep Sen, Tommy Andreasen, Johann Mittelhammer, Marcell Assan, Frank-Ruediger Poppe, Johannes Lorenz, Axel Kummer, Rainer Göttmann, Rainer Janssen, Paul Kolp, Peter Barthuber, Markus Berghofer, René Roider, Thorsten Kolwe,, Christian Guehrs, Peter Kempf, Sven Lorenz, Johannes Wechsler, Herbert Marchetti, Kenan Isgor, Robert Wagenleitner, Elisabeth Geyer-Schall, Karl Astecker, Martin Sturm, Abel Archundia Pineda, Arnold Aschbauer, Jens-Uwe Schlötel, Georg Schoenafinger, Armin Pfoh, Simona Tonella, Vincenzo Contento, Gerd Nierlich, Lissimahos Hatzidimoulas, Cristoph Auerbach, Karl Schwabel, Walter Fraissler, Thomas Mannmeusel, Jürgen Sturm, Christian Kramer, Sebastian Weigert, Viktoria Danzer, Marcus Grausam, Jan Brecht, Marcus Schulz, Stefan, Danckert, Mattias, Ulbrich, Samir Fadlallah, Johannes Schubmehl, Klaus Straub, Joachim Reichel, Elisabeth Hoeflich, Wolfgang Gaertner, David Thornewill, Edgar Aschenbrenner, Axel Schulte, Alexander Bockelmann, Claudia Dill, Martin Hofmann, Jean-Claude Krieger, Guido Vetere, Daniele Pagani, Dominique Geeraert, Sourabh Purkayastha, Anthony Headlam, Martin Beaver, Andrew Hovell, Justin Bushby, Adam Edwell, Jane Moran, David Edwards, Paul Evans, Mark Fabes, Rakesh Gupta, Jean-Michel Garcia, Richard Buckley, Andrew Elphic,

Mike Sackman, Chris Michael, Anthony Roberts, John Knowles, Lisa Gibbard, John Hiskett, Richard Wainwright, David Madigan, Matt Hopkins, Gill Lungley, Simon Jobson, Glyn Hughes, John Herd, Mark Smith, Guy Lammert, Steve Blackledge, Jacky Lamb, Simon McNamara, Kevin Hanley, Anthony Meadows, Rod Hefford, Stephen Miller, Willem Eelman, David Bulman, Neil Brown, Alistair Hadfield, Rod Carr and Neil Dyke, Jose Olalla, Javier Fonseca, Joaquin Reyes, Alu Rodriguez, Jose Maria Tavera, Angel Mahou, Juan Andres Pro Dios, Francisco Leon, Pablo de la Puente, Ivan Mateo, Oscar Gomez, Maribel de la Vega, and Julian Gonzalez.

I would like to gratefully acknowledge Gianluigi Viscusi at the College of Management (CDM) of EPFL, Lausanne, Switzerland, and Alan Serrano-Rico at Brunel University who provided me valuable suggestions and precious support in the coordination of the production process of this book.

Furthermore, I acknowledge the support of Business Technology Foundation (Fondazione Business Technology) and all the bright researchers at Business Technology Outlook (BTO) Research Program that have supported me in carrying out interviews, surveys, and data analysis: Florenzo Marra, Alessandro De Pace, Giovanni Roberto, Arianna Zago, Alessio Campi, Massimo Bellini, Andrada Comanac, Francesco Magro, Marco Castelli, Francesca Oberti, Andrea Zinzi, Francesca Donelli, Giacomo Giorgianni, Martino Scanziani, Luca Parravicini, Alessandro Scannapieco, Miguel Miranda, Valeria Lorenzi, Adrien Chatillon, Fabrizio Conte, Fabrizio Manzo, Gianluca Del Mastro, Marcello Manolio, Antonio Attinà, Mariya Terzieva, Giuseppe Vaccaro, Matteo Pistoletti, Daniele Durante, Antonio De Falco, and Eugenia Maggiore.

A special acknowledgment goes to the memory of Prof. Antonino Intrieri who provided precious comments and suggestions throughout the years.

Finally, I acknowledge my family whose constant support and patience made this book happen.

Vincenzo Morabito

Contents

Acronyms

3D	Three-dimensional
AD	Advertising
AI	Artificial Intelligence
API	Application Programming Interface
ATM	Automated Teller Machine
BYOD	Bring Your Own Devices
CEO	Chief Executive Officer
CIO	Chief Information Officer
CMO	Chief Marketing Officer
CPU	Central Processing Unit
CTO	Chief technology officer
DNA	Deoxyribonucleic acid
DNS	Domain Name System
GPS	Global Positioning System
GPU	Graphics Processing Unit
ICTs	Information and Communication Technologies
IO	Input/Output device
IP	Internet Protocol address
IS	Information Systems
IT	Information technology
NATO	North Atlantic Treaty Organization
RFID	Radio-frequency identification
SaaS	Software as a Service
TV	Television
URL	Uniform Resource Locator
US	The United States
VR	Virtual reality

Part I

Digital Systems Trends

associated with their development, training and utilization, researchers have combined regression decision tress and Artificial Neural Networks (ANNs) in hybrid system that benefits from the advantages of both of those techniques, simplicity and accuracy respectively [54]. The system thus produced higher temperature prediction accuracy required for optimal steel melting process.

1.5.2.4 Machine Intelligence Enhanced Robots in Manufacturing

Industrial robots play a vital role in nowadays factories. Throughout the years they became smarter, faster and more productive. The new generations of robots employed in manufacturing are capable of performing many tasks that used to be only achievable by humans, but with higher accuracy and in larger volumes of production [55]. Moreover, advancements in AI research have enabled industrial robots to adapt to new variations in working environment in order not to interrupt manufacturing process. These robots are enhanced with a trial-and-use algorithm that allows them to learn from experiences encountered in the production floor. Consequently, those smart machines have some form of humans' cognitive ability that enables them to plan future actions based on the recent changes in the production line [56]. Accordingly, factories equipped with mobile robots use AI's *Genetic Algorithms* and *Ant Colony Algorithms* to plan the optimal paths that the robots have to go through to accomplish all the production tasks in the production environment as well as to avoid known and unfamiliar obstacles they might encounter in their way [55].

1.6 Machine Intelligence for Smarter Industries

The significance of machine intelligence stems from its ability to have intelligent machines that can simulate human behaviors at work environment as well as to analyze large amounts of complex data from multiple resources. It helps organizations to apply human-like intelligence in order to solve problems, detect frauds, improve customer relationship management related processes, and most importantly to have the ability to learn from data and experiences or what is called *Machine and Deep Learning* [57]. AI has several applications in the business world. These usages can be categorized into:

1. *cognitive science* as the research of emulating the mind and its processes within business settings in order to achieve better management such the intelligent data analysis, data mining, and expert systems,
2. *robotics* as the application of AI in industrial automation such as the automated manufacturing lines and transportations robots within factories, and
3. *natural interfaces* as the study of improving user's interactivity with the machines by utilizing easy to use touch screens that have the capabilities of gesture recognition as well as speech recognition, which allows users to interact with a system through spoken commands.

From all the discussion above about AI's role in industry, it can be concluded that decision makers in many organizations use AI-enhanced smart systems for activities related to management, planning and manufacturing operations. Similarly, AI has an influential role to support researchers in Big Data analysis, biological taxonomies and robotics [58].

1.7 Challenges for Machine Intelligence

The achieved progress in AI development and applications will continuously be tested with many challenges that affect its success to simulate humans' intelligence. Skeptics of AI always doubt its ability to solve problems, accomplish tasks, learn from experience [59], exhibit self-awareness, simulate human-like interactions [60] and finally, the ability to absorb and use knowledge [61]. Additionally, in the work of Doyle [62] and Shi [63] the authors have identified other big challenges that face the development of AI as well as its application in different industries and contexts. These challenges include AI ability to reflect motivation, purpose, imagination, consciousness, human memory [62] as well as rationality and introspective learning [63]. The last two are the elements that represent mental attitudes such as consistency and completeness as well as the ability to learn from failures and experiences [63]. Researchers have managed to make AI capable of tackling some of the previous difficulties; however, the way for complete self-awareness and human-like intelligence is still long.

Moreover, there are some common risks and mistakes that need to be aware of when specialists apply machine intelligence in industry [64]. First example of these is the lack of enough data for all development lifecycle: training, optimization, calibration, verification and validation. Second factor that needs to be considered is the difference between the training data while designing the intelligent system and the actual data while using it. Third aspect that is important to appreciate is to establish reasonable expectations that could be achieved by data mining and modeling. Additionally, the complexity accompanying AI implementation has to be considered in AI adoption project. Finally, it is vital to expect errors, thus, it is essential to set criteria for performance evaluation and to discover problems in the systems [64].

1.8 Case Studies

In this section we investigate some case studies about the implementation of Machine intelligence at work environments and we provide explanation about its role for the business success.

The first case study is about applying AI's Machine Learning techniques and algorithms to optimize the measures for *Power Usage Efficiency* (*PUE*), which are utilized in modern Data Centers (DCs) implemented at *Google Corporation* [65]. DCs in huge organizations, such as Google and Amazon, need to have the

50. Milley A (2000) Healthcare and data mining. Health Manag Technol 21:44–45
51. Bravo C, Castro JA, Saputelli L, Ríos A, Aguilar-Martin J, Rivas F (2011) An implementation of a distributed artificial intelligence architecture to the integrated production management. J Nat Gas Sci Eng 3:735–747
52. Renzi C, Leali F, Cavazzuti M, Andrisano AO (2014) A review on artificial intelligence applications to the optimal design of dedicated and reconfigurable manufacturing systems. Int J Adv Manuf Technol 72:403–418
53. Xing B, Nelwamondo FV, Battle K, Gao W, Marwala T (2009) Application of artificial intelligence (AI) methods for designing and analysis of reconfigurable cellular manufacturing system (RCMS). In: ICAST 2009 – 2nd international conference on adaptive science and technology, pp 402–409
54. Kordos M, Kania P, Budzyna P, Blachnik M, Wieczorek T, Golak S (2012) Combining the advantages of neural networks and decision trees for regression problems in a steel temperature prediction system. Hybrid Artif Intell Syst 7209:36–45
55. Gigras Y, Gupta K (2012) Artificial intelligence in robot path planning. Int J Soft Comput Eng 2:471–474
56. Adami C (2015) Robots with instincts. Nature 521:426
57. Jones N (2014) The learning machines. Nature 505:146–148
58. Buckner GD, Shah V (1993) Future vision: impacts of artificial intelligence on organizational success. Kybernetes 22:40–50
59. Silver DL (2011) Machine lifelong learning: challenges and benefits for artificial general intelligence. In: Artificial general intelligence, pp 370–375
60. Taghizadeh A, Pourali MR, Shidfar D, Mirzapour J (2013) Artificial intelligence, Its abilities and challenges. Int J Bus Behav Sci 3:30–34
61. Reddy R (1996) The challenge of artificial intelligence. Computer (Long Beach Calif) 29:86–98
62. Doyle J (1988) Big problems for artificial intelligence. AI Mag 9:19–22
63. Shi ZZ, Zheng NN (2006) Progress and challenge of artificial intelligence. J Comput Sci Technol 21:810–822
64. Hurwitz E, Marwala T (2012) Common mistakes when applying computational intelligence and machine learning to stock market modelling. arXiv Prepr. arXiv1208.4429. 5
65. Gao J, Jamidar R (2014) Machine learning applications for data center optimization. http://static.googleusercontent.com/media/research.google.com/en//pubs/archive/42542.pdf. Accessed 15 Sept 2015
66. Anonymous (2008) Smart Manoeuvre: integrating an autonomous mobile robot into your facility. http://www.adamrobot.com/media/pdf/Adam_Integration1.pdf. Accessed 15 Sept 2015
67. Millner H (2007) ADAM' s era: a new age of adaptability in automation. http://www.adamrobot.com/media/pdf/Rmt_Adam_Casestudy_2011.pdf. Accessed 15 Sept 2015

Wearable Technologies

2

Abstract

This chapter introduces the reader to the basic terms and concepts of the wearable technology, its history, trends, implications and wide range of applications. Wearable technology is a rapidly evolving field and is expected to explode in the coming decade. It can be considered as a big umbrella term for any type of technological innovations that are used by wearing it on your body. Wearable computers are in fact connected devices always in the 'on' mode to make the appropriate measurements in real time. Furthermore, the use of assistive technology, e.g., by people with disabilities has also driven a continuing conversation about the use of tech to enhance human capabilities, for example, to track vulnerable people or using geo-location data for public health. Thus, wearable technology is a brand new world we are just beginning to uncover with never-ending opportunities and possibilities.

2.1 Introduction

Wearable computing, wearable computers, wearable gadgets, wearable tech or smart clothing, has recently moved from the realm of science fiction and military technology to being on the edge of everyday consumer technology [1–4].

It has become an interesting area of IT innovation that has received plenty of media attention over the past few years, but a reality check is necessary [6]. While some of these devices (e.g. Nike's FuelBand, Apple Watch or smart glasses to name a few) demonstrate the potential for wearable devices to change how we do daily routines or actually interact with information on a daily basis, many of these wearable technologies remain technologically limited. The good news, however, is that IT experts believe those limitations will be overcome in the near future as technology specialists work to address three main obstacles such as battery life problems, chipset limitations and design concerns [2, 4, 7, 8] (see Fig. 2.1). Global spending on wearable technology, which stood at $750 m in 2012, is expected to

V. Morabito, *The Future of Digital Business Innovation*,
DOI 10.1007/978-3-319-26874-3_2

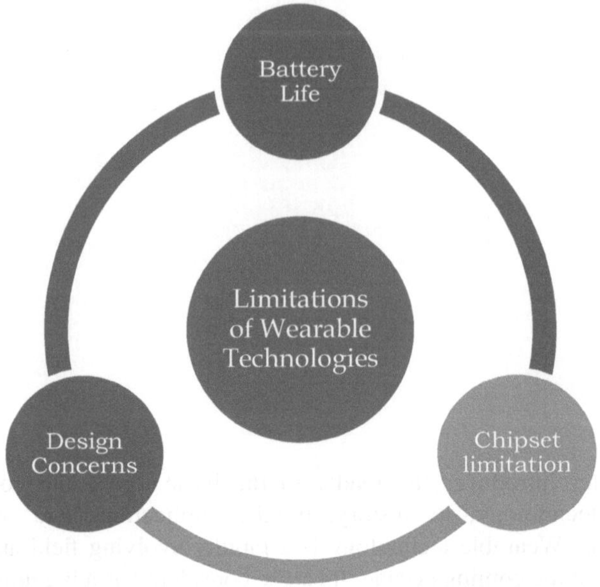

Fig. 2.1 Main obstacles for wearable technologies, adapted from [5]

reach $5.8 billion in 2018, according to Transparency Market Research [7]. So, what are the key areas of innovation that are helping to push developments in this fast-growing area?

2.2 Market Size and Outlook

Wearable Technology (WT) can now be considered as a massive global business [9–13]. From small start-up companies to major industrial companies, including Google, Samsung, Nike and Sony, everyone is seeing the opportunities for wearable systems to different degrees [14, 15]. Furthermore, online retail giant Amazon has also launched a dedicated wearable technology store in July 2014, confirming the importance of this product sector [16]. The Amazon store features over 100 different wearable devices currently, including products from big name brands and products from smaller emerging companies [17].

GfK [11], which is a trusted research group for relevant market and consumer information that enables its clients to make smarter decisions, has recently conducted an online interview with 1000 smartphone owners online in China, Germany, South Korea, the UK and the US to understand their usage of and attitudes towards 'smartwatches' and 'activity trackers'. This section briefly summarizes the findings of GfK's research, as it is insightful for the readers and researcher to note the current status of these two well-known wearables.

GfK's research highlights that WT consumers expect their devices to be controlled by touch rather than voice control. Accordingly, 67 % want to control their smartwatch with a touchscreen, 24 % say voice control and 8 % real buttons. Interestingly, nine out of ten also expect their smartwatch to run similar software as their smartphone, meaning that, they expect a similar experience on their smartwatches to that which they already have with their smartphones.

According to this report, when choosing a smartwatch, price, functionality and activity tracker functionality are considered as the most important criteria by 21 %, 14 % and 13 % respectively. Price is the number one criteria in all countries except China where it is not ranked in the top three. Instead, 'accuracy' is the most important criteria for Chinese consumers. Another notable difference is the emphasis placed on brand by respondents in China—15 % mentioned brand as being the most important criteria compared to just 8 % overall (see Fig. 2.2).

As to the question of, *which brand did you/would you buy a smartwatch from?*, results of the survey shows that tech brands are most favored by consumers. Almost two thirds (65 %) say they are most likely to buy a smartwatch from a tech brand, compared to 18 % who would choose a sportswear brand. These statistics show that amongst consumers there is a strong perception that wearables are first and foremost a technology purchase rather than a lifestyle accessory (Fig. 2.3).

Remarkably, when respondents were questioned on which functionalities were important for them when choosing a smartwatch, results revealed that smartwatch functionalities poorly understood by most consumers as activity tracking (29 %), taking phone calls (13 %) and telling the time (11 %) topped the list. The importance attached to activity tracking as functionality of a 'smartwatch' points to the fact that this is the function consumers are most able to understand, and there prioritize in any purchase decision. Evidently the full range of potential

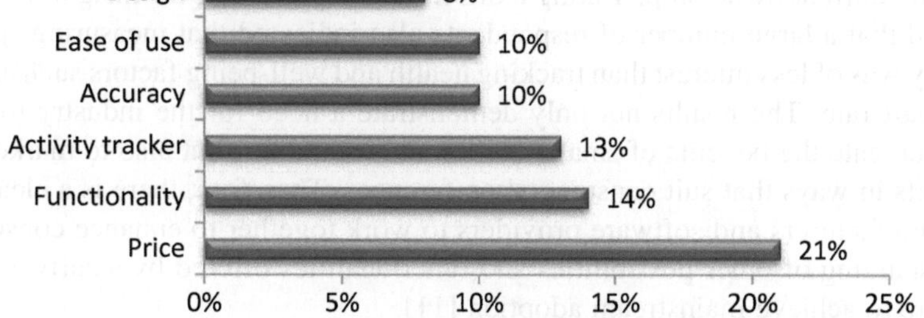

Fig. 2.2 Purchase criteria for WT devices, adapted from [10]

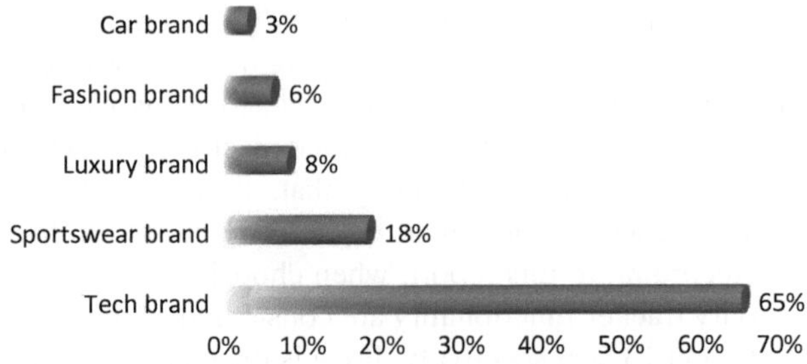

Fig. 2.3 Importance of brands in the smartwatch market

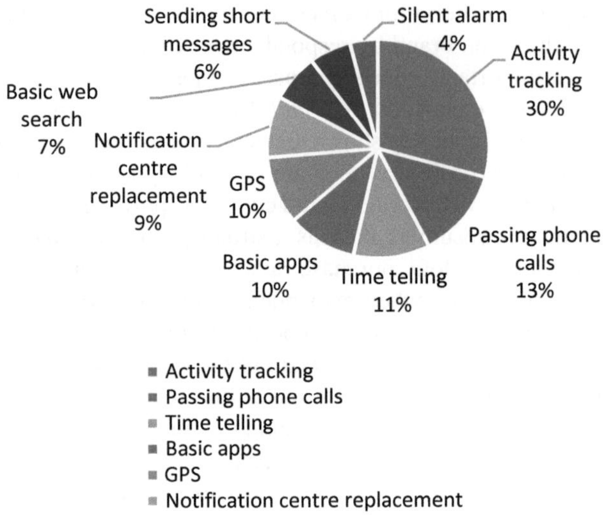

Fig. 2.4 Most important functionalities of smartwatches, adapted from [11]

applications of smartwatches and other wearables are, as yet, poorly understood (Fig. 2.4).

Tech analyst firm CCS Insight has also called on the consumer electronics industry to better articulate the advantages of smartwatches and wearable devices to the public if they are to survive the hype surrounding wearable technology [18]. The research included a survey of 4000 people in the UK, the US, China and Brazil on their views of wearable technology including usage patterns, awareness and current ownership. Taking a different perspective, CCS Insight's findings showed that a large number of respondents also indicated that measuring sporting activity was of less interest than tracking health and well-being factors such as sleep and heart rate. The results not only demonstrate a need for the industry to better communicate the benefits of smartwatches and wearables, but also to market their products in ways that suit consumers' preferences. Therefore, there is a clear need for manufacturers and software providers to work together to enhance consumers' understanding of other possibilities and functionalities offered by smartwatches if they are to achieve mainstream adoption [11].

Table 2.1 Percentage of luxury items with activity tracker by countries, adapted from [11]

Countries	Percentage of clothes/jewelry with activity tracker
USA	81
South Korea	72
Germany	73
China	71
UK	69

Table 2.2 Most relevant products for an integrated activity tracker, adapted from [11]

Type of products	Percentage
Bracelet	32
Shoes	29
Belt	15
T-shirts/shirts	11
Necklace	6
Trousers	4
Jacket	3
Ring	3
Underwear	3

Moreover, it is worth noting that 73 % of respondents in GfK's research also considered wearing clothes or jewelry with an integrated activity tracker which when divided by countries result as shown by Table 2.1.

And finally when respondents were asked on the type of product(s) they consider the most relevant to integrate an activity tracker bracelet, shoes and belt topped the list. The rest of categories were as shown in Table 2.2.

It is clear from the GFK research that there is huge potential for wearable technologies, both in terms of the size of this fast-growing market and the opportunities that this new technology offers to consumers. At the moment there is clearly a lack of understanding amongst consumers about the variety of applications for wearables and functionalities of such devices that can be improved through joint collaboration of WT device manufacturers and software developers via social media platforms.

2.3 Trends for Wearable Adoption

There are a number of technological and social trends that will play a crucial role in wearable adoption in the coming years. Below we summarize a number of these developments that will play a growing role in the wearable technology segment [14] (see also Fig. 2.5).

Advances in materials sciences will definitely be one of those critical areas, which may make new form factors and materials available for wearable computing and electronics. The University of Exeter in the U.K., for instance, recently

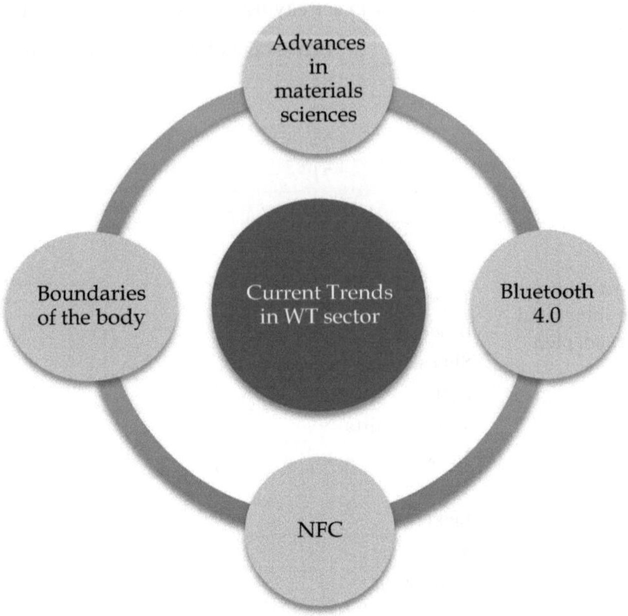

Fig. 2.5 Current trends in WT sector, adapted from [14]

announced the development of a new material called GraphExeter that can conduct electricity [14]. This material could be quite revolutionary in the Wearable Technology sector because the material is more flexible than the expensive materials currently used. Another key driver of wearables is the release of Bluetooth 4.0, which uses less power and can instantaneously pair with devices [14]. Bluetooth 4.0 is also a boost in the health market, due to connectivity with diverse medical devices and greater use with bracelets and watches, which are rapidly becoming important device platforms in the fitness and body-monitoring spaces. Furthermore, Near Field Communication (NFC) will also play a growing role in wearables too as it becomes a more commonplace technology used in mobile-money applications and services. There is already talk of embedding NFC technology in wearable devices so users can pay for different types of service from movie tickets, to subway tokens, to sporting events or simply a latte at Starbucks without even pulling out a card or phone, to name a few. This is provided consumers trust the technology to handle their financial transactions. Wearables are already causing a rethinking of the boundaries of the body and materials.

In her TED talk [14], Lucy McRae demonstrated some of the work Philips Electronics is researching and coined the term "*maybe tech*" for technologies that are not purely off or on the body and have the effect of blurring the boundaries of the body. Electronic tattoos that can conduct electricity and redefine the skin is an example of such efforts. In this way we can see how the body is becoming a platform or an API as nanotechnologies and computing converge in interesting ways.

2.4 Applications

Wearable technology is appealing to many consumers. In this section we summarize some of the current applications of wearable technologies.

2.4.1 Entertainment

2.4.1.1 Wearable Headsets

Workers in the digital age have become reliant on regularly checking their handheld devices to stay up-to-date with the surrounding environments, family and friends. Yet a new wave of technical innovation is likely to push knowledge right in front of faces. The most media-hyped example of wearable technology, Google Glass [19, 20] provides information on a head-mounted display and communicates with the Internet through natural voice commands. Glass can perform many of the tasks of a smartphone: it can take pictures, record video, give directions and send messages. At the lower-spec end of the spectrum, Oculus Rift [21–23], meanwhile, is a virtual reality (VR) head-mounted display. Thync is another company that creates wearable consumer products that make use of neuro-signaling to shift your state of mind by making on-demand shifts in energy, calm, or focus [8]. Thync in fact makes use of what they call 'Thync Vibes', which are intelligent waveforms delivered via neuro-signaling. These signals are targeted to specific neural pathways to achieve optimal results [24]. Augmented Reality (AR) offers a live view of a physical, real-world environment [25] whose elements are further enhanced by computer-generated sensory input such as sound, video, graphics or GPS data. The spread of smart mobile devices has led to rapid growth in AR with diverse from agriculture and architecture to education and medicine [13].

2.4.1.2 Smartwatches

Whereas smartphones has now become a normal part of life for millions of people globally, wearables are yet to achieve anywhere near this status for smartwatches. Computer-enabled wristwatches are not inherently new. Seiko and Casio developed data entry watches through the 1980s. What is new, however, is the ability to combine cheaper and smaller components in powerful and internet-enabled devices [7]. As far as buyers are concerned, smartwatches are not living up to their name. The widespread perception is that smartwatches are just activity trackers that tell the time. There is however the potential for wearable devices to overtake smartphones in terms of closer relationship between people and technology with innovations such as smartwatches, fitness armbands and data glasses that are generally used in conjunction with a smartphone [11].

2.4.1.3 Fitness Devices

Wearable technology has proved a popular adjunct to fitness routines—and it is not hard to see why. The potential to track and trace progress towards set fitness goals means individuals are prepared to invest money in technology that will provide real-time data of their health status. Nike's FuelBand, for example, is a smart pedometer that tracks steps, and provides motivational reminders and social connectivity. Fitbit, is another example, which offers a range of fitness tracking devices, and the minimalist Jawbone UP, which keeps interactivity to a minimum and does away with a screen [26]. As with smartwatches, reviews for fitness devices are mixed. Features on devices are limited, the initial cost is relatively high and connectivity with other technologies can be a concern, particularly when it comes to older or less popular smartphones.

2.4.2 Healthcare

Utilizing wearable technologies in healthcare sector brought forth many benefits for both patient and healthcare professionals (see Fig. 2.6) [25, 27]. Wearable technology could provide a platform to share patients medical data and to take necessary actions [5, 9, 10]. Thus, the availability and accessibility of patient's real time health records cold lead to better patient engagement with health and increased self-management in long term [28]. In addition to the remote access to the health data, wearable technology allows patients to keep an eye on their own health. Consequently, this could enable patients to make informed decisions on their own health.

Developments in smart healthcare technology are currently closely related to developments in smartwatches and fitness devices. Some of the companies pioneering developments in those areas already offer tools to monitor healthcare [9, 10, 29, 30]. Other firms are keen to gain a slice of a fast-growing sector [31]. Gaming specialist Nintendo recently announced its aim to target the

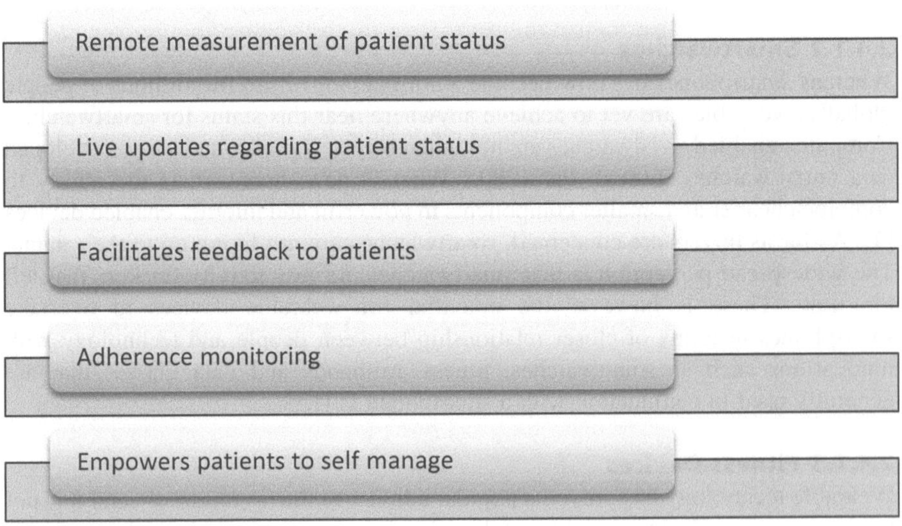

Fig. 2.6 Benefits of wearable technology in healthcare, adapted from [5]

healthcare market to help turn around its own economic fortunes [5, 10]. The advancement in the technology is likely to offer innovative solutions to some of the most healthcare's significant challenges. For instance, a recent innovative solution has been developed by the US-based company Proteus Digital Health to track patients' responses to medicine [5]. The device sends information wirelessly to the medical staff via pills stuffed with minuscule sensors. Electronic tattoos could be another solution as mentioned earlier. Other dedicated tools for conditions like diabetes are beginning to surface as well.

In the US the Food and Drug Administration (FDA) has recently approved Medtronic's MiniMed 530G, a wearable, artificial pancreas that monitors blood glucose levels and injects insulin to a defined threshold. Johnson and Johnson is also creating Animas, an external unit that monitors insulin levels automatically [13]. Remote monitoring of patients using wearable sensing technology may also mitigate the problems associated with access to healthcare.

2.5 Wearable Technology and Big Data

Over the past few years, healthcare research and development has relied on big data to advance medical science and create better diagnostics and drugs. Big data wearables capitalize on two huge trends: 'big data' and 'wearable technology' [32]. The fact that many well-known companies such as Google, Apple, Microsoft and a host of fitness-device manufacturers are making significant investments in this area reveals that we are on the verge of wearables becoming mainstream devices in the coming years [14]. With the health and fitness gadgets currently taking the lead in this sector, wearables will begin to occupy a growing role in the mobile-health sector, and data analytics as well as big data will become important services linked to their growth [14]. For example, Wearable technology such as the above-mentioned Google Glass, Nike+ FuelBand and the reported Apple Watch will not only enhance consumers' lives, but will also provide a new source of commercially exploitable data [15].

Call it wearable tech, the Internet of Things (IoT), or the quantified self—all terms reflecting a reality in which we collect as much data about our personal lives as we do (or should) about our sales figures. And what we do with that data could profoundly impact workplace culture and productivity [33]. The term 'Internet of Things (IoT)' usually refers to the interconnection of uniquely identifiable computing devices embedded in a whole host of things around you, such as heart monitoring implants, cars, thermostats, washing machines, etc. This interconnection of chips, means that practically everything will be connected to the Internet. Gartner predicts that there will be nearly 26 billion devices connected to the Internet by 2020 [26].

Another category closely related to wearable tech is the trend referred to as *quantified self-life*. As mentioned above, the computers that we wear make different types of measurements and analyze data in real time. Consequently, we can keep track of just about anything such as how many calories we've burned in s specific time frame, how many steps we've walked, for how many hours we slept, how we slept, what is our blood pressure, respiratory rate, etc. Since all these devices are connected, we can share all the information to be analyzed by other parties or in our own applications. The amount of generated information is so vast that experts are talking about a shift from big data to my data [12].

The numerous amounts of data collected via wearable devices could represent an issue of concern. For instance, health and fitness gadgets can capture sensitive data about users' health and make them available to the tech vendor via cloud technologies. Moreover, the captured data might be shared with third parties for 'big data' profiling. To comply with the law, wearable device manufacturers and suppliers will need to consider a multitude of data protection, privacy and security issues. These then need to be dealt with properly at design stage, at the point of data capture and once the data has been collected [34]. In other words, more collaboration between researchers in IT and medical fields as well as data scientist is highly essential at the design stage. The result of this collaboration would be a complete proper system including global networked computing environment of smart sensors, software, data centers and devises.

2.6 Challenges of Wearable Technology

Since 2008, wearable technology that can cover a broad range from measuring your heart rate to curating music based on your mood has been advertised as the next big moment in consumer electronics [6]. Nevertheless, the wearable technology market is not without its challenges. WT devices are typically divided into three categories: complex devices such as fitness trackers; smart accessories such as smartwatches, defined by their ability to run third-party applications; and fully autonomous smart wearables that connect directly to the Internet, such as Google's Glass headset (Fig. 2.7). It is believed that WT devices will reach 19 million units this year alone which will be more than triple last year's sales [6].

According to the study, a large segment of consumers (i.e. about 75 %) are generally aware of wearable technology gadgets however a very small portion of consumers (i.e. about 9 %) actually have any interest in buying and wearing it and even a smaller portion of 2 % admitted to essentially owning a wearable tech device, most of which consist of fitness trackers and smartwatches [6]. The question is why the number of adopters is small? According to [35] the research director of the US based benchmarking and education firm L2, Colin Gilbert, 'style' is not the only missing piece to the WT puzzle, but it's something to look forward to. More than half of the report's respondents want devices that feel more like jewelry while 62 % would like more than wrist-worn devices [6]. Nonetheless, the "cool" factor isn't the only issue. Security and privacy, particularly around the management of consumer data, remain a major issue as the tech industry seeks to bring more of our body parts online.

According to a report by [36] there are reasons many wearable devices fail to achieve long-term user engagement. Many consumers see obstacles to purchasing

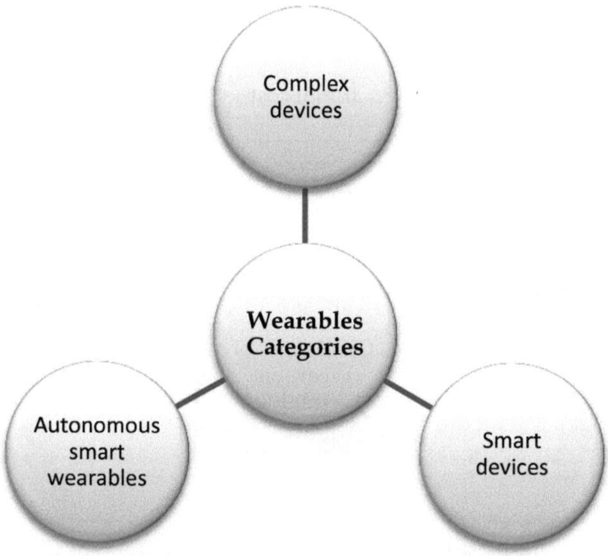

Fig. 2.7 Categories of wearable technology devices, adapted from [5]

wearable devices including the expense of devices and security and privacy of data, the look, comfort and health risks being other concerns among users [5]. As reported by Endeavour Partners while one in ten American adults now own an activity tracker, one third of users stop using the device within 6 months of receiving it [36]. According to this report, many wearable devices fail to achieve long-term user engagement due to a number of flaws [36]:

- They are easy to lose
- They break
- They are not waterproof
- They are a pain to sync with your smartphone
- The battery doesn't last long enough
- They are ugly
- They are uncomfortable to wear
- They provide no material benefit

Endeavour Partners believes that wearable technology companies need to really focus on real needs of consumers and develop devices that become an integral part of their day-to-day life. Devices need to address a wider and more interesting set of consumer problems than the existing designs.

As for these issues, Fig. 2.8 shows the main challenges of Wearable technology. Each challenge is now explained briefly but 'data security and privacy' due to their importance is explored in more detail.

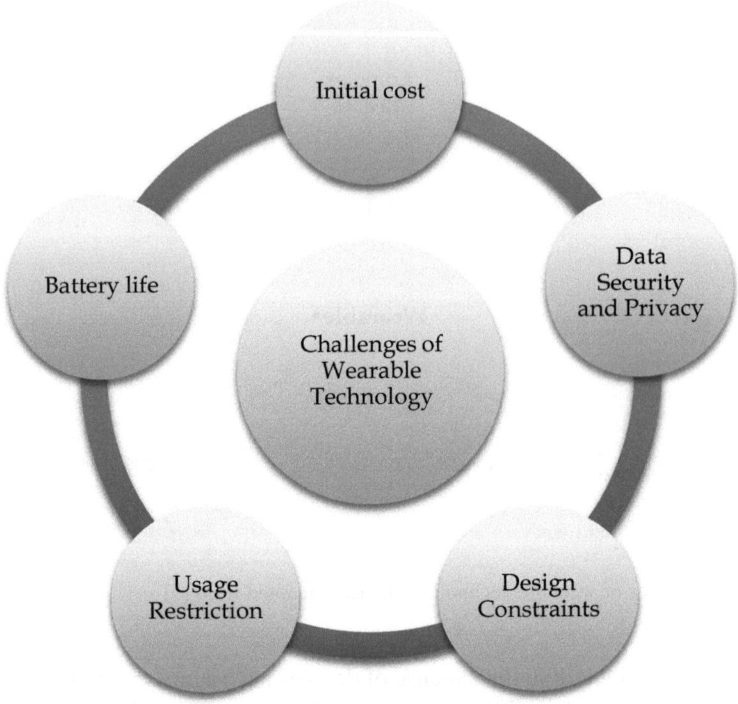

Fig. 2.8 Challenges of wearable technology

2.6.1 Design Constraints

The design of wearable technology is an important issue for the end users. In fact, most consumers use wearable accessories such as watches, jewelry and wristbands to make a statement about their personal identity and their fashion trend. Currently, however, most wearable device manufacturers give less consideration to the design of the WTs compared to the technology aspect. For instance, most of smartwatches use components that are designed for smartphones and thus they are bulkier than ordinary watches.

One of the major challenges in the Smart Wearable Technology market is the design constraint of wearable devices as most consumers use normal wearable accessories such as watches, jewelry and wristbands to make a statement about their personal identity. In other words the wearable item reflects the fashion trend of the users. Currently, however, most smart wearable device manufacturers have focused on technology aspect of WTs rather than on design. For instance, most of the smartwatches run on processors and components that are designed for smartphones so they are bulkier than a normal watch.

2.6.2 High Power Consumption

Another main challenge that may attribute to lack of usage and adoption of the WTs is high power consumption. This excessive power consumption is attributed to the fact that most wearable devices are supported with built-in features such as Wi-Fi, GPS and other technologies. As a result, the current battery life of wearable devices does not last for long. For instance, in case of intensive usage, the Google Glass battery lasts only for 4–8 h. So the issue of short battery life if not tackled may hinder the expected growth prospects of the market during the forecast period.

2.6.3 High Initial Cost and Usage Restrictions

The high cost of smart wearable devices is another challenge that is expected to limit the boom in the WTs market. Currently, most of wearable devices are launched in premium and luxurious product categories. Undoubtedly, this affects the affordability and therefore results in a very low mass adoption of wearable devices. Furthermore, though wearable technology hasn't been around for long, it has been on many companies' radars for a while. Thus, the possibilities in terms of functioning and applications are potentially endless for wearable technology. But while this is great for consumers, it isn't the best news for businesses that require strict laws and high security to operate. So far, wearable technology has been banned in casinos, movie theatres, and even some restaurants have disallowed their patrons to adorn wearables [37].

2.6.4 Lack of Data Privacy and Security

As WT devices grow in popularity, so do concerns over security and privacy of data. In this section we list some of these concerns. Most wearable devices are small in size, but they are able to store a huge amount of data. The small size of these devices means that the chance of them being lost or misplaced is high. Since they store a large amount of sensitive information, smart wearable devices can be disruptive for users. Wearable devices use GPS navigation systems to receive location-based information. Sometimes, users have to share their location to obtain certain information. For instance, Google Glass users have to share their location while checking-in at Foursquare, which is stored in its database. This information can be retrieved and used by advertisers as well. Moreover, the data about a subscriber's location is owned and controlled by the respective network operators, which includes mobile carriers and mobile content providers. Despite available legal frameworks [5, 10, 26, 37], WTs end-users are concerned about the intrusion on their privacy by other stakeholders. Furthermore, data privacy and security is considered as one of the main concerns for wearable technologies. No difference to computers and smartphones, wearable devices create an enormous volume of personal and detailed data that is extremely appealing to cybercriminals

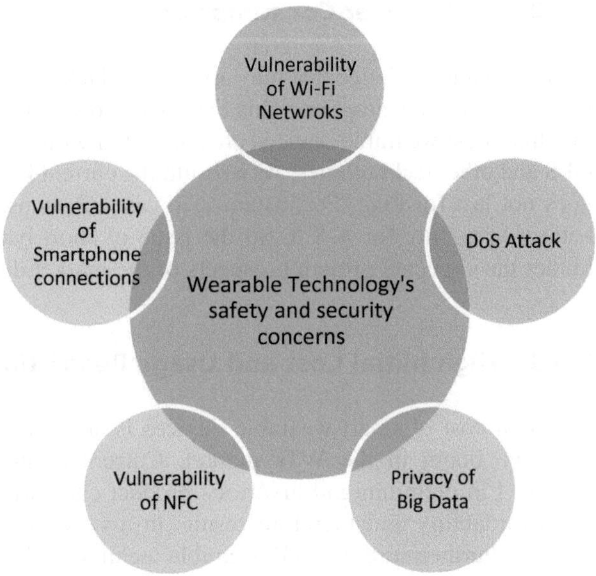

Fig. 2.9 Wearable technology safety and security concerns

[38]. Without the proper security, wearable devices with cameras, like Google Glass, could be hacked allowing the cybercriminal to gain information about where the user is, what they are doing, and who they are with [38, 39]. Even the data generated by activity trackers that use GPS could be used by cybercriminals to determine where the user lives and when they leave the home, office etc. The connection between many wearable devices and a smartphone is also another potential point that hackers can attack. For instance, Apple watch can be connected to other apple products such as iPhone, iPad and other Apple devices. With this in mind, such connection will definitely become a potential attack vector [39] (see Fig. 2.9).

Another issue with wearable technology is data ownership. Wearable devices like Fitbit and Jawbone have the ability to acquire huge volumes of data but the question remains as to who actually owns the data generated. The Federal Trade Commission in the US published findings of an investigation on 12 different health app and the result was that these apps transmitted information to 76 different third-parties, including consumer health metrics [30]. In order to overcome these safety and security concerns associated with wearable technology, devices need to comply with the necessary technology regulatory standards with most wearable device manufactures relying on the International Electro technical Commission's International Standards to operate reliably and safely. That in mind, we briefly take a look at how we can expect to be attacked in this sector [39].

2.6.4.1 Vulnerability of Google Glass on Public Wi-Fi

As for the vulnerability of Google Glass on public Wi-Fi, the well-known security firm Kaspersky decided to run a few tests on the technology to see how it performed on public Wi-Fi access points. The result showed that the security firm could determine what could and couldn't be seen from a user's activity. While almost all the traffic from Glass was encrypted, enough however was left in plain text to inform hackers what sites they had visited.

2.6.4.2 Denial-of-Service Attacks May Affect Doctors' Tools

The potential advantages wearable devices offer to improve medical technology have been one of the big selling points of the technology in the public sector. Doctors, for example, have long been using computers to aid the medical process, and wearables seem like a perfect fit. Unfortunately reliance on wearables opens up worrisome possibilities. As Trend Micro's well known senior threat researcher David Sancho wrote in a blog: "A simple Denial-of-Service (DoS) attack could prevent a doctor from operating on a patient or prevent a law enforcement agent from acquiring input data to catch criminals" [39].

2.6.4.3 Privacy Is at Risk as Wearables Collect Data

Consumers are now used to their smartphones doing research on them and wearable tech offers even more chances to take notes on our behavior, which is potentially useful but also potentially dangerous. Hackers have already become skilled at summarizing, and this trend is only set to get worse. Fitness bands, for instance, that monitor and capture information about our movement using GPS, can provide a malicious user with details about our daily routines and patterns, as well as our current location.

2.6.4.4 Digital Pickpocketing Is Likely to Rise

With the rise of contactless payments, thanks to near field communication (NFC), the security industry has warned about the risks to the user of having money stolen from them (their cards) in what is sometimes called "*digital pickpocketing*". One form can be used by converting a mobile into a radio frequency identification (RFID) scanner that once set up, the user can seek out payment cards with RFID chips, before exploiting them to steal money from unaware victims [39].

2.6.4.5 Smartphone Connections Could Be Exploited

It is very likely that at some point Apple Watch may become self-sustaining, but right now they need to be tied to an iPhone in order to work—this is also true for other tech companies such as Samsung. That connection also creates an additional point that hackers can attack. Ken Westin, security analyst at Tripwire for instance explains that the device connects to iPhones and other iDevices, so that connection will definitely become a potential attack vector [39].

2.7 Case Studies

In this section, a number of small-medium enterprises that have developed wearable technology solutions are outlined in a case study format, representing market and emerging trends.

In the first case considered, Charles Settles is a Product Analyst at Technology Advice (TA), a Tennessee-based company that provides unprejudiced research on business technology [40]. He believes that there are a number of exciting business applications for wearable technology on the horizon. He explains that in TA they educate, advise, and connect businesses with software solutions and one of the areas that increasingly our customers are asking for is related to software that will allow them to integrate wearable devices into their operations in the healthcare realm, which is one of the most promising areas for wearable technology. drChrono is one of the companies that experimenting with a Google Glass-based electronic health records solution that allows physicians to maintain eye contact with their patient while doing the routine procedures such as taking notes, recording orders, and even referencing patient history. This could therefore solve one of the biggest complaints made by providers and patients that is the documentation process for electronic health records kills the physician/patient relationship. Google Glass includes a camera, display, touchpad, battery and microphone, all built into display frames. Google Glass is controlled by a microphone and touchpad on one arm of the frame and the device syncs to Google Drive, and has in-built Bluetooth and Wi-Fi. Smart glasses thus may help healthcare professionals to work more efficiently allowing doctors to access healthcare records without having to break eye contact with the patient.

Point of Attention Wearable technologies such as Google's head-mounted glass can help physicians to overcome the challenges of the documentation process for electronic health records that kills the physician/patient relationship. It could even allow surgeons in the sterile environment of an operating room to document findings in a patient's medical notes and in real-time share this data with colleagues.

The increasingly usage of wearable devices by lay consumers may present a great opportunity for physicians to provide these devices to particularly at risk patients. Being able to monitor a patient's vitals in real-time without requiring a hospital stay could be a game-changer for heart patients, chronic disease sufferers, and their physicians.

In the second considered case scenario, it is noteworthy also to brief the viewpoint on the body worn camera by Tiffany Wang is the Vice President of Sales for Wolfcom Enterprises, a manufacturer of body worn cameras for Law Enforcement and consumers. According to her, businesses will be investing in various applications of WTs to expand their applicability. For instance, body worn cameras are becoming smaller and lighter. Already in use by police agencies across different countries and particularly US, these cameras are worn by police officers to record interaction with the public. This has resulted in a reduction of complaints and lawsuits saving cities across America millions of taxpayer dollars in payouts from false claims. Body cameras will be the next wearable technology and one southland company is betting on it.

To widen its applicability, body cameras manufactured by Wolfcom are designed to be light and wearable. Moreover, the founders stated that there is incredible opportunity to provide their cameras to a wide group including doctors, attorneys, social workers, process servers, and just about anyone exposed to the possibility of frivolous lawsuits. The camera, Wolfcom Vision', is characterized by high recording and storage capacity; store up to 36 h of video, take up to 56,000 photos and record up to 360 h of audio. Amazingly, the camera is integrated into a lightweight unit that is smaller than a business card and clips right onto either a shirt or belt.

Point of Attention At a flick of a switch, business professionals can now record interactions with their clients, monitor employee interactions with customers or record their everyday activities. The recorded videos can then be used to settle disputes and allegations as well as be used for customer service training.

External headset cameras is an addition to the 'Wolfcom Vision' which makes it perfect for those requiring Point of View (POV) recording such as a building inspector who needs to record where his eyes are looking and where chest mounted body cameras cannot see or record such as ceilings, pipes, floors, blueprints, etc. Therefore, body worn cameras are a promising technology for businesses and they will be here to stay.

2.8 Summary

This chapter has discussed wearable technology as a trend for business innovation. Once seen as a novelty, the area is ever expanding, with new devices been launched practically every week if not every few days. Wearable technology is per se, an umbrella term, that covers all types of technologies that are worn on the body, from sensors that measure fitness to accessories such as smartwatches, to fully autonomous smart wearable devices that connect directly to the internet, such as Google's Glass headset.

There are many advantages of using wearable devices. The advantages include measuring and monitoring physiological and biomechanical systems of the body as well body movement. In addition, wearable devices allow users or external parties to capture data on individuals' behaviour and to monitor their health and fitness.

Besides that, wearable devices enhance individuals' engagement with the external environment. Such advantages are not limited to healthcare professionals and patients rather they appeal to other stakeholders such as athletes and their trainers as well as the average consumer. According to Global Web Index [2], 64 % of global internet users aged 16–64 have worn a piece of wearable technology already, or are keen to do so in the future.

Many wearable devices are wireless and this feature, combined with the small size of many of the sensors used, makes them easily integrated into wearable systems. Sensors have so far been integrated into garments, hats, wristbands, socks, shoes, eyeglasses and other devices such as wristwatches and headphones making them truly wearable [9]. Advances in sensor technology, microelectronics, telecommunication, and data analysis techniques have also been attributed to the huge increase in wearable technology. According to Robert Scoble, startup liaison officer at Rackspace Inc., the transformation in wearable technology is being fuelled by cloud computing. "It allows the data generated by wearable devices to be captured, analysed and made readily accessible whenever users need it" [41]. Johan Svanberg, Senior Analyst with Berg Insight says, "A perfect storm of innovation within low power wireless connectivity, sensor technology, big data, cloud services, voice user interfaces and mobile computing power is coming together and paves the way for connected wearable technology," [1].

References

1. Reed B (2013) Wearable computer shipment projection: 64 million in 2017. BGR. http://bgr.com/2013/10/25/wearable-computer-shipment-projection/. Accessed 8 Aug 2015
2. Mander J (2014) 71 % of 16-24 s interested in wearable tech. Globalwebindex. http://www.globalwebindex.net/blog/wearable-tech-age-gender-income. Accessed 8 Aug 2015
3. The Market for Smart Wearables (2015) WiFore Consult. http://www.nickhunn.com/wp-content/uploads/downloads/2014/08/The-Market-for-Smart-Wearables.pdf. Accessed 3 Aug 2015
4. Howard (2015) Wearable technology trends in 2015 – Apadmi. Apadmi. http://www.apadmi.com/wearable-technology-trends/. Accessed 3 Aug 2015
5. ICT: Wearable Technology – KARIM Foresight Report (2014) http://www.karimnetwork.com/wp-content/uploads/2014/11/Wearable-Technology-Final_November2014.pdf. Accessed 11 Aug 2015
6. Reed B (2014) 2014 is not the year of wearables, according to report – fortune. http://fortune.com/2014/06/20/2014-not-year-wearables/. Accessed 6 Aug 2015
7. Jon C (2013) Future thinking with EE. Mobile and technology expert opinions. EE. http://futurethinking.ee.co.uk/machine-to-machine-m2m-and-the-internet-of-things-iot-ready-for-business/. Accessed 3 Aug 2015
8. How far would you go with wearable technology? (2015) Narrative. http://blog.getnarrative.com/2015/01/how-far-would-you-go-with-wearable-technology/. Accessed 3 Aug 2015
9. Wearable Technology & Preventative Healthcare (2014) TechnologyAdvice. http://technologyadvice.com/medical/blog/study-wearable-technology-preventative-healthcare/. Accessed 10 Aug 2015
10. Graham C (2014) Trends in wearable technology & preventative healthcare. TechnologyAdvice. http://technologyadvice.com/medical/blog/study-wearable-technology-preventative-healthcare/. Accessed 8 Aug 2015

11. Wearables: Geek Chic or the Latest "Must Have" Consumer Tech? (2014) GFK. https://www.gfk.com/Documents/whitepaper/GfK_wearables_report-digital_low_res.pdf. Accessed 12 Aug 2015
12. hatalska.com (2013) Trend book 2013 http://hatalska.com/trendbook2013/. Accessed 18 Nov 2015
13. Udhas P, Jha S (2013) Six converging technology trends. KPMG. http://www.nasscom.in/six-converging-technology-trends-driving-tectonic-shift-businessconsumer-ecosystem. Accessed 8 Aug 2015
14. Ranck J (2012) The wearable computing market: a global analysis. https://research.gigaom.com/report/the-wearable-computing-market-a-global-analysis/. Accessed 11 Aug 2015
15. Shah S (2013) Wearable technology "will be powerful for big data analytics" says Rackspace. http://www.computing.co.uk/ctg/news/2272640/wearable-technology-will-be-powerful-for-big-data-analytics-says-rackspace. Accessed 9 Aug 2015
16. Gill C (2014) The rise of wearable technology. Fashionbeans. http://www.fashionbeans.com/2014/the-rise-of-wearable-technology/. Accessed 9 Aug 2015
17. Todd L (2014) Amazon launches wearable technology store. FashionBeans. http://www.fashionbeans.com/2014/amazon-launches-wearable-technology-store/. Accessed 11 Aug 2015
18. Deacon H (2014) Clear marketing needed to drive sales of smartwatches and fitness trackers. CCSinsight. http://www.ccsinsight.com/press/company-news/1957-clear-marketing-needed-to-drive-sales-of-smartwatches-and-fitness-trackers. Accessed 10 Aug 2015
19. Glauser W (2013) Doctors among early adopters of Google glass. Can Med Assoc J 185:16
20. Hong J (2013) Considering privacy issues in the context of Google glass. Commun ACM 56:10–11
21. Oculus VR (2015) LLC: private company information – Businessweek, http://www.bloomberg.com/research/stocks/private/snapshot.asp?privcapid=241782536. Accessed 10 Aug 2015
22. The Oculus Crescent Bay is a two-screen VR headset. The Verge. http://www.theverge.com/2015/3/13/8212205/oculus-crescent-bay-two-screen-vr-headset-palmer-luckey. Accessed 10 Aug 2015
23. A Brief History of Oculus. http://techcrunch.com/2014/03/26/a-brief-history-of-oculus/. Accessed 10 Aug 2015
24. Thync: How good feels (2015) Thync. http://www.thync.com/. Accessed 3 Aug 2015
25. Chai P, Ranney M, Babu K, Boyer EW (2014) The virtual toxicology service: wearable head mounted devices for medical toxicology. J Med Toxicol 10:382–387
26. Wearable Technology: What You Need To Know (2014) Greenlight digital. www.greenlightdigital.com. Accessed 7 Aug 2015
27. Ianata A, Nardelli M, Gentili C, Scilingo EP (2014) Complexity index from a personalized wearable monitoring system for assessing remission in mental health. IEEE J Biomed Heal Inf 11:1–7
28. Doherty AR, Hodges S, King AC et al (2013) Wearable cameras in wearable cameras in health: the state of the art and future possibilities. Am J Prev Med 44:320–323. doi:10.1016/j.amepre.2012.11.008
29. Jee K, Kim G-H (2013) Potentiality of big data in the medical sector: focus on how to reshape the healthcare system. Healthc Inf Res 19(2):79–85
30. Sweeney L (2014) Consumer generated and controlled health data. Spring Privacy Series. https://www.ftc.gov/news-events/events-calendar/2014/05/spring-privacy-series-consumer-generated-controlled-health-data. Accessed 8 Aug 2015
31. Skiba DJ (2014) The connected age and wearable technology. Nurs Educ Perspect 35:346–347
32. Wearable Tech: The Next Big in Big Data. PromptCloud. https://www.promptcloud.com/blog/wearable-tech-the-next-big-in-bigdata-part-1. Accessed 10 Aug 2015
33. Dearborn J (2014) Big data gets personal: wearable tech in your workplace. Forbes. http://www.forbes.com/sites/sap/2014/08/01/big-data-gets-personal-wearable-tech-in-your-workplace/. Accessed 9 Aug 2015

34. Taylor L (2014) Wearable technology in business: big data benefits bring legal and privacy risks. V3. http://www.v3.co.uk/v3-uk/opinion/2329804/wearable-technology-in-business-big-data-benefits-bring-legal-and-privacy-risks. Accessed 9 Aug 2015
35. L2: Business Intelligence for Digital (2014) http://www.l2inc.com/research/wearables-2014. Accessed 10 Aug 2015
36. The Future of Activity Trackers: The Secret to Long-Term Engagement Endeavour Partners (2014) Endeavour. http://endeavourpartners.net/the-future-of-activity-trackers-part-3-the-secret-to-long-term-engagement/. Accessed 8 Aug 2015
37. The brave new world of wearable tech: what implications for IP? (2014) WIPO Magazine. www.wipo.int. Accessed 6 Aug 2015
38. Curtis S (2014) Wearable tech: how hackers could turn your most private data against you. Telegr. http://www.telegraph.co.uk/technology/internet-security/10925223/Wearable-tech-how-hackers-could-turn-your-most-private-data-against-you.html. Accessed 8 Aug 2015
39. Wearables hacking and cybercrime on the rise. How secure are you? http://wtvox.com/2014/09/wearables-hacking-cybercrime-rise-secure/. Accessed 6 Aug 2015
40. Stanley R (2014) 24 experts share the best new uses of wearable technology, wearable devices, and smart clothes for business & field service management. ClickSoftware. http://blogs.clicksoftware.com/index/24-experts-share-the-best-new-uses-of-wearable-technology-wearable-devices-and-smart-clothes-for-business-field-service-management/#Settles. Accessed 15 Oct 2015
41. Brunson B (2013) Rackspace investor relations. Rackspace. http://ir.rackspace.com/phoenix.zhtml?c=221673&p=irol-newsArticle&ID=1827146&highlight. Accessed 8 Aug 2015

Digital Currencies and Distributed Ledgers 3

Abstract

This chapter explores the concept of Digital currencies and distributed ledger. Digital currencies have become the alternative medium of exchange and are a true reflection of innovations in payment systems. While retaining the functions of money—a store of value, a unit of account, and a medium of exchange—these new Digital currencies have incorporated the concept of a 'distributed ledger' which allows a digital currency to function in a decentralized payment system. One example of Digital currency is Bitcoin. Today, Bitcoin is gradually becoming the most widely used digital currency. It is very flexible in its use as it does not require any centralized vetting procedures or incur any fee to create an account. However, the uniqueness of Bitcoin also creates peculiar risks that vary from other payment methods; therefore grasping the strengths and weaknesses of Bitcoin is key for businesses willing to understanding its business value. Actually, one common thing associated with any new technology is the unforeseen risks and digital currencies are no exception. They can leave an organization vulnerable. It is therefore advisable to evaluate all changes presented by these currencies so that organizations can be equipped with necessary tools to mitigate the risks.

3.1 Introduction

In the past, digital currencies were perceived as a futuristic innovation. Digital currencies now exist and are accepted by a variety of business cutting across online business to public trading companies [1]. Payment technologies have evolved remarkably, allowing users trade digital currencies or goods and services amongst each other in without the involvement of any third party such as banks. In line with this thought, Ali et al. [2] attribute the success of digital currencies to the brilliance of its "distributed ledger" which enables payment systems to function in a decentralized way. Table 3.1 displays some of the recent innovations in payment

V. Morabito, *The Future of Digital Business Innovation*,
DOI 10.1007/978-3-319-26874-3_3

Table 3.1 Types of innovation, adapted from Ali [2]

Category	New payment system	New currency
Wrappers	No	No
Mobile money	Yes	No
Credits and local currencies	No	Yes
Digital currencies	Yes	Yes

technologies. They are categorized into whether or not they propose a new payment method and currency.

Wrappers focus is on improving user interface and access to existing fund. It is neither a new currency nor a new payment method. *Mobile money* provides a new payment method in which money is converted as mobile credit on a smart card however it is still reliant on the existing national currency, a good example is M-Pesa which is popularly used in Kenya [2]. *Credits* also make use of existing payment systems; it is a scheme usually run by private companies where an agreed unit amount is given to a customer in exchange for money. The received unit amount can be spent in any form preferred (e.g. within an online game account). *Local currencies* similarly work on the same principles. People trade national currencies for a local equivalent, which can be used as a medium of transaction within specific geographical area. Yet, *Digital currencies* scheme propose both a new currency and payment system [2].

The motivation behind the adoption of digital currencies can be narrowed down to three major factors namely: *ideology*, *financial returns* and the *desire for lower transaction costs*. Ideologically, digital currencies were designed to achieve decentralization of financial control as well as to minimize trust issues that accompanies the involvement of financial third parties such as central banks. Secondly, the perception of digital currency as financial assets with profitable investment opportunity also drives its adoption. Finally, the possibility of lower transaction costs offered by digital currency makes it a preferred medium of exchange [2].

3.2 Understanding Digital Currencies

To the Economists [3], the concept of 'money' can be explained by the role it serves within the society. By implication, the concept of money can be understood as the degree to which an asset serves as a medium of exchange for payment settlements or a store of value, which enables purchasing giving the ability to buy services and goods. Furthermore, it can be considered also a unit of account that can be used as a scale of measurement for valuing a particular item for sale, may determine its acceptance as a legal tender (money) [2]. However, money and payment systems are closely entwined. Hence, if an asset is to serve as money, there should be a secure payment system through which it could be transferred. Likewise, a ledger is required to document the values of physical mediums of payment, e.g., notes or coins [2].

In recent times, payment systems have evolved significantly and the bulk of money typically exists as digital files on banks' accounts. These innovations in payment technology have enforced exchange platforms and digital currencies, which are fast becoming the preferred legal tender of the retail market. One distinct feature of the innovation of digital currency is its functioning 'distributed ledger'. It functions in an autonomous way by operating in a decentralized way with no need for banks as intermediaries. Thus, digital ledgers cut across global markets, enabling swift transfer and receipt of money without the complexities that come with conventional banking exchanges. This innovation actually leverages on game theory, cryptography and peer-to-peer networking [2].

While digital currencies may sometimes be perceived to be volatile and high-risk, their supporting technologies are considered secure [4]. These modern payment technologies are a resultant evolution from early payment systems, being that certain characteristics are adapted. In the past, payments were made by exchanging valuable assets like gold coins. Things evolved in the sixteenth century as customers could deal with each other only if they used the same goldsmith bank, and ledgers were used to keep customers' deposits. This enabled payments to be made by making changes in the ledgers rather than physically exchanging assets. Over time cross-bank payments became necessary, and this could be realized with the establishment of a central clearing bank. All member banks were required to have accounts with the central clearing bank, and this enabled easier inter-bank transactions.

With modern payment systems, if a payment is to be made to a customer, the sender's account is debited with the specific amount while the receiver's account is credited with that same amount. This is basically the same process that was used in the sixteenth century, however: what makes it differ is the advancements in technology used to record and effect the transactions. Over the past five decades technological advancements have affected the world globally and have also led to simplification and automation of many processes. One of such process that evolved was the change from using hard copy (paper) ledgers for recording transactions to the use of electronic form. This has helped reduce risks and has drastically improved the speed at which a transaction is processed [2].

The computerization of payment systems did not alter its foundational process significantly; however, distributed ledger is a game changer. It presents a totally different way of how payment systems will work with its decentralized approach. Interestingly, the decentralized approach not only affects payment systems, other financial assets like bonds and shares exist as digital records and are stored on centralized databases [2]. Bitcoin was the first digital currency to solve double spending in a decentralized way using the decentralized public ledger which can also be referred to as the *blockchain* [5]. It functions by retaining values of bitcoins in an indirect manner by linking transactions. A clear benefit of this design decision which makes it stand out is the fact that the value enclosed in a single transaction

Table 3.2 European Central Bank categorization of digital currency, adapted from Raj [6]

Characteristics	Electronic money schemes	Virtual currency schemes
Money format	Digital	Digital
Unit of account	Traditional currency (US dollars, Euros, etc.) with legal tender status	Invented currency (Linden dollars, Bitcoins, etc.) without legal tender status
Acceptance	By undertakings other than the issuer	Usually within a specific virtual community
Legal status	Regulated	Unregulated
Issuer	Legally established electronic money institution	Non financial private company
Supply of money	Fixed	Not fixed (depends on issuer's decisions)
Possibility of redeeming funds	Guaranteed (at par value)	Not guaranteed
Supervision	Yes	No
Type(s) of risk	Mainly operational	Legal, credit, liquidity, and operational

which is also related to a single bitcoin address will need to be paid out entirely [5]. It is understandable that when digital currency is mentioned, the focus moves towards Bitcoin. This is due to the fact that Bitcoin has gained a lot of popularity.

However there are other digital currencies in existence. McAfee Labs agrees with the European Central Bank (ECB) [6] in the way they categorize digital currencies: *electronic money* schemes such as for example US dollars, Euros, etc. (their units are traditional currency) and *virtual currencies* which are defined by units that are invented currency. Table 3.2 presents the characteristics of both categories.

A clear distinction between electronic money and virtual currencies lies on the unit of account. Electronic money, which is bound by the traditional money format, has a grounded legal foundation as oppose to virtual currencies. The demand for digital currencies is on the rise. Yankee Group projects a virtual market growth of US$47.5 billion as at 2012 and expected further growth of 14 % within the next 5 years with an expected figure of about US$55.4 billion by 2017 [6]. At this point it will be good to look at a few digital currencies but before we do so, lets understand the role of a *miner*. Information for crypto currency transactions are collected or embedded in data blocks. Each data block is interlinked with many others, which in turn creates a chain of blocks. The process of verifying transactions involves the analysis of these blocks in the shortest possible time; however, this will involve large processing power that makes it difficult for issuers of digital currency.

The miners step in at this point, they are investors who make available computer space and devote time into analyzing the data blocks. As their mining hits the right hash, a complex mathematical formula puzzle is resolved and thereby a transaction is verified and a new currency is created [7].

Table 3.3 Summary of the properties of a sample of available digital currencies

Coin	Algorithms	Properties
Litecoin	Scrypt	• Coin limit: 84 million • Mean block time of 2.5 min • Difficulty retarget of 2016 blocks • Block reward details: Halved every 840,000 blocks • Initial reward: 50 LTC • Current block reward: 50 LTC • Market cap: $540,274,528.26
BBQCoin	Scrypt encryption algorithms	• Each block generates 42 coins • Difficulty adjustment 60 blocks • Block generated every 1 min • Coin Cap is 88 million
ChinaCoin	Scrypt encryption algorithms	• 60 s block targets • Subsidy halves in 2628k blocks (5 years) • ~462.5 million total coins • 88 coins per block • 5040 blocks to retarget difficulty • Default Port:8106, RPC port:8108
Feathercoin	Scrypt encryption algorithms	• Current Gen ASIC resistance • 80 Coin reward per block • 336 million coins total • Block target is 1.0 min • Block reward halves every 2,100,000 blocks • Enhanced hash rate compensation (eHRC) • Advanced checkpointing (ACP)
Ixcoin	SHA-256 Algo	• 21 million total coins • 96 coins per block • Re-target every 2016 blocks • Merge mined with Bitcoin

In what follows we discuss examples of Digital Currencies (Table 3.3 provides a summary of the properties of a sample of the key available one). However, it will be nice to understand one common terminology which is found amongst digital currencies: "blockchain".

Blockchain helps in enforcing integrity of transactions by acting as a repository that holds records of every transaction executed in the currency [8]. Each and every block contains a hash of its preceding block, which then creates a chain of blocks starting from the genesis block (first block) to the current block. The blocks are formed in a chronologically order and the hash is simply an algorithm and its function is to convert arbitrarily-large amount of data into a fixed-length hash. Hashes are large numbers mostly written as hexadecimal [8].

3.2.1 Litecoin

Litecoin has been created for easier mining than bitcoin. The transactions of Litecoin are more quickly verified compared to the verification period of bitcoin transactions. The verification period of transactions for bitcoin (10 min) is four times that of the verification period for litecoin (2.5 min). Litecoins have an ultimate limit, which is four times the ultimate limit for bitcoin [9]. Litecoin is another peer-to-peer currency. It enables instant, close-to-zero cost payments to just about anyone in the world. Litecoin is not just a global payment network but also an open source currency which is fully decentralised without any central authorities [13]. Individuals can control their own finances while employing the use of mathematics to ensure a secure network. Owing to the substantial industry support, liquidity and trade volume, Litecoin has carved its mark as a proven medium of commerce and is even complementary to Bitcoin [13].

3.2.2 BBQCoin

BBQCoin, which is usually abbreviated to BBQ or BQC is defined as a scrypt based blockchain fork of the original bitcoin source code, which is quite identical to Litecoin. In other words, BBQCoin is a form of peer-to-peer internet currency which rides on the Bitcoin protocol, allows payments to be made as at when required to people across the world [9]. BBQCoin was launched a short while after the launching of Litecoin [10]. As at May 2013, the BBQ block reward was 42BQC with an Hash Algorithm called Script. Moreover, the block time for BBQ is 60 s with a coin cap of 88 million [10].

3.2.3 Chinacoin

In May 2013 Chinacoin (CNC or CHNCoin) which is a currency based on Litecoin, made its debut into the market. It makes use of the scrypt password-based key derivation function. It has 88 coins per block. The concept of Chinacoin is tailored to generate 462.5 million coins. It's produced in 60-s blocks with 88 coins per block at the moment [9].

A few notable features of CHNCoin include: 60 s block targets, 88 coins per block, subsidy halves in 2628 k blocks (5 years), approximately 462.5 million total coins and 5040 blocks to retarget difficulty [11].

3.2.4 Devcoin

Devcoin can be said to be a bitcoin fork, which was created to inspire various projects of programmers and developers from inception to completion. Within the Devcoin economy, participants such as marketers, developers or even writers earn

Devcoins in ratio to their project development. For instance: the writers will earn Devcoins by writing, developers will earn by developing, administrators earn devotions based on time spend and effort put in to help manage the DevCoin project [12]. It is easy to mine devcoin. Indeed, for every devcoin new block that is generated, 50,000 devcoins are provided in which 45,000 devcoins and 5000 devcoins for developers and miners respectively while writers and other participants do a split of 10/90. On the average, 144 devcoin blocks are generated per day and this implies that in a day, about 7.2 million devcoins are generated [9].

3.2.5 Feathercoin

Feathercoin, which is mined through the use of a scrypt-based hashing algorithm made its debut in April 2013. Feathercoin produces four times the number of coins Litecoin produces [9]. Feather coin is a digital currency that was created in 2013 and it makes use of unique Application-Specific Integrated Circuit (ASIC) resistant algorithm. It uses peer-to-peer technology. It has a block time of 150 s and a coin cap of 336 million. Also, it has a block reward of 200 coins [14, 15].

Feather coin is a unique digital currency with similar monetary properties like those of Bitcoin, Litecoin and other alternative coins. Feathercoin has a higher level of customization in its software development compared to Bitcoin and Litecoin protocols. Indeed, it has been further developed with the intent to expand, experiment, and build onto the blockchain technology in a manner open to all for participation [16].

Feathercoin is based on NeoScrypt and implements many features not seen in the majority of crypto coins. It has open source projects for ATMs, Point of Sales equipment as well as laser etched physical Feathercoins [16].

3.2.6 PPCoin

PPCoin was launched in 2012 to be an energy-efficient crypto-currency and keeps the original bitcoin's properties. It Is mined through the use of proof-of-stake [9]. PPCoin is another peer-to-peer crypto-currency which also originated from Bitcoin. Proof-of-state which replaced the proof-of-work is centered on coin age and which is generated by each node by a hashing scheme. The coin age is described as the currency amount multiplied by holding period. While a form of proof owning the currency refers to "proof-of-stake". For PPCoin, the transaction settlement and block chain history are given additional protection by a centrally broadcasted checkpoint mechanism [24].

3.2.7 Novacoin

Novacoin is both a hybrid scrypt Proof-of-Work (PoW) and a Proof-of-Stake (PoS) based crypto currency. It is identical to PPcoin except that it makes use of a marginally distinct emission model [9]. Proof-of-stake in simple terms refers to the use of currency itself i.e. ownership to achieve certain goals [25]. The mixed Coin-Age/CoinDayWeight approach is used by Novacoin to provide Proofs of the stake. Within Novocain mining and transaction processing are kept on par with proof-of-work with the help of Proof-of-stake. Proof-of-work can be explained as the solution for a difficult mathematical problem. Novacoin utilizes the hashcash method to provide proofs of the work [26].

3.2.8 Groupcoin

Groupcoin was created as a backup plan (backup currency) for Devcoin. It was created to generate 50 coins per block. Groupcoin is another peer-to-peer, open source and also a decentralized digital currency. This provides users the ability to achieve near instant transactions, which are actually free to people across the world. It is quite identical to Bitcoin except that it has a smaller coins supply. It is a proof-of-stake-based crypto currency [9, 17]. The creator of this digital currency had an objective to create a coin that is purely distribution oriented. It was therefore built as a Proof of Stake (PoS) coin that acquires its strength via its distribution [18].

3.2.9 Ixcoin

Ixcoin is a form on digital currency and functions as a low cost peer-to-peer currency, which is also like Bitcoin. Presently, it is not so active and generates 96 ixcoins per block. It is an open source and decentralized digital currency, which was created in 2011 and has a speed of 10 min [9, 19]. iXcoins are referred to as the unit of currency of the iXcoin digital currency, and the shorthand for this is "IXC" which is used to refer to an amount for example: "100 IXC" [20].

3.2.10 Namecoin

Namecoin can be defined as a decentralized peer-to-peer currency and Domain Name System (DNS). DNS is the way domain names are located on the internet and then translated into internet protocol addresses. It works as a handle for an internet address [21]. Namecoin uses technology which is similar to that of Bitcoin. Namecoin also functions in a decentralized manner and operates on the Bitcoin crypto currency [9]. It handles secure recording and transfer of arbitrary names (keys). Being the first fork of Bitcoin it still stands out as one of the most innovative coins. As said above, it has implemented decentralized DNS and merged mining

[22]. In summary, what Namecoin does is to securely record and also transfer arbitary names (keys), assign a value (data) to the names up and transact namecoins. Thus, it helps in webs more resistant to censorship [23].

3.2.11 Terracoin

Terracoin, which had its first mine in October 2012 can be described as a digital currency, which was created to end up with a maximum of 42 million coins. It has a confirmation of transaction time of 2 min. It experienced a few troubles, which includes difficulty in retargeting, hashing power spikes among others and has also experienced some fixes [9]. Terracoin is accessible by anyone anywhere in the world for payments. It is another peer-to-per technology and it operates with no central authority by allowing the management and issuing of money to be collectively carried out by the network. Transactions are broadcasted to the network by the end-user node initiating the payment, verified and grouped together as entities called "blocks" [27]. As we have seen above, this is the process of mining, and "this mining process" can simply be explained as the process of grouping transaction together as blocks involving multiple nodes in the network, then validating the transactions and propagating the created blocks back to the network [27].

A transaction would usually consist of one or several "inputs" (*coins origin*), and one or several "outputs" (*coins destination addresses*). End-user nodes which are configured for mining constantly help in validating the transactions, making sure a given input matches a previous transaction output and then also shielding malicious nodes from double-spending coins. At this point, once validated by "miners" all previously broadcasted transactions gets included in blocks of data and then propagated to all nodes in the network. Those blocks are then aligned together in a chain ("blockchain", as we have seen above) which originates from the very first block that existed referred to as the "genesis block" [27].

3.2.12 Ven

This is a digital currency, which was launched in 2007. It was created for the community within the *hub culture* to enable commerce among its members, international travelers and so on [9]. Actually, the Hub Culture, founded in 2002, is a global collaboration platform, using a rich variety of tools for knowledge sharing. Hub Culture operates within three functions namely: *Knowledge brokerage* (deal services and consulting), *Pavilions* (locations to collaborate) and *Ven* a global digital currency which powers the entire network [28]. Ven leverages on reserve funds in order to minimize inflation risks. A number of banks such as Citibank have purchased Ven for internal use, and the currency is indexed by Thomson Reuters [9].

3.2.13 Zen

Zen can be described as a digital currency that can be used to obtain different items from the "zen" market and pay for particular extended game capabilities [29]. Furthermore, it operates without any central authority and is neither attached to any commodity or any currency. It is anti-bitcoin and publicizes itself as the fixed digital currency. This is due to the fact that it has properties of both centralization and decentralization, but it was created to have the properties of centralization [29, 30]. By having both elements of centralization and decentralization the currency functions by being overseen by a transparent democratically managed organization with an open-book accounting system, which is tasked with the responsibility to regulate the money to prevent deflation or inflation. Membership to this organization is kept open to the public [31].

Actually, Zen was intentionally created to function in a centralized way. It allows agents act as banks, thereby holding accounts on behalf of users; then, users can create personal bank-like accounts and wallets can be stored by third-party apps. Using the Zen APIs gives users the ability to create wallets, issue as well as verify vouchers, check exchange rate and even transfer Zen [31].

3.3 Digital Currencies Versus Distributed Ledger

Digital currencies are becoming more acceptable as an alternative form of money as seen from the growing types and options of digital currencies as seen above. As seen in previous Sections, a digital currency is a web-based medium of exchange with features that bear semblance to physical currencies, which enables on-the-spot transactions and seamless transferals [32]. Today, the bulk of conventional money exists as e-records in banks. Accordingly, it could be implied that our progressively "cashless societies" provides for the conversion of all currencies into e-moneys [32]. In the era when barter system was the medium of exchange for goods and services, it became more difficult to keep track of debts. Then, the ledger has been introduced as a more efficient way of keeping track of debts with the use of a ledger. Indeed, the ledger was a physical book that kept detailed records of debts. Over the years, the ledger has evolved into an electronic form [33].

Furthermore, in recent years, advancements in payment technologies have emerged with the aim of making payments easily available to a mixed set of users through decentralized structures rather than a central authority: *distributed ledger technology*. By implication, digital currencies such as Bitcoin are neither run by a sole authority or organization that oversees, validates and authorizes transactions and controls the flow of money [34]. In a nutshell, a digital currency scheme is an embodiment of a new currency and a new payment system that is decentralized. The scheme operates a publicly visible ledger, which is accessed across a computing network.

However, in principle, a digital currency does not exist in a vacuum but is underpinned by distributed ledger technology through which diverse financial instruments can be equipped and processed on a universal decentralized peer-to-peer system. Distributed ledgers are basically e-records of who-owns-what. However, in contrast to conventional database technology, there is neither a central control over it, nor a central data warehouse. This is a pivotal innovation as it enables payment systems to run exclusively, without "middlemen" [35]. To this end, the distributed ledger technology is considered as a means to establish safety measures that were rife in liquid markets. Hence, there is a rapidly growing interest in the use of distributed ledger technology with the recognition of its significance in the establishment of trusted networks to enable swift and cost-effective trade and manage financial transactions [36].

One of the many advantages of using digital currencies stems from the fact that the transfer of money between financial institutions is completely avoided, as digital currencies are instead dependent on the transference of encryptions across the Internet. This is arguably faster, more secure and economical than conventional payment systems, in addition to being able to make payments through an e-wallet from any device and location [35]. E-wallet (*electronic wallet*) functions by supporting automated handling of customer information and associated transactions. For example, e-wallet can be used to store personal information on a cloud platform that facilitates easy integration access [37]. Information collected from a publication on the views of the benefits of digital currencies in the UK suggests that cheaper transaction fees and speedier processing times are major advantages of this technology [35].

Likewise, digital currencies center on a decentralized payment system, without middlemen thereby offering more security and privacy as opposed to bankcards for example, that are tied to customers' bank account. Besides, digital currencies cannot be faked and are easier to track owing to the underpinning digital ledger technology.

As also noted in previous sections, one common feature of cryptocurrency is "mining". Mining refers to the use of high computational power to process transactions of a cryptocurrency blockchain in order to gain reward for the effort. This computational power is the one of CPU processing or GPU processing. Thus, "miners" payment comes as a result of successful computation [38]. Indeed, miners are individuals who set out their computer space and time as a form of investment to sorting through data blocks. When their mining resolves the right "hash" (a complex mathematical formula puzzle that verifies transactions and also creates new currency), they submit the solution to the currency issuer. Upon proper verification of the hash, the miners receive a reward of a specific number of coins [39].

3.4 Digital Currencies Advantages, Limitations, and Risks

One of the profound advantages of digital currencies is that it offers a cheaper value for exchanges and transactions than other traditional currencies. For instance, to transfers funds from one for traditional currency to another would normally incur an exchange rate cost, which could be a loss. This is not so which digital currencies, funds can be transferred between several accounts without any transactional cost [40]. When considering moving money internationally such transactions usually take time (in most cases a number of days) and the fact that it attracts fees makes it expensive for regular customers handling small transactions: these issues create even a more valid option for customers to engage with digital currencies [41]. Further advantages are the ease of transaction as well as the possibility of earning good income if the value of digital currencies appreciates [40].

Actually, the fact that digital currencies are subject to lesser regulatory influence makes it a very attractive option for transaction, but also a source of potential risks as we are going to see in what follows. Yet, while digital currencies are beneficial and seemingly invaluable, some limitations exist. Owing to the fact that digital currencies are stored in e-wallets, users such as consumers and merchants are open to fraud and hacking. Likewise, the unstable price of digital currencies leaves users exposed to loss of value of the currency. Unfortunately, there are currently no measures in place to help users recover lost funds [35].

Moreover, the level of anonymity may be instrumental to their use in criminal and fraudulent activities as transactions are carried out without any monitoring financial systems. Research suggests that the major crime risks that stem from the use of digital currencies include fraud, money laundering, buying of illicit goods and services; anonymous extortion and terrorist financing [35]. Limitations of digital currencies can be summarized around three issues namely:

- Risk of abuse
- Exchange rate fluctuations and
- Consumer Protection

Thus, the unique properties of digital currencies make it easily susceptible to abuse. Criminals and their associates who engage in suspect businesses can very easily take advantage of the anonymity associated with digital currency to continue to carry out their shady business. They can conveniently have reliable banking/ transaction facilities without the hassle of providing identifying information [35]. In addition to this, the fluctuations in exchange rate represent another challenge to the adoption and transaction power of digital currencies. It was reported that during the first few years of the introduction of Bitcoin the exchange rate fluctuated drastically between $5 and $15, it has however been stable since the start of the year 2013 [35]. Lastly, the lack of regulatory control over digital currencies poses a huge threat particularly to consumers. Unlike physical transactions, digital transactions are designed to be irreversible hence in the event of any financial misappropriations; victims are left with no possibility of getting their monies back. It is only a matter of time before hackers will begin to target huge digital currency accounts [35].

Thus, however digital currencies have the capability to potentially lead to an improvement in the financial system by stepping down the cost of payment-transactions for small businesses, consumers and nonprofits, it is critical that

Digital-Currency firms must outline plans, e.g., for mitigating Anti Money Laundering (AML) risk [42]. A few things to consider while addressing AML risks include:

- Create strong AML programs.
- Work hand-in-hand with other digital-currency firms so as to enable a good information-sharing mechanism on user identities in a way that transactions remain private but no longer anonymous.
- Acquire licenses from state regulators of money transmitters and also register with institutions such as, e.g., FinCen (a bureau of the U.S. Department of the Treasury in charge of the safeguard of the financial system from illicit use).

Yet, industry wide AML standards should be established, and then over time it will be wise to have a self-regulatory organization to oversee industry adherence to standards. Due diligence will need to be performed by banks providing services to digital-currency firms including evaluating the firm's AML controls. On the other hand, Digital currency firms should [42]:

- Have a clear strategy on how to convince customers of the security of all the firms' services and also the currency.
- Anticipate any action made by securities and derivatives regulators towards treating of digital currencies.

Having discussed the advantages and limitations of digital currencies, it is necessary to discuss how improvements can be made in the regulatory aspect of digital currencies. Two regulatory influences that have been identified include consumer protection laws and possible limitation of criminal activities that can likely plague digital transactions. It is envisaged that in order to encourage consumers in the use of digital currencies, consumers have to be assured of the safety of their monies [40]. It is also expected that in order to make the use of digital currencies more attractive to consumers, there need to be more cooperation between digital currency operators and the government to reduce criminal activities. Seeing that the original of digital currency and transactions fosters anonymity, which in turn provides criminals with the much need cover for activities, the cooperation of the government and operators in this regard would be greatly impactful [40].

3.5 Case Studies

In this section it will be good to look at two prominent types of digital currency schemes: Linden dollars (*The second life scheme*) and Bitcoin.

Leveraging on the large appetite for gaming, CEO Philip Rosedale created a virtual community under the umbrella Linden Research Inc. The multiplayer online role-playing game was lunched in June 2003, it gives users the ability to create 3D virtual objects. A user will initially need to install software on its computer and then create a free second life account which gives them access to the virtual world. Membership options are in different categories—per month, quarterly or yearly, which attracts a fee, e.g., of USD9.95, USD22.50 and USD72. In the year 2011, over 26 million recorded users were registered in the community. Once resident users are logged in, they can take on any form they choose like animals, humans, vegetable, their real life image or a combination of options etc. Residents have the ability to earn money, sell assets or even win prizes in events. An automatic grant of 300 Linden dollars is paid to avatar accounts belonging to premium members weekly [32].

Thus, the Linden Dollar is a virtual currency that can be purchased with PayPal or a credit card through Linden Lab's currency brokerage. It can be converted back to real money and has been observed to be stable in value "L$260 = USD1". Yet, *Second Life* is not just an online game, most companies are developing their virtual presence for merchandising their goods, the real estate market for instance has grown and has been profitable etc. [32]. The economy in the second life is similar to any other economy in the world, however it is distinct in three ways:

- It is self-sufficient i.e. no external interactions with the outside world
- Focused on the virtual world i.e. virtual goods and services
- Exists only within the Linden Lab's infrastructure

Point of Attention CEO Philip Rosedale's idea of creating the virtual community also created the market and environment to use the Linden dollars. In the second life scheme, for instance, users can interact with each other, have meetings, buy virtual houses, purchase a car, and basically have interactions like in everyday life; whereas they use the virtual currency for all the transactions and dealings.

Consider now the case of Bitcoin, which currently stands out as one of the most prominent of the digital currencies. It was created by a Japanese programmer known under the pseudonym of Satoshi Nakamoto in 2009 and it functions on a peer-to-peer network. The Bitcoin scheme holds an updated database of providers (organizations) that offer goods (e.g., clothing and accessories, books, electronic gadgets, etc.) and businesses that accept Bitcoin as a payment form [32].

With Bitcoin, the exchange rate is influenced by the supply and demand within the market. Mt.Gox is one of several exchange platform which avails users the service of changing from US dollars to Bitcoin and vice versa. Bitcoin doesn't require a central clearing house, also there is no central authority that handles money supply. However money supply is achieved with a specific type of "mining "activity. A Bitcoin first time user simply needs to download the free open-source software. Any money purchased by the user is then stored on the users computer within a digital wallet. The risk level with this is very high because if proper

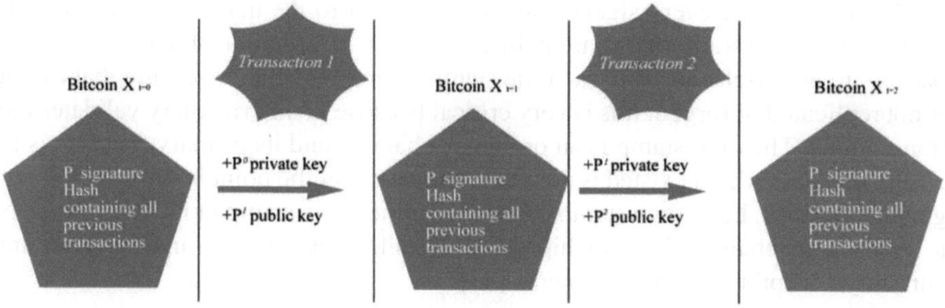

Fig. 3.1 Chain of Bitcoin transactions, adapted from Europe Central Bank [32]

security measures are not in place such as anti-virus and periodic backup all the information can be lost. Yet, as said above, there are numerous benefits that can be highlighted with Bitcoin such as [32]:

- Bitcoins are sent from one computer to another because transactions are anonymous.
- Transactions can be differentiated by multiple Bitcoin addresses.
- The delay observed during a transaction is highly reduced and cheaper than traditional payment methods.
- No banking fee is charged and very low transaction fees are obtained if any exist.

Furthermore, Bitcoin and its supporters argue the following:

- Bitcoin is perceived to be instrumental to stopping the monopoly of central banks in issuance of money.
- Hold strong views against current fractional-reserve banking system.
- Strongly opine that the former gold standard birthed the Bitcoin scheme.

Figure 3.1 shows a chain of Bitcoin transactions, following a same Bitcoin at different points in time. The transaction is initiated by future owner P^1 sending his public key to original owner P^0. Then the owner makes a transfer of the Bitcoins by digitally signing a *hash* of the former transaction and the public key of the future owner. Each Bitcoin holds the entire history of the transactions, while transfers between owners become part of the code. The hash value can be described has the value which was returned by the algorithm which maps the sets of data to smaller sets of a fixed length. The Bitcoin is then stored allowing only the new owner access to spend it.

Point of Attention Bitcoin is accessible globally and can be used to transact as a currency for the exchange of goods and services physically or even virtually, thereby standing as a competitive substitute for typical currencies like the US dollar or Euro.

Considering that every signed transaction is sent to the network, this is a clear indication that all transactions are public; however, information about the involved parties are not disclosed. Thus, a "time stamp" is implemented to ensure that a coin is not replicated or forged: this is very critical because no intermediary validates the transactions. The time stamp is an online mechanism and its primary function is to ensure that data which existed is not altered since a specific point in time, in order to get into the hash. Each time stamp carries its former time stamp in its hash, which is a build up of chains of ownership. Major retailers like Target and Amazon are currently accepting Bitcoin payments [43].

3.6 Summary

This Chapter has explored the concept of Digital currencies and distributed ledger. Digital currencies have become the alternative medium of exchange and are a true reflection of innovations in payment systems. While retaining the functions of money—a store of value, a unit of account, and a medium of exchange—these new Digital currencies have incorporated the concept of a 'distributed ledger' which allows a digital currency to function in a decentralized payment system. Furthermore, the cases of Linden dollars (within the second life scheme) and Bitcoin have been discussed as examples digital currencies use.

Notwithstanding the risks associated to their unique characteristics, the benefits associated to Digital currencies make them potentially have a far-reaching spread from the private to public sector and even organizations such as, e.g., charities [44]. However there is a school of thought that most digital currencies are unlikely to replace traditional payment systems in any significant way, it is also believed that majority of the digital currency platforms introduce their currencies to boost and promote their business model and increase profits [45]. Consequently the online industry will continue to evolve and lead to development of innovative products e.g. new digital currencies.

References

1. Hoelscher JL (2014) Digital currency risks. Intern Audit 71:24–25
2. Ali R, Barrdear J, Clews R, Southgate J (2014) Innovations in payment technologies and the emergence of digital currencies. Bank Engl Q Bull Q3:262–276
3. Moffatt M (2015) What is money? About education. http://economics.about.com/od/termsbeginningwithm/g/money.htm. Accessed 14 Oct 2015
4. The Economist (2014) Why Bitcoin may herald a new era in finance. The Economist http://www.economistinsights.com/technology-innovation/analysis/money-no-middleman/tab/1. Accessed 28 Jul 2015
5. Oberhauser A (2014) Decentralized public ledger as enabler for the gift economy at scale (Literature Study). https://www.alex-oberhauser.com/papers/blockchain_gift_economy.pdf. Accessed 19 February 2016

6. Raj Samani E (2013) Digital laundry: an analysis of online currencies, and their use in cybercrime. McAfee Labs, Beaverton
7. CoinPursuit (2014) What is digital currency mining? CoinPursuit. https://www.coinpursuit.com/articles/what-is-digital-currency-mining.137/. Accessed 19 Aug 2015
8. BitcoinWiki Block chain (2015). https://en.bitcoin.it/wiki/Block_chain. Accessed 25 Oct 2015
9. Siluk S (2013) What other digital currencies are there? CoinDesk. http://www.coindesk.com/what-other-digital-currencies-are-there/
10. CryptoSource (2015) Crypto source. CryptoSource. http://cryptosource.org/coins/alt-coins-other/bbqcoin-bqc/. Accessed 5 Aug 2015
11. Criptomonedas.tel CHINACOIN (CNC). http://chinacoin.criptomonedas.tel/. Accessed 26 Oct 2015
12. Belovachap (2014) Devcoin Official Site. http://www.devtome.com/doku.php?id=devcoin. Accessed 19 Aug 2015
13. Litcoin (2014) What is Litecoin? https://litecoin.org/. Accessed 26 Oct 2015
14. CryptoSource (2015) Feathercoin. CryptoSource. http://cryptosource.org/coins/alt-coins-other/feathercoin-ftc/. Accessed 5 Aug 2015
15. Feathercoin (2015) An Internet currency free from any central bank or institution. Feathercoin. https://www.feathercoin.com. Accessed 5 Aug 2015
16. Feathercoin (2015) About feathercoin. https://www.feathercoin.com/about/. Accessed 26 Oct 2015
17. Groupcoin (2014) Groupcoin. http://groupcoin.com. Accessed 5 Aug 2015
18. Cryptocointalk (2015) GroupCoin GPC information. https://cryptocointalk.com/topic/13968-groupcoin-gpc-information/. Accessed 28 Oct 2015
19. Coinwik (2015) IxCoin. Coinwik. http://coinwik.org/IxCoin. Accessed 5 Aug 2015
20. Cryptocointalk (2015) IxCoin IXC information. https://cryptocointalk.com/topic/124-ixcoin-ixc-information/
21. TechTarget (2015) Domain name system (DNS) definition. http://searchnetworking.techtarget.com/definition/domain-name-system. Accessed 28 Oct 2015
22. Namecoin (2015) A trust anchor for the Internet. Namecoin. https://namecoin.info. Accessed 5 Aug 2015
23. Namecoin (2015) Freedom of information. https://namecoin.info/. Accessed 28 Oct 2015
24. King S, Nadal S (2012) PPCoin: peer-to-peer crypto-currency with proof-of-stake. Ppcoin.Org
25. GitHub_Inc (2015) Proof of stake. https://github.com/novacoin-project/novacoin/wiki/Proof-of-stake. Accessed 28 Oct 2015
26. GitHub_Inc (2015) Proof of work. https://github.com/novacoin-project/novacoin/wiki/Proof-of-work. Accessed 28 Oct 2015
27. Terracoin (2013) Terracoin. http://terracoin.sourceforge.net/about.html. Accessed 30 Oct 2015
28. Hub_culture (2002) Hub culture. https://hubculture.com/groups/hub/projects/62/wiki/. Accessed 30 Oct 2015
29. Ziff Davis (2014) Zen. Ziff Davis, LLC. http://www.ign.com/wikis/neverwinter/Zen. Accessed 10 Nov 2015
30. Truong A (2013) Zen – Bitcoin's polar opposite. CoinDesk. http://www.coindesk.com/zen-bitcoins-polar-opposite/. Accessed 5 Aug 2015
31. CoinDesk (2015) Zen – Bitcoin's polar opposite. http://www.coindesk.com/zen-bitcoins-polar-opposite/. Accessed 30 Oct 2015
32. Europe Central Bank (2012) Virtual currency schemes. Europe Central Bank 21. ISBN 978-92-899-0862-7
33. Bitcoin_coin_live (2015) History of Money. http://bitcoinpricelive.com/history-of-money/. Accessed 30 Oct 2015
34. The Economist (2011) Virtual currency bits and bob. The Economist. http://www.economist.com/blogs/babbage/2011/06/virtual-currency. Accessed 10 Nov 2015

35. HM Treasury (2015) Digital currencies: call for information. Government of UK. https://www.gov.uk/government/consultations/digital-currencies-call-for-information/digital-currencies-call-for-information. Accessed 5 Aug 2015
36. Symbiont MS (2015) Distributed ledgers: a FinTech innovation. Markets Media. http://marketsmedia.com/distributed-ledgers-a-fintech-innovation/. Accessed 28 Jul 2015
37. Al-fedaghi SS, Taha MM (2006) Personal information eWallet. In: IEEE international conference on systems, man, cybernetics, pp 2855–2862
38. Ahamad S, Nair M, Varghese B (2013) A survey on crypto currencies. In: Proceedings of international conference on advances in computer science, AETACS, pp 42–48
39. CoinPursuit (2014) What is digital currency mining? https://www.coinpursuit.com/articles/what-is-digital-currency-mining.137/. Accessed 30 Oct 2015
40. Dwyer G (2015) The Economics of Bitcoin and similar private digital currencies. J Financ Stab 17:81–91. doi:10.1016/j.jfs.2014.11.006
41. Shin L (2014) Susan Athey on how digital currency could transform our lives. Forbes. http://www.forbes.com/sites/laurashin/2014/11/24/susan-athey-on-how-digital-currency-could-transform-our-lives/. Accessed 7 Aug 2015
42. Shapiro A (2013) The way forward for digital currencies. Promontory sightlines infocus, pp 1–12
43. SlotoBit (2015) Companies that use bitcoin. http://carnavalcasinos.com/companies-that-use-bitcoin. Accessed 30 Oct 2015
44. Dodgson M, Gann D, Wladawsky-Berger I, Sultan N, George G (2015) Managing digital money. Acad Manag J 58:325–333
45. Fung B, Halaburda H (2014) Understanding platform-based digital currencies. Bank Canada Rev (Spring):12–20

Data Visualization

4

Abstract

Nowadays, different types of technologies are driving an exponential increase in the amount and complexity of transactional and operational data. Additionally, millions of networked sensors embedded in physical devices such as mobile phones, smart energy meters, automobiles, and machines in the factories are sensing, creating, and communicating the data to servers and data warehouses. The challenge now is how to make sense of all these collected data and how to make the decision making process easier for users within organizations. This is where data visualization is increasingly taking its rightful place as an important part of the business intelligence systems. Data visualization enables decision makers to examine large amount of data and to communicate and share ideas more efficiently. Moreover, interactive data visualization provides more capabilities than static graphs by allowing managers who are seeking more details to drill down into charts and graphs to gain better understanding of the data. Hence, many industries have started to utilize data visualization to achieve the insights they strive for. This chapter will illustrate and discuss the latest trends in data visualization as well as its applications in different industries.

4.1 Introduction

The constant increase in the amount of data that is generated from various resources has provoked researchers from different backgrounds to understand it, define it, and to develop technologies that are capable to make use of such an explosion of data. This is especially recognizable in the research of computer science, where researchers in this field are trying to improve how to visualize large sets of data by presenting them in a graphical format, which makes it easier and quicker for managers and data scientists to understand data and obtain useful information. Consequently, data visualization tools, which enable decision makers to (i) find relations and connection between various variables, (ii) discover patterns, (iii)

V. Morabito, *The Future of Digital Business Innovation*,
DOI 10.1007/978-3-319-26874-3_4

visualize analytical results, and (iv) communicate these findings, are of major interest in every day's successful business. It is even more important for those tools aimed to enable the prediction of future market trends and customers' behaviors. Actually, visual display of data makes the whole process of data analytics a lot easier and less complicated, adding an extra dimension to our understanding of data.

The importance of data visualization tools originates from the fact that it is usually considered easier and faster for the human brain to conclude useful insights when numbers are portrayed in graphs and charts in comparison to lengthy spreadsheets with thousands of rows and tens if not hundreds of variables [1]. In other words, data visualization allows users to discover interesting facts that are not obvious when there is just a collection of numbers. This is particularly true and important when patterns can be detected quickly while analyzing very large volumes of data.

Consequently, data visualization provides several opportunities for today's competitive businesses. For example, it enables analysts to discover the weak points that need improvements in the industry. Also, it helps to understand the dynamics that affect customers' behavior. Additional examples of the advantages that data visualization delivers are to help with the positioning of products in the market, to predict sales forecasts, and to be able to determine the areas that allow the business to increase profits and to diminish expenses.

4.2 The Power of Data Visualization

It is acceptable that having more information is influential to the quality of the decisions we make, however, the more data is generated, the more the complexity it causes for communicating the desired results. Therefore, the explosion of data described above poses an additional challenge to the communication of the analyses' results and the information concluded. This is where data visualization plays an important role in communicating and sharing the discovered facts and ideas between analysts and managers. In the work of Pandey et al. [2], the authors studied the impact of charts on communicating the required results, and they discovered that graphs could have high persuasion power in comparison to tables when they are used as means of sharing findings.

However, in such a dynamic world that we live in, static diagrams or graphs have several limitations. One example of these restrictions is the constant need and dependency on data specialists to continuously update the static values on the charts to match latest numbers. Another example is when graphs are loaded with huge volume of information to the extent that they are hard to interpret and understand. Consequently, the necessity for more advanced visualization has emerged [3]. Therefore, the complexity and the velocity of the generated data require visualization tools that can produce interactive reports and dashboards.

4.2.1 Interactive Data Visualization

Interactive data visualization tools are computer enhanced systems that give the power for the users to not only visualize and present information, but also, to select specific parts of the graphs to view in more details, update the contents of the charts simultaneously with live data, examine relations between different variables, discover new trends and patterns in the data, and change presentation formats as needed [4]. In simple words, interactive data visualization tools provide the means to explore the data by interacting and manipulating charts or graphs.

Moreover, interactive data visualization tools can empower non-statisticians as well as users not acquainted with technical issues of data management to produce productive reports. Actually, users can replace complicated SQL code with simple clicks such as zoom, resize, align, drag and drop graphics to produce the same results. Consequently, non-technical business users can leverage the advantages of such systems to focus on the interesting and important information. They can drill down and up to better understand business data and make informed strategic decisions [3]. The ease of use of the interactive data visualization systems enables managers and executives at the organization to have meaningful data that can be shared by publishing dashboard via emails. Few [5], for example, highlights that interactive visual analysis, allows the simultaneous presentation of several graphs that are organized together for easier comparison. Such arrangement provides significant expansion to data visualization which is reflected by the increased number of variables or dimensions that can be examined together, compared and associated.

The advantages of interactive visualization mentioned above are based on the flexibility of the tools that allow different kinds of interactions and distortions. The following categories have been identified [6]:

- ***Dynamic projections***: This category encompasses projections driven randomly for the purpose of exploring a multidimensional data set.
- ***Interactive filtering***: This category allows user partitions by restricting data displayed and by highlighting specific subsets of the data.
- ***Interactive zooming***: This category provides the users with the ability to view the data in multiple resolutions and provides details about the data in higher level zoom.
- ***Interactive distortion***: This category involves showing specific areas of data in greater detail while other areas are provided with less detail.
- ***Interactive linking and brushing***: This category involves the combination of multiple visualization methods to overcome the failure of single methods. Actually, a change is made to the visualization by linking subsets of points in different projections.

Thus, interactive data visualization delivers several benefits such as the improved collaboration, better insights and the ability to manipulate data as needed.

These capabilities are only possible thanks to the recent and improved visualization techniques and algorithms that will be discussed in the following sections.

4.3 Data Visualization: The State of the Art

The advancements in data visualization depend on the new algorithms that support the different display types of data [1, 36]. However, issues like proximity measurements, overlap of interests, rendering resolutions, scale of axis, colors and parameters weights are of important architectural concerns for the success of visualization [5]. Figure 4.1, illustrates a very good example for demonstrating different kinds of visualizations for the same data, in which four different types of maps represent the support for United States presidential candidates Bush and Kerry during their campaign in 2004. The presentations in the Fig. 4.1 vary from

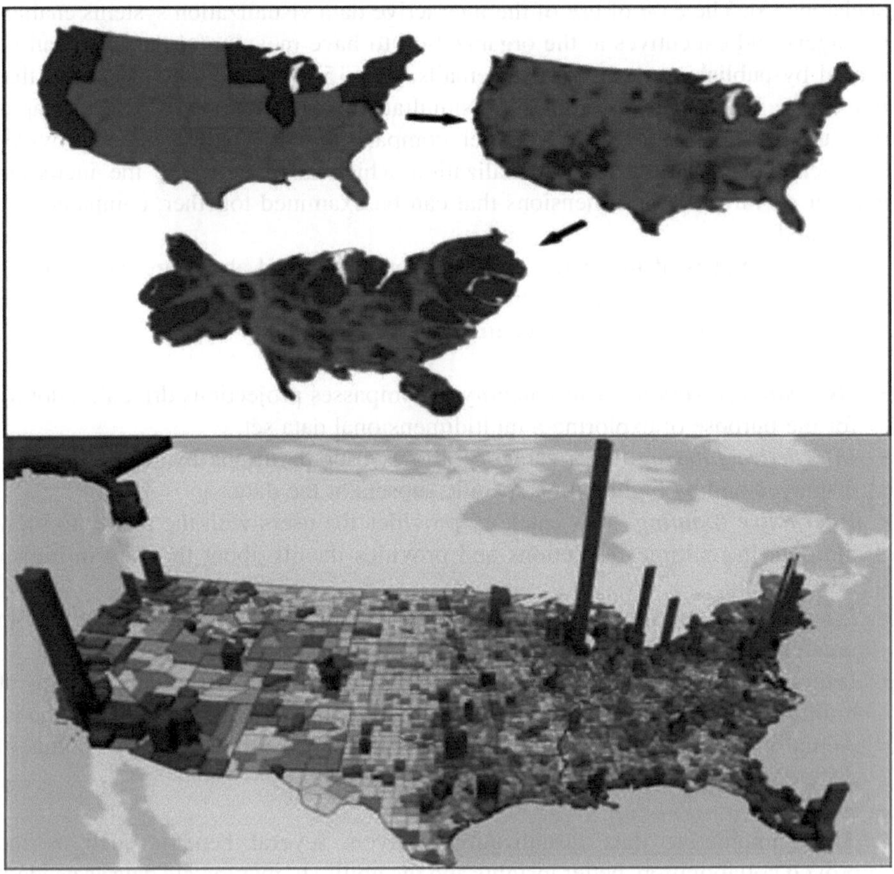

Fig. 4.1 Four visualizations of the same elections data, adapted from [1]

the state level to the country level. However, users can further manipulate these figures by scaling the map up and down in order to depict realistic results or by adding an additional axis or dimension that could reflect the number of voters per county [1].

These manipulations as well as the different styles of charts can only happen because of the progress in the algorithms that enable the interactivity in the visualizations. Businesses can benefit from the ability to manipulate and interact directly with the data in order to have actionable insights in contrast with one-dimensional tables and charts that can only be "viewed".

Engaging executives with data visualization can open up new ways of looking at business and operational data, enabling senior management to scale new heights in business performance while enabling a much broader audience of analytics users in the quest for greater performance. Yet, the progress mentioned here depend on the visualization techniques that are explained in the following Section.

4.4 Visualization Techniques

The different categories of data require different visualization techniques. These techniques are used along with multiple interaction and distortion methods to promote visualization manipulation [6]. Furthermore, the visualization techniques can be classified into the following types:

- ***Standard displays***: Standard displays include *x-y* plots or *x-y-z* plots which are presented in 2D and 3D. These displays also include bar charts, line graphs and pie charts [6].
- ***Geometrically transformed displays***: Geometrically transformed displays play a vital role in the transformation of multidimensional data. These displays use exploratory statistics including scatterplot matrices, prosecution views, parallel coordinates and hyper-slices [7].
- ***Iconic display***: Iconic display is a type of visualization method where the use of symbols and icons is vital in mapping an attribute of a multidimensional data set. This attribute is then mapped to the attributes of an icon using colors, geometric shapes, faces and sticks [6].
- ***Dense pixel displays***: Dense pixel displays help in mapping every dimension to colored pixels and grouping these pixels into different areas. Dense pixel displays are found to make use of one pixel per data value to promote presentation of large volumes of data [6].
- ***Stacked display***: According to [6], staked displays make use of embedding one coordinate system in another. In this method, an outer coordinate system is formed, within which other attributes are embedded. A good example of stacked displays is the dimensional stacked displays [8].

The aforementioned techniques form the backbone for all data visualization methods and trends. The following part will explain five important examples of the new trends in interactive data visualization [1]. Nevertheless, there are many other methods that can be used to present and communicate data in order to conclude information. That includes funnel chart, scatter plot, pie chart bar graph and bubble chart.

4.4.1 Radial and Hyperbolic Tree

We now consider radial and hyperbolic tree, which are two data representations that aim to enable the user, manger or analyst to explore and easily understand the context of large related data sets by focusing on the center of the hierarchy, but with the ability to interactively change the focus between the nodes in the center and the surroundings [1]. These data representations can be used in a business context as good visualization techniques that can support statistical treatment of data. Also, they can be used as communication tools to report insights that inform decisions. For example, managers can use these representations in order to visualize products and sub -products related to specific customer.

In radial tree, when the user changes the focus from one node to another, the tree tries to equally split the rest of the branches from the chosen node and collapses the successive layers as possible as displayed in Figs. 4.2 and 4.3, which are created using the demo section of an online interactive data visualization toolkit that can be accessed at http://philogb.github.io/jit/, and illustrate the connections between people and other people or objects.

In Fig. 4.2, which shows connections for the US rock band Pearl Jam, it can be seen how the node on the inner circle (*Jack Irons*) is connected to the node in the center (*Pearl Jam*), while in Fig. 4.3 it can be noticed how the connections have rearranged themselves in order to project the focus on the node (*Jack Irons*) that reallocated to the center and its branches have reallocated to the inner circle.

On the contrary, the hyperbolic trees would reallocate the branches on the Euclidean plane by using a nonlinear focusing procedure [1] as displayed Figs. 4.4 and 4.5, which are developed using the same website used for Figs. 4.2 and 4.3, while focusing on connections related to the US rock band Nine Inch Nails.

In Fig. 4.4, it can be seen how the node on the inner circle (*Nine Inch Nails*) is connected to the node in the center (*Danny Lohner*), while in Fig. 4.5 it can be noticed how the connections have rearranged themselves in order to project the focus on the node (*Danny Lohner*) that reallocated to the center, while its branches have reallocated to the outer circle.

4.4.2 Treemaps

Another way to display large collections of quantitative data in a limited area such computer screen or printed report is by using a Treemaps visualization technique [5]. In this type of visualization, the center of the data is broken up into several nested colored blocks that exemplify the parent-child relationship while using space

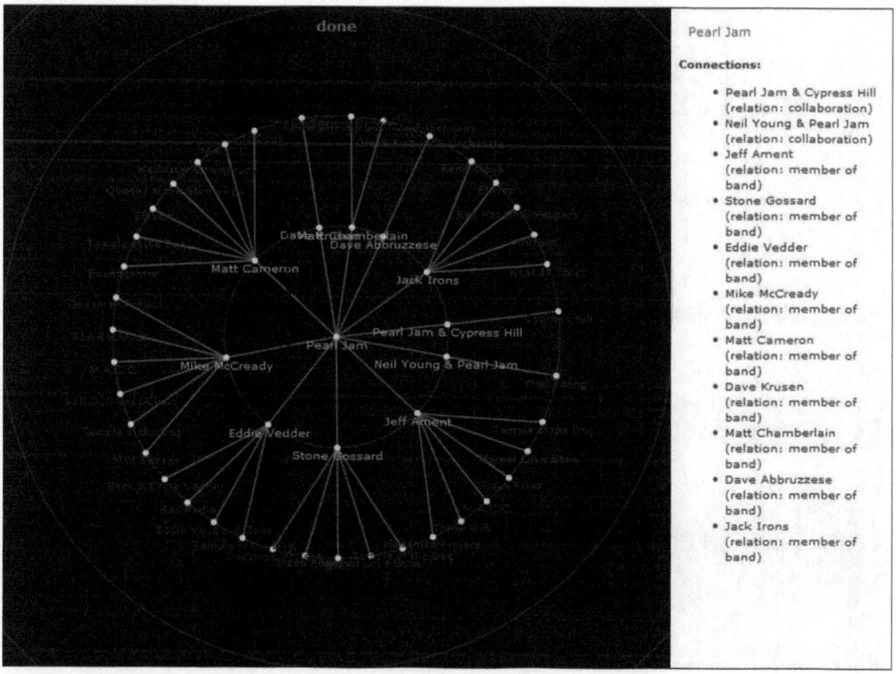

Fig. 4.2 Radial tree with the focus on the node in the center

filling algorithms to fill in empty areas [1]. With this method, correlated color and size measurements play an important role to portray different kinds of data as displayed in Fig. 4.6, which is created on Tableau data visualization software using superstore sample data, and illustrates an example of the superstore sales categories and shipping types. It can be seen in Fig. 4.6 how the different rectangles sizes depict different sales amounts, while different colors portray various shipping methods. Also, it can be noticed how by hovering the mouse on one of the categories, the user can view the additional information about that category.

4.4.3 Geo-spatial Visualization

The esteem for this type of data presentation stems from the popularity of Google Earth and similar web services that provide geographical related information. Geo-spatial visualization refers to a set of tools and techniques supporting geospatial data analysis through the use of interactive visualization. For example, businesses started to take advantage of such models to depict sales numbers categorized by the sales area [5]. Customer-oriented services that are based on the consumers' post codes are also used.

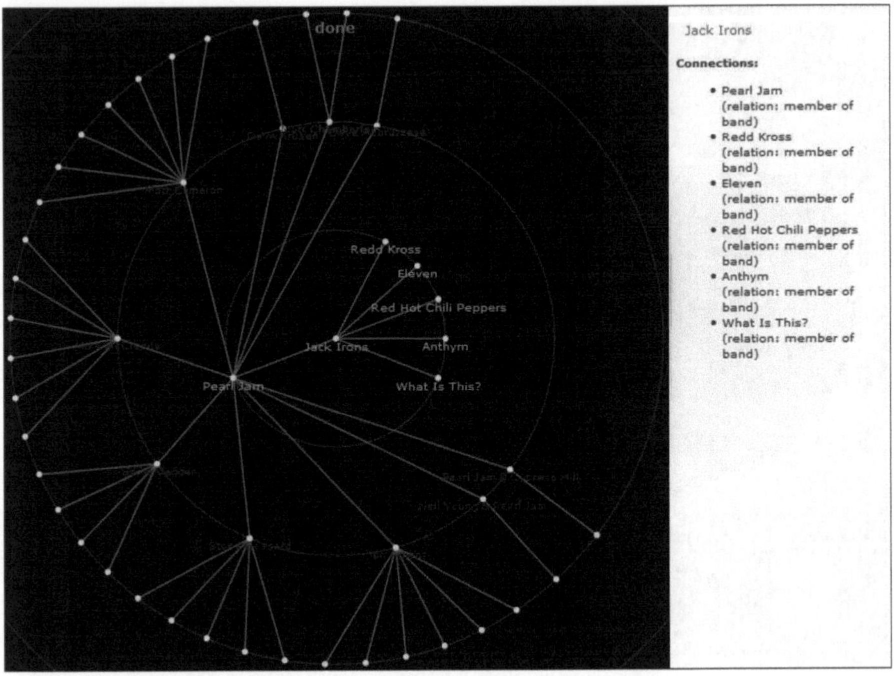

Fig. 4.3 Radial tree with the focus on a surrounding node

4.4.4 Animated Data Visualization

Animations provide means to convey changes over time, transitions between states, or the unfolding of a narrative. Through animations we can show processes, tell stories and evoke emotions where it is difficult or impossible with static graphics and text alone. However, it is important to be careful not to distort the data or introduce unnecessary complexity. This visualization technique combines the beauty of a photo with the wonder of a film. It is a new trend in business intelligence for displaying information, in which moving objects represent the changes of the numbers, such as sales figures, over a period of time or to illustrate live variations or fluctuations of numbers such as stocks' prices [5]. This is particularly important when the focus is on time-based data. For example, for portraying the changes in the correlation over the time between the numbers related to marketing campaign and the resulting sales figures. In such situation, the best way is to use animated scatterplot visualization.

4.4.5 Networks Visualization

This type of visualization is concerned with portraying relationships between different entities and it started to take a lot of attention with the spread of social

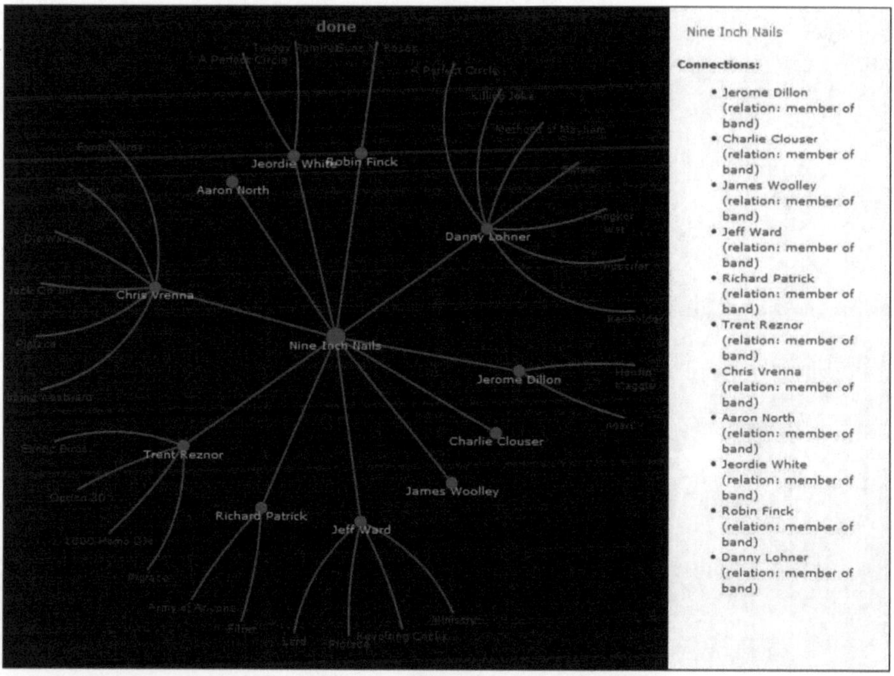

Fig. 4.4 Hyperbolic tree with the focus on the node in the center

networks. One example is to depict the relations between people in a social network, which can help in studying interactions patterns or to portray how people communicate within companies by examining their emails. Another example is to illustrate websites' communications dependencies [5]. Figure 4.7, which is also created on Tableau by the author, shows a random example of the network visualization and the relationships between groups of people. Networks visualization provides methods to identify the dynamics of the network, which helps to understand the spread of information and people thoughts as well as the sources of news and ideas.

Such method of visualization provides many opportunities for businesses as it can be used to identify the people who can influence others with their ideas or to predict customers' expectations and requirements. Also, it can be used in the security domain to discover and predict dangerous activities by monitoring the behaviors of suspect who are in the same network [9].

4.5 Applications of Data Visualization in Industry

In today's competitive market, data analysts are becoming of big value for several industries since they are the people that can detect weak areas in the business and promote the profitable sectors [3, 10]. However, these data experts need powerful

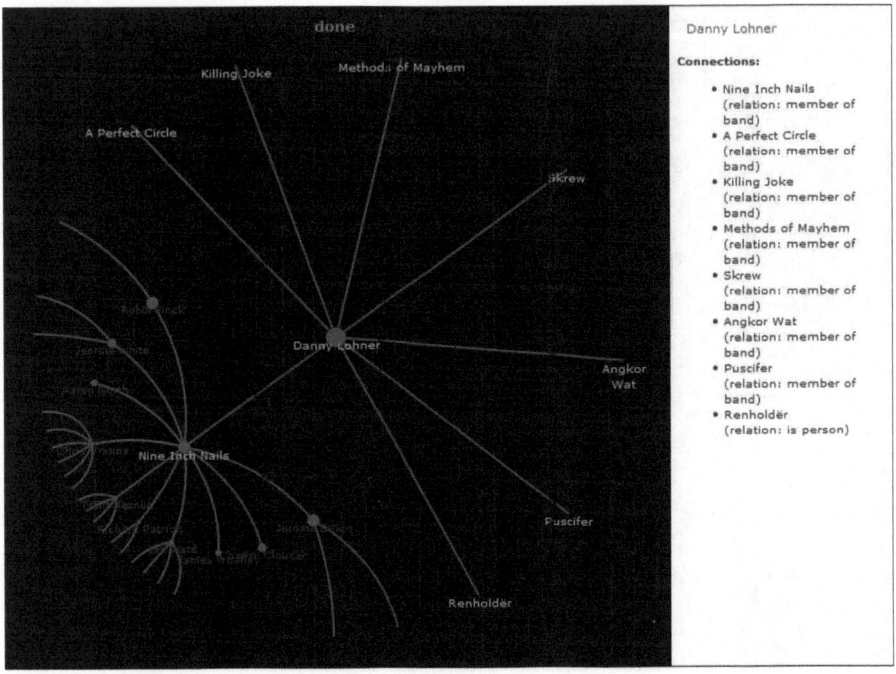

Fig. 4.5 Hyperbolic tree with the focus on a surrounding node

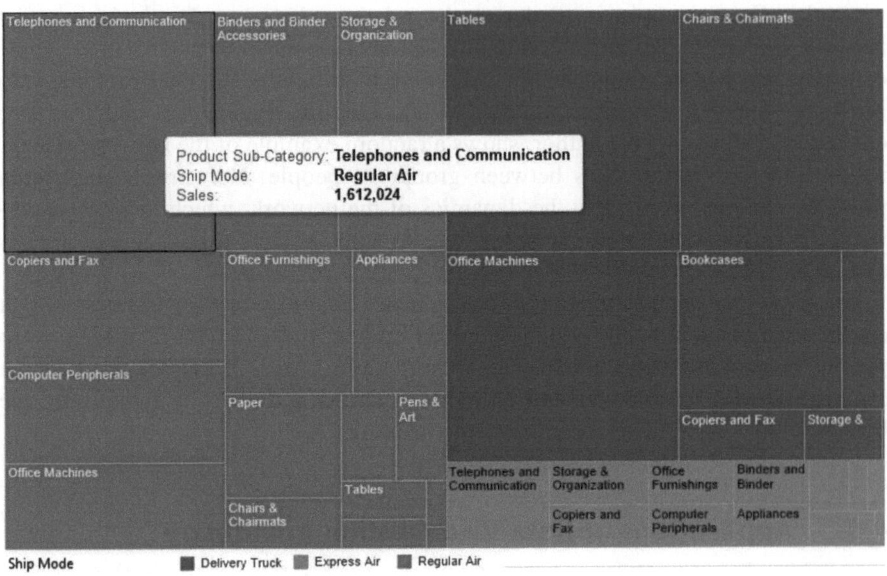

Fig. 4.6 Example of Treemap for products export category

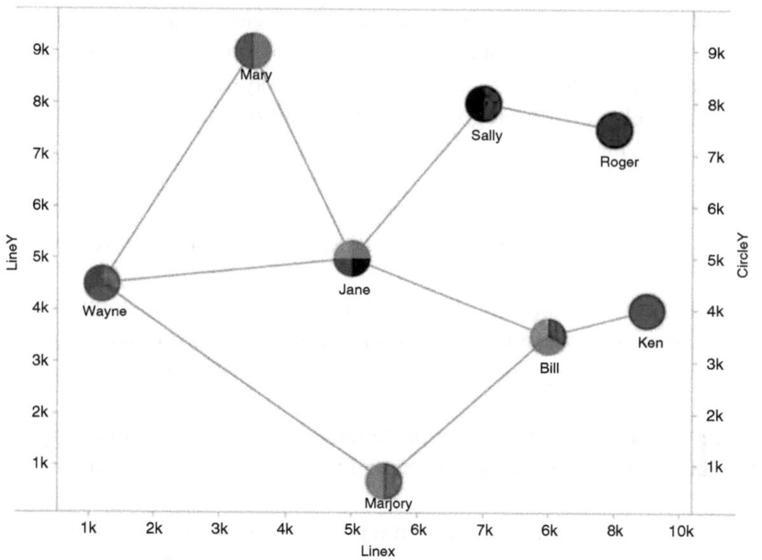

Fig. 4.7 Example of network visualization

tools to produce meaningful presentations, visualizations and dashboards. Such tools enable decision makers to examine large amounts of data and to communicate and share ideas more efficiently in order to make better decisions [1, 4]. That is how and why the utilization of data visualization is increasingly taking its rightful place as an important part of business intelligence systems in most if not all industries. This section will discuss specifically the role of data visualization in two business sectors:

- *Bioinformatics*, because of its importance as the heart of the biological research, which is the main driver for a number of significant business sectors such as pharmaceutical industries and crops improvement research [11], and
- *Social Sciences*, particularly with regard to social networks because of its role in studying users' behaviors and preferences which enables companies to better understand customers' needs, thus producing better products as well as to optimize their processes including customer relationship management [12].

4.5.1 Data Visualization in Bioinformatics

Bioinformatics is the field that is concerned with applying and utilizing computing power to the research in the field of biology. It is an interdisciplinary domain where researchers combine expertise in computer science, statistics and engineering to develop algorithms and software applications to facilitate gathering, storing and analyzing biological data in order to improve, develop and discover better medicines [13]. In such an important industry, data visualization is becoming exceptionally vital for the research in the field of biology to make sense of the scientific data [14]. However, data visualization systems have to address some issues that are related to biological data presentations to be effective. According to [13, 14], these include the ability to:

1. *Encode* data into colors with various intensity and gradients, such as distinguishing tissues with different characteristics using different variations of colors.
2. *Map* biological data into images by normalizing and processing the raw data in order to clean any possible abnormalities, and then, by constructing images.
3. *Convert* data into 3D graphs, which is the more advanced level of data to image mapping.
4. *Interact* with the biological data presentation, so the users can change the view of the data or to pan the object to examine the neighboring tissues.

Data visualization helps scientists in the field of biology to accomplish different types of biological data visualizations. The following three parts provide examples of these analyses:

- ***Sequence Visualization***: Sequence data in the field of biology represent two types of protein sequences, Amino Acid or DNA [15]. Powerful data visualization applications provide the user with the ability to perform Multiple Sequence Alignment (MSA), which is very useful to overcome the standard textual presentation of the four basic molecules of the DNA. For example, [14] provides figures of visualization tools that illustrate how each line denotes to a specific protein sequence, and it can be noticed how various colors are used to differentiate between the different amino acids. Additionally, such tools can be used to do phylogenetic analysis that helps in constructing the evolutional trees as well as to define the characteristics and features for protein families [14].
- ***Protein Structure Visualization***: The structure of the protein, which is mainly composed of amino acids that are linearly encoded by the DNA code, is divided into three levels, primary, secondary and tertiary structures. The analysis of these levels is more advanced than the previously explained *Sequence analysis*. Biological specialized visualization tools have the capability to show the 3D structure of these levels. For one instance, Visual Molecular Dynamics (VMD) visualization tool can be used to render and visualize the 3D structures of a protein molecular [16]. Additionally, biologists have the ability to choose different combinations such as the coloring and drawing methods as well as the material to construct the required visualization of the protein domains [14]. Another example is a dedicated website *bioinformatics.org* which provides a simple tool for macromolecular visualization, in which the user can enter the code of the protein or the molecule that needs to be visualized and the website would generate the required visualization.

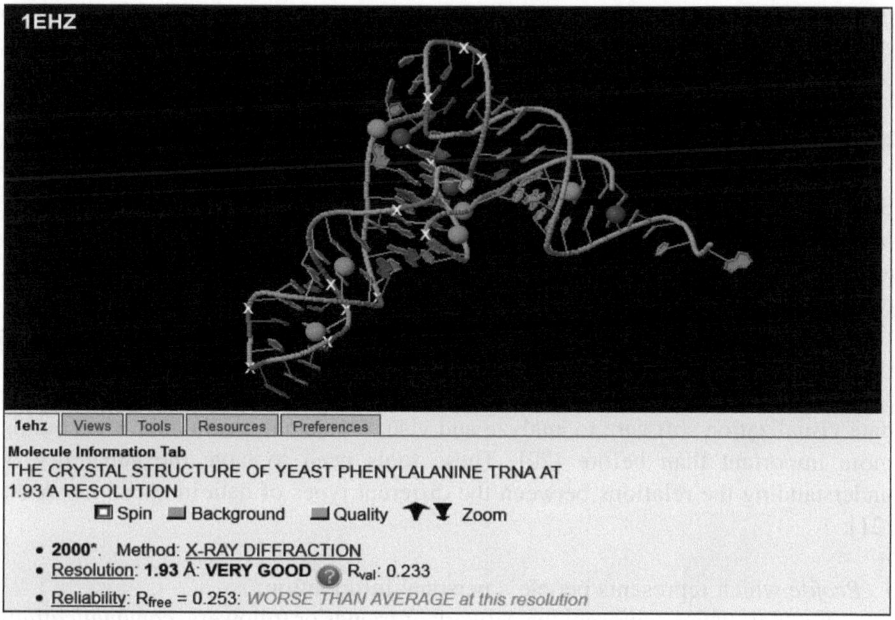

Fig. 4.8 The crystal structure of (Yeast Phenylalanine tRNA) 1EHZ

Figure 4.8, illustrates visualization of the crystal structure of (Yeast Phenylalanine tRNA) with Protein Data Bank (PDB) Identification Code (1EHZ) generated by *bioinformatics.org* website.

The additional importance of the visualization illustrated in Fig. 4.8, is that biologists can compare different 3D protein structures, make prediction based on that comparison and discover where medicines might affect those structures. Moreover, visualization tools can access online database for the protein 3D information such the Protein Data Bank (PDB), which contains the 3D structures for large molecules of proteins and nucleic acids [17].

- ***Numeric Data Analysis***: Biological experiments yield a plentiful of numeric data. Making use of such data, by employing specialized visualization tools, enables scientists to perform advanced analyses and produce different kinds of visualizations such as histograms, animations, colored bars and 3D images. Thus, it would be possible for biological specialists to make important scientific conclusions. For instance, histograms help in finding patterns in a set of scrambled numbers. In general, using various types of visualizations assists in interpreting raw data and producing scientific conclusions [14].

In addition to the visualization methods discussed above, there are also other ways of presenting biological data such as animations, colored bars and 3D surface images. It can be noticed that with the assistance of these visualization techniques, the original biological raw data could be transformed in a more understandable and perceivable way and so the conclusions drawn can be not only scientific but also easily understandable.

4.5.2 Data Visualization in Social Sciences

Social Sciences are nowadays challenged also by the understanding of humans' interactions in forms such as emails, phone calls, instant messaging as well as posts and entries in social networks [18]. Actually, considering areas such as, e.g., *computational social science* [18], the research in the field is currently hugely linked with Big Data analysis since the outset of the social networks and the enormous amount of data they generate [12, 19]. Indeed, social media play important roles in the marketing campaigns of big companies. Therefore, the necessity for data visualization software to analyze and visualize social media data is becoming more important than before [20]. These tools need to have the capability of understanding the relations between the different types of data in social networks [21]:

- *Profile* which represents people's personal information,
- *Individuals* which represent the network of friends or followers, *communications* between network members, and
- *Content* this comprises texts, audios and videos.

Thus, in summary, social networks visualization provides the opportunity to understand the dynamics between connected people. These relations are portrayed by using a *node-link* diagram, in which nodes with different characteristics such as color, size and shape are used to depict people or objects with varying attributes. Moreover, social networks visualization is illustrated by a combination of three elements, which are *attribute*, *time* and *location* [22]. These combinations depend on the type of the network, static or dynamic. On the one hand, for static social networks only the *attribute* and *location* elements are used. On the other hand, dynamic networks use all of the three elements. The following Section provides examples of the main social-link visualizations including *random*, *force direction*, *circular*, and *tree layout*.

4.5.2.1 Social Node-Link Visualization

Graph Layout it is the simplest representation of a static social network [23], in which *Random*, *Force-directed* and *Circular layouts* can be used to represent the people and the connections among them. We now provide a brief discussion of each of them.

1. ***Random Layout***: In this layout, the positions of the nodes are randomly calculated, and it could have one of the following forms Binomial random graph, random grid graph or random geometric graph [24]. These graphs are efficient when the goal is to depict large social network in linear time, however, when

relationships cross heavily, it could be a disadvantage. Random Layouts are the basic form of networks graphs that are useful to portray people's associations with other people or favorite products.

2. ***Force-Directed Layout***: This layout uses nodes to represent people or objects and links to represent the relationships. Additionally, it also assigns forces to the links to pull or push the related nodes towards or from the main node until they balance [25]. Although this graph provides flexibility in representing the nodes and the links, it might take some time until reaching stable state. Force-Directed graphs can do the same presentation as random layout; however, it could be of additional interest for businesses, since it can also highlight the products with highest importance (force) for the business.
3. ***Circular Layout***: It is a very common way of illustrating social networks nodes and connections, in which, the nodes are located on the circle and the connections go through the circle to the other side of the relation [26]. This layout is good in relatively small social networks; however, such graph is not practical when the social network includes thousands of members or products since it would be hard to trace the origin and destination of a connection or relationship.
4. **Tree Layout**: It is another representation of static node-link graphs that portray a hierarchical structure in which the parent node is located in a different level than the child node [27]. It can take the forms of radial, balloon and wedge layouts [28]. The hierarchical form of this graph helps with analyzing the network because it easily portrays the social distance between the nodes. However, it is not very effective for complex networks [29]. Nevertheless, graph and tree layouts as well as their variations are useful in depicting static social networks; yet, *time* perspective too needs to be considered while dealing with dynamic networks in order to demonstrate changes happen in the other two elements, attribute and geo-location, over a period of time [30].

Consequently, the advances in data visualization have provided several options that can be used to present information. Choosing the proper graph representation depends on the business needs and the required value of such visualization.

4.5.2.2 Geographic Based Social Networks Visualization

Geographic location is one of the most important aspects in visualizing social networks. Therefore, in addition to the node and link representation of a relationship between people or objects, maps can be additionally used to indicate to the geographical location of a network member. To generate such visualization, *nodes* and *links* are used on a map to portray the geographical locations of the nodes and the connections among them [27, 28]. The explained visualizations so far are very good examples of the variations that data visualizations can provide depending on the industry and the required presentation. However, none of them can portray dynamic social networks where the above mentioned time element, which reflects the change over time, can be displayed. Indeed, the time element would be very useful in order to discover, for example, trends related consumers' behaviors or products consumptions.

4.5.2.3 Geo-temporal Based Social Networks Visualization

Geo-Temporal Based Social Networks visualization combines both the geographic location and the time element to illustrate the changes that happen over time. One way to demonstrate this is by using a series of static maps with slight changes between two consecutive maps. The other technique is to use animation maps such as the weather report, which illustrates changes of the atmosphere's meteorological conditions according to a preset frame rate [31]. Additionally, a space-time cube can be used to present a series of events throughout a period of time. In this cube, the Z axis represents time, and the X and Y axes are for the two-dimensions geographical map.

4.6 Key Factors for Good Visualization

Data visualization includes *data*, *processes* and *relationships between variables*. These elements may have the basic format such as dots, lines, charts and shapes in graphs. Additionally, they might be enhanced by adding interactivity to those illustrations, which allows the users to manipulate, compare and to have multiple views for the same [14]. However, in order for the visualization to have a good value, certain issues regarding interface design have to be considered. According to Ren et al. [14], These issues are related to key factors for data visualization that concern:

1. ***Effectiveness***. Data visualization needs to be easy to use and to be understood by viewers. To address this issue, visualization tools developers have consider several factors such as lighting conditions, visual perception, surrounding items, color, culture and scale.
2. ***Accuracy***. Data visualization has to be accurate and correct quantitative calculation.
3. ***Efficiency***. Data visualization tools must be capable to achieve the required visualization task quickly and accurately. In bioinformatics, for example, efficiency means that users would have better scientific perception of the biological data.
4. ***Aesthetics***. The interface of the visualization tool has to be appealing and enjoyable for users. Therefore, it is highly recommended that expert interface designers or aestheticians would participate in the designing process of the visualization software's interface.
5. ***Adaptability***. It is important for such tools to serve more than one type of visualization requirement.

The design principles consequent to the above listed factors are of a great importance for the development of data visualization tools and they need to be followed in order enhance the human perception of the business information presented by charts and graphs.

4.7 Challenges Facing Data Visualization Software Development

The previous discussed issues and factors impose several challenges related to data visualization software development. These challenges fall in several categories which include parallelization while exploring huge datasets, the architecture of the computing power, rendering of the generated graphs, and the interactions with visualization software's interface [32]. In what follows these relevant categories are summarized together with the main challenges they encompass.

Category 1: Parallelization While Exploring and Visualizing Big Data
The challenges under this category are:

1. *Handling* the required structure that is capable of utilizing the techniques for addressing both the distributed and shared memories.
2. *Managing* and supplying the required energy for a computing infrastructure that is capable of decomposing the analysis tasks into multiple independent smaller ones in order to save processing time.
3. *Tackling* parallelization over trillions of records.

Category 2: The Architecture of the Computing Power
The challenges under this category are:

1. The ability of visualization software developers to cope with the varying data structures and new computing architectures with the multiple processing cores.
2. Teaching the required visualization programming skills to handle the multiple graphical processing units.

Category 3: Rendering the Required Visualizations
The challenges under this category are:

1. The necessity to develop rendering subsystems to quickly adapt with the different and new rendering choices.
2. The ability to develop visualization systems that can separate the *server* (where large datasets are located), from the *clients* (where the rendering happens).

Category 4: Interactions with the Visualization Software's Interface
The challenges under this category are:

1. Visualization software's ability to handle interactions from a wide variety of devices such as tablets, smartphones and handheld tracking devices.

Table 1.1 Challenges facing data visualization software development

Category	Challenges
Parallelization while exploring and visualizing Big Data	• Memory handling during data visualization • Managing and supplying the energy required for computing • Managing parallelization over trillions of records
The architecture of the computing power	• Visualization of varying data structures • Teaching visualization programing skills
Rendering the required visualizations	• The ability to cope with different rendering choices • Separating data layer from processing layer
Interactions with the visualization software's interface	• Ability to handle interactions from different platforms (Laptops, Mobile, Tablets, . . .)

Generally, data visualization techniques and software need to be able to identify the state-of-the-art with respect to these challenges and to discuss possibilities to meet these demands with modern techniques. Table 1.1 provides a summary of the previous categories and challenges.

4.8 Review of Data Visualization Tools

Visualization tools help analysts and decision makers analyze data, generate graphs, discover patterns, and infer valuable results. However, determining the differences between the several visualization products available in the market and choosing the best software is not an easy task [33]. This part of the chapter will explain the features of some of the most common visualization tools (see also [34]) such as, e.g., Tableau, JMP (SAS), QlikView, IBM Cognos and Tibco Spotfire.

4.8.1 Tableau

Tableau software is one of the leading vendors in the data visualization market. It provides the users with a wide variety of presentation options. In addition to connecting to relational or multidimensional database to perform the required analysis, both beginners and advanced users of Tableau can take advantage of its powerful features such as the in-memory data analysis, discovery and exploration by using simple drag and drop [10]. The clients of Tableau range from large organizations to small firms. Customers of Tableau can publish and share dashboards and reports they create to be seen and used online on different web browsers and mobile platforms. Moreover, Tableau proved to be very effective with geospatial visualizations [33]. Furthermore, it has the ability to analyze Big Data by connecting to multiple Hadoop distributions. Additionally, Tableau has a unique feature in which it can construct a story that represents a specific event by analyzing and connecting the changes of the data throughout the life of that event such as marketing campaign.

4.8.2 JMP (SAS)

JMP software was developed in the 1980s to take advantage of the graphical user interface introduced by Macintosh. Later, it has since been made available for the Windows operating system. JMP is used in applications such as Six Sigma, quality control and engineering, design of experiments and scientific research. There are five different versions with different usages: JMP, JMP Pro, JMP Clinical, JMP Genomics and the JMP Graph Builder App for the iPad. Additionally, scripting language is also available to extend its functionalities. The software is focused on exploratory analytics, whereby users investigate and explore data, rather than to confirm a hypothesis.

JMP provides its customers with the ability for easy self-service visualization and exploration of large data sets [35]. Users of JMP can perform all kinds of statistical analyses and data visualization. Moreover, they can interact with the produced analysis reports and graphs to change the view and gets more details [10]. Furthermore, it is possible to use a query builder feature of JMP to write complex queries to get the required advanced insight.

4.8.3 Qlik

Qlik is ranked among the highest visual analytics vendors that offer analytics platforms that are capable of addressing users' needs from reporting and dashboarding to analysis and application creation. This product offers several versions, QlikView and QlikSense among others, with different price range depending on customers' needs. It can suite the needs of novice users as well as skilled analysts. QlikView helps its users to not only perform conventional statistical analysis and visualization, but also to discover hidden information and trends in the data as well as to gain unexpected business insights by understanding how data are associated and what data are not related [10].

Additionally, similar to Tableau, QlikView can either connect to the relational database or to load all the data into the memory to perform the required analysis and visualization [10].

4.8.4 IBM Cognos

It is IBM's Business Intelligence (BI) platform, in which, users can perform advanced in-memory data analysis and visualization, and have the ability to perform the "what-if" scenario modeling. IBM Cognos enables managers to produce views that reflect the past, the present and the future of the organization's operations and performance. These views can be used to comprehend the effects of the decisions that potentially cover complex interrelated factors [10].

Moreover, it features a powerful predictive analysis capabilities powered by the engine of IBM's statistical analysis software, SPSS. Additionally, it facilitates access and analysis for both structured and unstructured data [10]. Consistent snapshots of business performance are provided in enterprise-class reports and independently assembled dashboards based on trusted information. As a result, executives and managers as well as technical Business Intelligence (BI) users can respond quickly to rapidly changing business needs.

4.8.5 Tibco Spotfire

Tibco Spotfire software is one of the leading enterprise-class data analytics, discovery and exploration platform, providing unrivaled performance, scalability, and security. The software's differentiating hybrid in-memory/in-database analytics architecture supports the most demanding enterprise needs, supporting thousands of users and limitless of records and variables. Tibco Spotfire software is currently implemented in the world's largest energy, manufacturing, consumer packaged goods and life sciences companies, working within existing IT systems, and backed by a global domain expertise as well as 24 × 7 customer service [10].

Tibco Spotfire software helps enterprises to anticipate opportunities and risks seamlessly by integrating predictive models and real-time event streams. Additionally, its capabilities include supporting collaborative decision-making process by capturing moments of insight, ideas, and hypotheses with peers, advisers, and customers. These rich discussions can be captured through collaborative bookmarks, guided analytic apps, corporate portals and social platforms to provide visually compelling context to accelerate the decision making process.

4.9 Case Studies

In this Section we investigate some data visualization environments related case studies and we provide explanation about their role for the business success.

The first case is based on [34] and analyzes a technological service supplier company established on 2004, called Zyme, which provides its almost 2000 clients with services related to processing and analyzing their sales and inventory transactions that occur through other retailers [34]. By doing so, Zyme offers its customers critical information related to revenues, incentives, sales commissions as well as the important data required for planning supply chain processes. Zyme used to do this by collecting, validating and providing the information to its customers so they can feed them into their own business intelligence suites and perform the needed analysis.

However, some clients started to realize the difficulties associated with loading, analyzing and visualizing the supplied data from Zyme in order to get the required insight and generate the valuable outcomes from the data. Consequently, they demanded Zyme to provide the required analysis. Therefore, in 2009, Zyme implemented a data analysis and visualization software, called QlikView, and provided a web-based access to it for its customers, which required minimum training. Additionally, Zyme, designed a series of customized dashboards that can provide additional insights and would relieve its customer from developing them internally [34].

Point of Attention The ease of use and adaptability are the key factors when it comes to implement and adopt data visualization systems. By choosing to implement QlickView for its customers, instead of make them loading, analyzing, and visualizing the supplied data, Zyme was able to increase its services offerings, while focusing on developing advanced dashboards.

The second case study is based on a case history by [3] and discusses insights from the experience of a Texas based microfinance institution, established in the 1960s and called ACCION. This organization is specialized in providing loans for companies that do not qualify for financing plans offered by other financial institutions like banks [3]. The business model of ACCION is based on assessing 35 different criteria in order to find whether a business is capable to pay the loan back or not. To achieve the required flexibility while evaluating applicants' profiles and without requiring extra programming experience, the ACCION Company decided on 2008 to utilize SAS Visual Analytics to develop a scorecard.

Point of Attention Choosing the right visualization tool plays a very influential part in the success of the implementing organization. Such tools can help with several management aspects such as risk management, and can be a significant support to achieve better services for customers.

The scorecard helped the company in many ways. First, it assisted in reducing the number of the eligible candidates for loans by 50 % (which means having a fewer number of applicants to evaluate). Second, it played an important role in helping the officers responsible about approving the loans to easily score the applicant and provide an evaluation based on the 35 criteria. Third, it was essential in reducing the approval time substantially, from 2 weeks to 3 days. Moreover, the success of the scorecard was one of the main factors that attracted larger organization such as Citigroup to have successful partnership with ACCION [3].

4.10 Summary

The unprecedented increase in the amount of the generated data of all kinds has put external requirements on the researchers and developers to introduce new algorithms and develop more advanced data analysis and visualization systems. Now, it is up to the users to choose the tool that suits their needs and generate value. However, such a task is not easy, because of the many distinctive features that each vendor offers. Therefore, it is important to consider all the factors related to business needs such as the additional training, continuous support, individual departmental requirements, and the overall business objectives.

In this chapter, detailed explanations about the definitions, latest visualization techniques as well as the variety of tools that can generate values for customers, have been provided. Moreover, the chapter has discussed some of the data visualization applications in two of the most vital industries nowadays, Bioinformatics and Social Sciences. Yet, as pointed out in this chapter, researchers and developers of data visualization software have to consider important success factors and challenges in order to keep meeting the explosion and variations of data generated from all kinds of resources. Finally, the chapter has discussed two case studies, showing the importance and benefits associated with selecting and implementing the right visualization system that meets business requirements.

References

1. Wallis JC (2005) Databases and data visualization the state of the art. Center for Embedded Networked Sensing. Center for Embedded Networked Sensing, Data Management Team, UCLA. http://www.moebiustrip.org/CENS/DataVisTechRep.doc. Accessed 10 Sept 2015
2. Pandey AV, Manivannan A, Nov O, Satterthwaite M, Bertini E (2014) The persuasive power of data visualization. IEEE Trans Vis Comput Graph 20(12):2211–2220. doi:10.1109/TVCG.2014.234641920
3. Tilton S (2011) Harness the power of data visualization to transform your business. IT Business Edge and SAS Corporation. http://www.tentonmarketing.com/wp-content/uploads/2014/12/SAS-Data-Visualization_WP.pdf. Accessed 7 Sept 2015
4. Dilla W, Janvrin DJ, Raschke R (2010) Interactive data visualization: new directions for accounting information systems research. J Inf Syst 24:1–37
5. Few S (2007) Data visualization: past, present, and future. IBM Cognos Innovation Center for Performance Management, pp 3–11. ftp://public.dhe.ibm.com/software/data/sw-library/cognos/pdfs/whitepapers/wp_data_visualization_past_present_future.pdf. Accessed 10 Sept 2015
6. Keim DA (2002) Information visualization and visual data mining. IEEE Trans Vis Comput Graph 8(1):1–8
7. Erbacher RF, Frincke D (2000) Visualization in detection of intrusions and misuse in large scale networks. In: IEEE conference on information visualization. An international conference on computer vision and graphics, pp 294–299
8. Peng W, Ward MO, Rundensteiner EA (2004) Clutter reduction in multi-dimensional data visualization using dimension reordering. In: Proceedings of IEEE symposium on information visualization. INFO VIS, pp 89–96
9. Cruz JD, Bothorel C, Poulet F (2013) Community detection and visualization in social networks. ACM Trans Intell Syst Technol 5:1–26
10. Evelson B, TaKeaWays K (2012) The Forrester Wave™: advanced data visualization (ADV) platforms, Q3 2012. https://www.tableau.com/sites/default/files/whitepapers/the_forrester_wave__advanced_data_visualization_adv_platforms_q3_2012.pdf. Accessed 31 Oct 2015
11. Bevan MW, Uauy C (2013) Genomics reveals new landscapes for crop improvement. Genome Biol 14:206
12. Buckley S, Ettl M, Jain P, Luss R, Petrik M, Ravi RK, Venkatramani C (2014) Social media and customer behavior analytics for personalized customer engagements. IBM J Res Dev 58:1–12

13. Gibas C, Jambeck P (2002) Developing bioinformatics computer skills. O'Reilly, Cambridge. ISBN 1565926641
14. Ren J, Lu J, Wang L, Chen D (2012) Data visualization in bioinformatics. Adv Inf Sci Serv Sci 4:157–165
15. Watson JD, Crick FH (2003) Molecular structure of nucleic acids. A structure for deoxyribose nucleic acid. 1953. Rev Invest Clin 55:108–109
16. Humphrey W, Dalke A, Schulten K (1996) VMD: visual molecular dynamics. J Mol Graph 14:33–38
17. Bergeron B (2002) Bioinformatics computing. Prentice Hall/Professional Technical Reference. ISBN 0131008250
18. Lazer D, Pentland A, Adamic L, Aral S, Barabási A-L, Brewer D, Christakis N, Contractor N, Fowler J, Gutmann M, Jebara T, King G, Macy M, Roy D, van Alstyne M (2009) Computational social science. Science 323:721–723
19. Becker RA, Eick SG, Wilks AR (1995) Visualizing network data. IEEE Trans Vis Comput Graph 1:16–28
20. Healy K, Moody J (2014) Data visualization in sociology. Annu Rev Sociol 40:105–128
21. Hansen DL, Shneiderman B, Smith MA (2011) Analyzing social media networks with NodeXL – insights from a connected world. Morgan Kaufmann, Amsterdam. ISBN 9780123822291
22. Li X, Kraak M-J (2008) The time wave. A new method of visual exploration of geo-data in time–space. Cartograph J 45:193–200
23. Du X, Ye Y, Li Y, Wang X (2014) Social network visualization oriented multi-level layout method. Adv Sci Technol Lett 50:32–37
24. Díaz J, Petit J, Serna M (2002) A survey of graph layout problems. ACM Comput Surv 34:313–356
25. Chen IX, Yang CZ (2010) Handbook of social network technologies and applications. Springer, New York
26. Gansner ER, Koren Y (2006) Improving circular layouts. In: 14th international symposium. Springer, Berlin, pp 386–398
27. Reingold EM, Tilford JS (1981) Tidier drawings of trees. IEEE Trans Softw Eng SE-7:223–228
28. Wills GJ (1999) NicheWorks—interactive visualization of very large graphs. J Comput Graph Stat 8:190–212
29. Hong L, Meng F, Cai J (2009) Research on layout algorithms for better data visualization. Science 7:369–372
30. Erten C, Harding PJ, Kobourov SG, Wampler K, Yee G (2004) GraphAEL: graph animations with evolving layouts. Graph Draw 2912:98–110
31. Kraak M, MacEachren A (1994) Visualization of spatial data's temporal component. In: Spatial data handling. Advances in GIS research, pp 5–9
32. Childs H, Geveci B, Schroeder W, Meredith J, Moreland K, Sewell C, Kuhlen T, Bethel EW (2013) Research challenges for visualization software. IEEE Comput Soc 46:34–42
33. Henschen D (2012) How to choose "advanced" data visualization tools. Informationweek 14–17
34. Wise Analytics (2009) Data visualization – market landscape report. http://www.wiseanalytics.com/uploads/library-research_2_866469864.pdf. Accessed 10 Sept 2015
35. Okerson BB (2013) I'm a SAS® programmer. Why should I JMP®? Abstract. SESUG. 1–12
36. Guo D (2009) Flow mapping and multivariate visualization of large spatial interaction data. IEEE Trans Vis Comput Graph 15:1041–1048

Digital Security

5

Abstract

Malware attackers have been creative in manipulating the susceptibilities in desktop and server operating systems, thereby bypassing detection from anti-virus softwares as well as other complex security mechanisms used by business organisations. As attackers continue to use social networks to distribute their malicious programs business organisations are facing the enormous challenge of coping with evolving threats. In addition, they seldom integrate in their security strategies a provision for sufficient preventive measures in order to mitigate these threats. Also, modern malware has become more sophisticated; dangerously spreading speedily due to the escalating use of social networks in business environments. Consequently, it is also becoming extremely difficult to control and eliminate this misdemeanour. This chapter presents the security implications of malware attacks on business organizations. Moreover, the disaster recovery approaches employed by organisations to control and prevent the propagation of malware attacks are also discussed.

5.1 Introduction

Catastrophes can occur at any time and threaten the technical and operational permanence of a business activity. Increasingly, the accessibility and dependability of IT infrastructure has been constantly compromised by various forms of malware such as; viruses, Trojans, and worms intended to harmfully impact business organizations and reduce employees' productivity [1, 2]. Malware can be described as a purposeful malicious discharge of software that is intended to reduce or destroy the efficiency and productivity of individuals and businesses [3].

Malware attacks are growing exponentially with the United States, Asia and Europe as three major malware hotspots. According to a report from an online information security corporation [4], malicious users otherwise known as attackers are taking advantage of new methods, such as exploiting social networks to

V. Morabito, *The Future of Digital Business Innovation*,
DOI 10.1007/978-3-319-26874-3_5

proliferate undetected. Social networking giants, Facebook, have now become the major target for attackers searching for vulnerable users to become actors in proliferation of their malicious softwares [5]. According to Faghani and Saidi [6], the rationale for the distribution of malicious softwares through social networks is due to the enormous population of potential victims, and also because social networking-based worms are not expelled through Web proxies and network address translation (NAT) processes.

This chapter does not present a technical analysis of malware variants from an information security view point; the aim is to highlight the management issues involved with the propagation of malware on business organizations. Thus, we argue that what is presented in this chapter may provide insights and perspectives suitable to enhance the improvement of malware defense systems for business organizations so that they may have more control over the spread of malware from a social engineering perspective.

5.2 Digital Security Challenges Facing Business Organizations

Employees now are divulging sensitive information on social networks and therefore, becoming easy links for targeted attacks against their organization [7, 8]. The sensitive information they reveal on social networks are been used by attackers to launch sophisticated targeted social engineering attacks. Recurrently, targeted attacks have severe implications such as; intellectual property theft or corporate espionage [9, 10].

According to a new investigation on cyber-attacks conducted by Enterprise Strategy Group [11], many organizations are not equipped to keep up with the level of speedy distribution and sophistication of malware today's attacks. The main conclusions of their survey on cyber-attacks, which was sent to 315 Information Technology professionals in North American organizations, are summarized in what follows:

- 72 % of respondents acknowledge that the characteristic organization is vulnerable or extremely vulnerable to malware attacks. Since 2011, 49 % of respondents experienced at least an attack, 32 % faced between two and five attacks, and 6 % experienced 100+ attacks.
- 58 % of the research participants, faults deficiency of user awareness for their organization's malware susceptibility, 31 % faults sophisticated malicious strategies such as the Spear Phishing attacks; 29 % blame more use of social networking sites, and 26 % blame increased problems in detecting malware that uses compound attack vectors.

Social networks represents the next frontline of threats for IT security specialists as well as the organizations they protect. A study conducted on Fortune 100 businesses and their social network channels found that illegal social network accounts, content threats and account hijackings are three primary issues plaguing business organizations. For example, an average of 40 % of Facebook accounts presented as a Fortune 100 brand were illegal, and 20 % of Twitter accounts were also illegal.

5.3 The Rise of Malware Attacks

In the last three decades, information systems have seen the evolution of malware and its exponential growth [12, 13]. Initially, malware was created as proof of some security perception and then malware was created for financial gains which have led to malware created to damage business infrastructures.

Malware attacks continue to grow, not just in size but in complexity, according to a recent report from security outfit McAfee [2], more organizations are being targeted by more intelligent cyber-attacks. The amount of Trojans intended to steal passwords rose 72 % in the fourth quarter of 2012. A number of these Trojans are components of modified threats, whereas others are packed with more forms of malware. For example, the 'Citadel Trojan' was chiefly created to strike financial services companies [12].

Rootkits malware, are one of the worst classifications of malware intended to escape detection and take complete control of systems for long-lasting periods. Subsequent to rising all through most of the past years, the number of new rootkit samples took a vertical decline in the fourth quarter of 2012 as seen in Table 5.1.

Over the last decade, malware propagation has become a recurrent online criminal story [14]. The estimated figure of known computer malwares such as viruses, ransomware, worms, Trojan horses, exploits, rootkits, keyloggers, dialers, backdoors, password stealers, spyware, adware and other variations of malicious programs range into millions. Repetitively, malware developers are using client and server polymorphism (the capability for malware to create different forms of itself dynamically in order to impede anti-malware programs) [15].

Table 5.1 Top ten malware threats on the internet in the fourth quarter of 2012 (Adapted from: [31])

	Top 10 WAV	% of all attacks	Change in ranking
1	Malicious URL	87.6	0
2	Trojan.Script.Iframer	2.9	0
3	Trojan.Script.Generic	2.4	0
4	Trojan.JS.popupper.aw	0.4	4
5	Trojan.Win32.Generic	0.3	−1
6	Trojan.JS.Agent.bxw	0.3	New
7	Exploit.Script.Blocker	0.3	New
8	Trojan-Downloader.Script.Generic	0.2	New
9	Trojan-Downloader.Script.Generic	0.2	−4
10	Trojan.JS.Redirector.uk	0.2	New

In 2010, social networks became the favorite medium of information sharing for users, with the average user spending more 40 min a day on Facebook alone, thus making this platform an ideal malware distribution target [16]. In regards to social networking and business network security, some executives have no in-depth understanding about the implications of their employees' poor online behaviors. The impact of a business network's disruption from malware attacks affects all devices or components that are connected to the networks such as email, web, file, database, print servers, as well as desktop and remote employees' use of laptops [7].

According to a study from security experts at Panda [17], almost a third of small businesses have been affected by social media malware. Even as this is currently motivated by the fame of Facebook, malicious users are now exploiting online social networks as their core malware distribution domain. In particular, it has emerged that 77.5 % of businesses use social networks as an advertising medium and 52 % affirmed that they had experienced a rise in malware as a result of employee use of social media (see also Fig. 5.1). As for these issues, Table 5.2 presents the analysis of the most common malware types and their attack techniques synthesized from various sources [10, 12].

5.4 Digital Security Challenges Facing Business Organizations

As stated previously, the rise of social networks has led to increased security risks for many organizations and if a security breach occurs from an employee's social networking activity, the compromised organization may face severe consequences [18]. The successful execution of malware attacks mostly begins when an employee falls for a phishing trick and then downloads malware onto an organization's network website through the use of social networks. The victim usually does this by clicking a malicious link posted on social networks (e.g., Facebook) while using a computer belonging to the organization. Moreover, due to the Bring Your Own Devices (BYOD) policies of some organizations, employees may also compromise the infrastructure of their organization by using their personal devices (which also contains the organization's resources) for social networking activities, which further compounds the problems (see [19] for more details on BYOD business challenges).

In today's business environment, the social networking-security policies, procedures, and technical safeguards are struggling to cope with exponentially growing variances of malware attacks. Additionally, *social engineering*[1] within social networks, as well as "spoof" social network profiles or pages provide other means of entry for attackers and poses legal risks for business organizations. A spoof site is one where attackers design profiles or fan pages to reproduce an

[1] Social engineering is a non-technical method of intrusion used by the hackers, which is based heavily on human interaction and often implies cheating people into breaking normal security procedures.

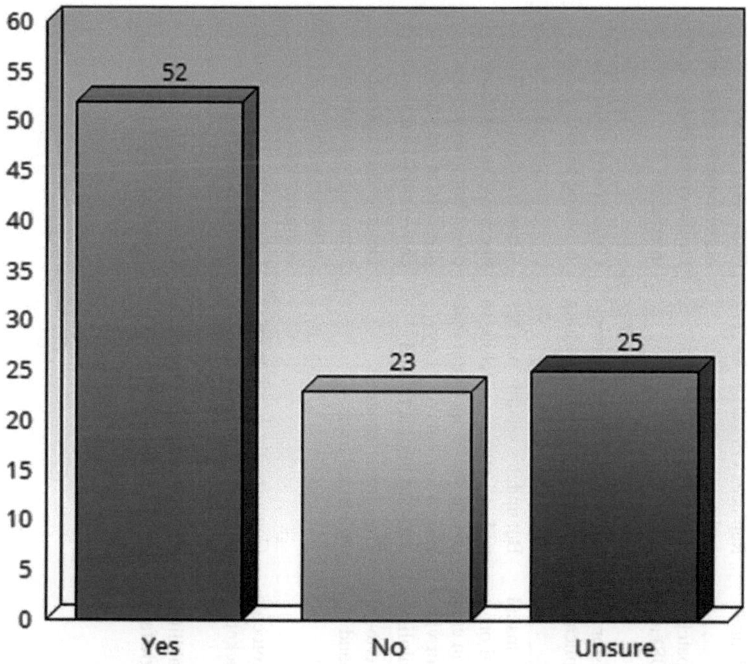

Fig. 5.1 Percentage of employees who experienced malware from social media use in the workplace (Adapted from: [17])

organization's own original page. With social engineering becoming more sophisticated, customers or novice employees may be tricked into providing sensitive information or personal information which the attacker can utilize to successfully launch a targeted attack based on such information [20].

5.5 Threat Implications on Business Organizations

This Section discusses the implications of malware attacks on the business organizations, which are revenue loss, brand damage, data loss and huge recovery costs.

5.5.1 Revenue Loss

The outcome of successful malware attacks often leads to the loss of revenue; this could take place as a result of a tarnished performance by the compromised hardware or software infrastructure of the affected business organization or costs incurred due to repairs of the infected system [21, 22]. Furthermore, social networks have escalated such loses to a greater proportion. For example, the attack on

Table 5.2 Common malware types and techniques of attack (Adapted from: [10, 12])

	Proliferation pattern	Infectivity	Self-defense	Potential
Rootkit	Through infected websites or installation on servers by hackers or malicious users working within the organization	Exploited trusted admin access, browsers vulnerability, or unpatched operating system (OS) and client applications	Replaces OS kernel-level API routines	Collects data and impersonates user activity for the entire device and its interfaces
Keylogger	Through Infected websites and/or USB or other media	Vulnerable browsers or unpatched OS or application	Replaces IO device drivers or application programming interfaces	Collects user keystrokes including sensitive data
Bot (identical bots on numerous devices from the same malicious attacker is called a botnet)	Bots are commonly distributed through infected websites, or links to malicious websites embedded in Phishing email	Users may willingly install individual bots based on deceptive messages in email or web instruction, or via Browser/OS vulnerabilities	Bot updates security patches and anti-virus on machine to ensure stable operation and keep other bots out. Lays dormant until activated	When triggered by botnet operative, the operative may direct bot to execute a diversity of standard or conventional functions
Flaw exploits	They execute unforeseen commands to flawed software by remote hackers	Susceptible software-to-database and command execution interfaces	They impersonate authorized users	Download or upload data from data repositories between target and malware operator site
Denial of service attacks (DOS)	Delivery of IP packets	Through Internet protocols that computerize packet processing	Concurrently attack from numerous sources	Chomp through computing resources on targets
Phishing	Phishing are commonly executed through malicious URLs to malicious websites embedded in most social networking sites	Exploits the vulnerabilities associated with single factor authentication	Replicates the user interface design of most Web applications	Collects private and sensitive data from its victims

Click-jacking	Within the context of social networking, attackers lures the potential victim into clicking on a link, mostly posted on the victim's wall and then spam the victim's 'friends' with attractive words like "check it out," or "view my photos"	When a victim clicks on the link, they unintentionally install malware (code or script) that can be used to steal information or take control over their computer	Click-jacking utilizes the dynamic nature of social networking and a willingness to click on 'catchy' links from those the victims know, and even other users unknown to quickly reach a large audience	Click-jacking, cajole the user into revealing private information (for example through surveys), collect hits for ad revenue, and eventually allow access to the user entire social network

Associated Press (AP) Twitter account shows that social networks are now intertwined with the profitability of businesses in the real world.

When Associated press were attacked, the attackers posted on the compromised account that President Barack Obama was hijacked and the White house had been bombed. According to TechCrunch, Washington Post and many other independent online news agencies, the false 'breaking news' led to the instant dropping of the stock price of many organizations with a consequent estimated one hundred and thirty six billion dollar loss ($136,000,000) [23].

5.5.2 Brand Damage

A successfully executed malware attack may also negatively impact the business by damaging the organization's brand [19]. This sole impact has now been amplified with the involvement of various business brands on popular social networking sites. For example in February 2013, Burger King's Twitter account was hacked and had its logo replaced with the one of McDonalds. The attackers also tweeted that the organization has been sold to McDonalds which resulted to an increase in 30 % of followers from 83,000 to 110,000 [24]. Although the real cause of the attack remains unknown, however, the main point is the reputational brand damage an organization encounters when malicious users compromise its social network identity. In addition, when the software and hardware infrastructures of organizations are compromised, they normally do not perform to full capacity which could adversely lead to irritated clients seeking for better services [20].

5.5.3 Data Loss

One of the most significant effects of malware attacks is the loss of information and/or data that might be very critical to the operations of the business. Unfortunately, many businesses often risk losing vital data due to weak preparation or control based security measures employed for the ever-increasing sophisticated malware attacks. Malware can also have distressing effects if allowed to penetrate a business network; this is because access to sensitive information about a business or its clients/partners by permitted persons may lead to legal ramifications and a fatal business collapse [5, 9, 10].

As hideous as it is for an individual to have its data infected and/or destroyed by malware, the gravity is far worse for the data belonging to business organizations. Depending on the business, data with sensitive customer information, financial information about the company, passwords, account numbers, and other information that one would not want any outside individual to see, are all potential targets for malware. If an organization experiences a security breach and its customers' data were stolen, the cost of recovery would be the entire responsibility of the organization (see Table 5.3 for examples of costs of stolen data and [22]).

Table 5.3 Costs of stolen data (Adapted from: [22])

Costs of stolen data	
Router credentials	$12.50
Rich bank account credentials	$750.00
US/UK passport information	$800.00
CCV	$3.25
FTP exploit	$6.00
OS administrative login	$2.50
Full identity information	$5.00

A famous example of a gap in data security that happened within the last year was with Sony when the PlayStation Network users had their name, date of birth, address, credit card numbers, and passwords for the network stolen. This information was estimated to be worth more than 100 million dollars. Needless to say, the loss of data can cause a tremendous financial burden for a company [25]. Actually, the company's public image would also suffer, causing a loss in consumer confidence that could send the company into bankruptcy if the situation is not appropriately dealt with.

5.5.4 Recovery Costs

Businesses are spending an astounding amount of money in the repercussions of an attack. According to reports from Solutionary [26], up to $6500 per hour to recuperate from distributed denial of service attacks (DDoS) and more than $3000 per day for up to 30 days to recover from malware attacks.

Security specialists, disaster response teams, mitigation softwares and other instant investments make up the cost effects for malware attack recovery. However, some other costs should be considered as well. Most times the financial recovery figures reported do not include money lost due to systems interruption, or misplaced productivity. In addition, intellectual property-related costs are not included. Malware attackers are also targeting business organizations with advanced threats and attacks intended to drain off treasured corporate internet IP and regulated information, deny online services to millions of users and destroy brand reputation.

It is reported that that 80 % of efforts to infect businesses with malware are focused at financial (45 %) and retail (35 %) sectors [27]. These malware campaigns are now frequently posted as enticing social network video and image links, which attempts to compel a victim to execute an attachment or click on the malicious driven link. Notwithstanding the number of detecting security solutions being developed by academic and the industrial sectors, it is still challenging for many business organizations to keep up with the exponentially evolving variations of malicious programs targeted against them. This makes total dependence on technical solutions for controlling and preventing malware infiltration on the IT infrastructure of business networks not efficient. Besides, from the report by [27] a full 54 % of malware normally evades antivirus or anti-malware detection. Only

46 % of samples tested through VirusTotal by Solutionary were detected by antivirus which indicates a clear need for business organizations to invest in an innovative system for malware attack awareness, control and mitigation [27].

5.6 Existing Techniques for Disaster Recovery

Having a Disaster Recovery (DR) agenda which consists of a knowledgeable team and a pre-emptive plan is vital to effectively cope with the outcome of an occurrence [28]. The DR team of an organization is normally gathered from key employees within the organization with special training in DR set of guidelines and are familiar with the DR plan. It is uncommon for an organization to have a dedicated DR team, even for large financial services institutions that have fraud and conformity departments. The rationale of the DR plan is to provide a pre-approved and clear set of strategy of actions needed in the event of a security violation, which can be followed during a distress period [10].

Organizations have to know that there may be two incongruous goals (1) whether to alleviate the impact of the disaster and recover the organization to a satisfactory position as promptly as achievable, or (2) whether to collect and substantiate evidence in a manner that facilitates detection of an executor and their prosecution. Furthermore, when dealing with a virus or worm outbreak, returning to regular operation is mostly the priority, but when a rootkit action is detected then the latter approach may be more suitable.

In what follows the disaster recovery techniques shown in Fig. **5.2** are discussed:

1. *Identification*: This involves evaluating the impact of the disaster on the business either internal, on partners, and/or on customers. In addition, determining the source and nature of the disaster is done in this process.
2. *Containment*: This involves containing the disaster such that it ceases to spread to previously unaffected systems, or impact systems or processes elsewhere.
3. *Annihilation*: The next step having contained the disaster is the eradication of its effects from the affected networks and restoring those systems to a trustworthy state both operationally and in regards data reliability. Thus, generate as well as pre-test value propositions utilizing advanced and discovery analytics.
4. *Knowledge*: The next step for a successful disaster recovery is evaluating the learning outcome from the unfortunate occurrence because this is crucial in preventing further happenstances [22].
5. *Improvement*: Next, is the application of this learning to improve the security posture such that future attacks, be they of this type or other, are less likely to lead to an incident.

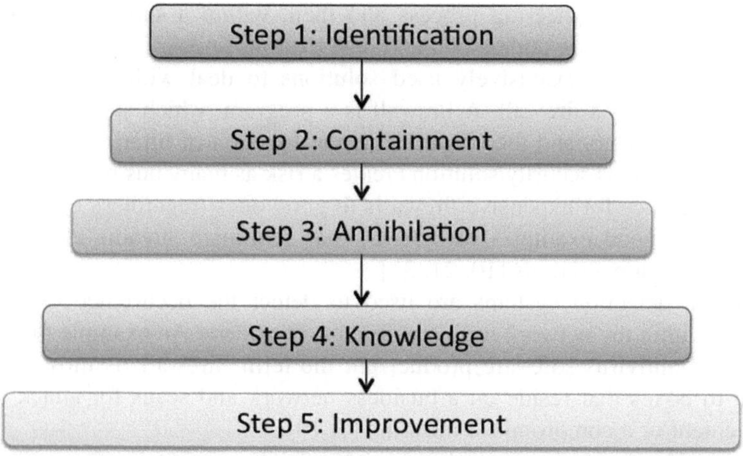

Fig. 5.2 A model of malware disaster recovery

Remediation of malware attacks are becoming more complicated due to a number of factors such as the varieties of malware found that exploit "zero-day" vulnerabilities [29]. "Zero-day[2]" modifies the word vulnerability to mean that likely victims do not yet know the vulnerability, and as a result victims usually have no effective security measure or adequate prevention strategies in place before the attacks occur. Unfortunately for most individuals and business organizations, modern malware variants are now been designed with polymorphic capabilities [6, 30]. A polymorphic malware changes certain features of itself for each infection and it circumvents signature-based detection mechanisms because they typically use a hash algorithm to fabricate a unique signature from a file containing malware. Any remote alteration to the malicious files changes its signature. A polymorphic malware can also change its own filename on each infection, and this also makes detection more difficult by traditional means. Taking these issues into account, the following section describes some existing techniques used by some business organizations to prevent malware attacks.

5.6.1 Configuration Management

Popular malware attacks on systems usually exploit previously identified bugs or vulnerabilities. The characteristic process is that the software vendor releases a set of security patches at once a month; thereafter after release, malicious attackers

[2] Zero-day vulnerability is an unknown exploit in the wild that exposes vulnerability in software or hardware, which can create complicated problems well before anyone realizes something is wrong.

launch a reverse engineering process and then, within a short while, the bugs/vulnerabilities fixed are understood and new exploits appear [21].

One of the most extensively used solutions to deal with the challenges of malware attacks is a firewall. A firewall is a program, which stands amid a local system and the Web, and then it performs the function of filtering out potentially harmful traffic. This security solution creates a risk as many business organizations have a preference for expensive firewalls to good ones (regardless of the quality). Firewalls are good examples of systems that scrutinize streams of packets and perform filtering operations [10, 21, 31].

Intrusion detection systems are used to detect the occurrence of malicious activities within the network infrastructure of a business. An example of a firewall is a typical antivirus software product but the term 'firewall' is most frequently applied to boxes that reside on a business network and scans for attack signs in advancement or a compromised machine [7, 10].

In preventing malicious attacks on networks encryption has been the easiest approach used by many business organizations. Encryption regularly does not provide the adequate level of security that most business organizations need to resist the level of sophistication of malware attacks, however, it can sometimes be useful. Some of the four most significant network encryption scenarios includes; secure shell (SSH), the local link security provided by Wi-Fi (wireless fidelity), Bluetooth and HomePlug, IPSec and TLS [22].

5.7 Case Studies

In this Section we discuss two cases of malware attacks through online social networks as well as their consequent impact on the business world.

The first case study is based on [32] and discusses a malware attack at Dutch Financial Market through Twitter users. In April 2013, IBM founds out a financial malware which attacked Twitter users [32]. A *Man-in-the-Browser*[3] attack was executed by the attackers through the browser of infected personal computers, thus, gaining access to the Twitter account of victim's and then created malicious tweets. Apart from stealing the users' credentials and their financial transactions, the attackers' goal was also to ensure that malware was distributed via online social networks.

Although the Dutch financial market was targeted, due to the diverse demographics of Twitter users, such attacks could have been utilized against any business industry in any geographic location. Table 5.4 shows some of the tweets posted by the malware attackers from victims' accounts (tweets having explicit

[3] Man-in-the-browser is a security attack where the perpetrator installs a Trojan horse on a victim's computer capable of modifying that user's Web transactions as they occur in real time.

Table 5.4 Tweets posted by malware attackers from victim's account

Original text (in Dutch)	English translation
"Onze nieuwe koning Willem goat nog meer verdienen dan Beatrix check zijin salaris"	"Our new King will earn even more than Beatrix. Check his salary"
"Beyoncé valt tijdens het concert van de superbowl, zeer funny" "Topman [Dutch Bank] gaat"	"Beyoncé falls during the Super Bowl concert, very funny!!!!"
"Topman [Dutch Bank] gaat ervandoor met onze milojoenen!! De minister heeft weer het nakijken. . .zie"	"CEO of [Dutch Bank] is off with our millions!!" The minister is inspecting again. . .see"

content were omitted from this chapter). The tweets include the following malicious links, adapted from [32]:

hXXp://yix.be/b18e9
hXXp://yix.be/11efb
hXXp://ow.ly/hr6a6
hXXp://01.nl/rohvj9

The texts in Table 5.4 shows how malware attackers easily deceived Twitter users using social engineering, making it extremely difficult for anti-virus to detect. With online social networks like Twitter, users have a high tendency to trust other users and very often attackers easily exploit these trust-based relationships to deceptively spread their malware. Due to the fact that the malware automatically generates malicious posts and sends them through an infected account of a trusted person or organization, followers are most likely to trust and engage with them. Though, an abbreviated URL can be used to mask the original URL so that users have no way of perceiving that the link is malicious. The fact that the tweets include shortened URLs is not the major security concern because Twitter has restrictions on the number of characters in a message, so followers expect to get interesting news bits in the form of a short text message and a shortened URL. Nonetheless, these types of attacks point out the need for business organizations to exploit a more innovative prevention technology to beat the attackers.

A useful technique for anti-malware companies to deploy against these forms of attacks is to increase the security of end-users through security plugins for browsers in order to prevent unaware users from unknowingly downloading malware to their systems. External sources like social network contents, which may contain an unseen inserted code, should be carefully observed by end-users while they engage with them. Most malicious URLs triggered by users of social networks have certain characteristics, which distinguish them from legitimately working URLs. These characteristics can be largely explored by researchers and disseminated to naïve users' in order to enhance more effective threat avoidance.

Point of Attention Most malicious URLs triggered by users of social networks have certain characteristics, which distinguish them from legitimately working URLs. Thus, organizations developing anti-malware softwares may need to look beyond purely technical systems and start developing effective security awareness solutions based on the context of the attacks.

The Second case is based on [33] and discusses the Zeus malware re-launched against Facebook users. Indeed, the Trojan horse malware that was initially reported in 2007 resurfaced and attacked Facebook users in 2013 [34]. Using fake Facebook fan pages and compromised accounts, the Zeus malware was able to drain bank accounts and steal private information such as Social Security numbers. The Zeus malware was camouflaged as a URL with posts pressing users to check videos or products. On clicking the URL link, the malware contaminates the computer but halts in the background. It then monitors the banking Web browsing activities of the victims. When the victim performs an online banking activity the malware is activated, sending the login information to a remote server. Furthermore, the attackers were able to remotely initiate the malware to hijack the bank account. Some variants of the malware were able to create a counterfeit of the bank's website with functionalities to request private information such as Social Security, credit card and ID numbers.

The malware stole numerous Facebook accounts, sending messages with malicious links to all the connections of the victims. The New York Times reported that the advocacy group *Fans Against Kounterfeit Enterprise* (which raises awareness on the importance of the protection of user privacy data on social networking sites) also detected links serving up the Zeus malware on fake Facebook pages, notably ones for National Football League (NFL) fans. Pages such as "*Bring the NFL to Los Angeles*" post links claiming to be football news, but actually infecting computers with Zeus. The malware infected millions of computers, with most cases happening in the US. The new version of the Zeus malware version has been steadily on the rise according to security firm Trend Micro. "*Peddling stolen banking and other personal information from users is a lucrative business in the underground market*," Jay Yaneza wrote on Trend Micro's Website [34]. The security specialists at Trend Micro suggested that it is vital for social network users to be more vigilant while clicking links. Furthermore, frequently used trusted sites should be bookmarked in order to avoid visiting unfamiliar ones.

Point of Attention Many malicious softwares created are usually being recycled to launch further dangerous attacks in the future. The Zeus malware case triggers the need for information security specialists to improve on their malware predictive analytical tools in order to understand and predict the goals of future malware attacks.

Malloy Labs (which offers "Smart solutions for security issues" by developing state-of-the-art cyber security toolkits for professionals and NATO states alike) were able to connect the Zeus malware to Russian servers belonging to a crime organization known as the Russian Business Network. In addition to malware, the gang has been linked to numerous online crimes, including identity theft. There have also been versions of the Zeus malware found which attacked Android and BlackBerry phones. Taking the above issues into account, information security specialists' experts suggest that the preeminent method to remain secure is prevent clicking links also from 'trusted' users, being suspicious of messages encouraging users to click a link without a personal message as well as ensuring that antivirus applications are updated regularly.

5.8 Summary

The chapter has provided insights concerning the issues involved with securing individuals and business organizations from malware attacks. Despite the sophisticated and costly security infrastructures implemented by business organizations to deal with various malware threats, attackers are always finding clever ways to compromise these security measures. Furthermore, we see from the reported cases that the rise of social networks have introduced new ways of delivering malware to business organizations, while employees are divulging more sensitive data on these networks. This implies that practitioners and stakeholders need to implement a multi-pronged tactic towards dealing with malware attacks from social networks rather than employing only mechanical remedies. Security practitioners' have made great improvements in applying security technologies and procedures, but there is a gap in integrating these efforts with employees' behaviors, which are the weakest link in the chain of security. Indeed, with regards to hardware and software-based information security processes, the prevalent weakness is not essentially the computers or software flaws but the end-users. Actually, important errors are sometimes made by users such as, e.g., storing their passwords where others can see them, downloading malware by triggering malicious social network URLs that contain viruses. Because human actions can greatly affect computer security, therefore creating an efficient up-to-date security awareness system for end-users, the information technology employees as well as senior management should be included as a core segment in the security plans. This may ensure that users may start developing good security behaviors. However, these tactics are relatively cost efficient for organizations in the long run. Security awareness should provide users with recommendations for avoiding malicious activities so that they are able to escape potential threats and manage any occurrence. Some safe online behaviors, which users need to adapt, are listed below:

- By no means reply to email requests for financial or personal information.
- Under no circumstances should one password be used for all the online accounts.
- Suspicious email file attachments should not be open.

- Do not reply to any suspicious or unwanted emails.
- Do not install unauthorized applications.
- A firewall should be active at all times.
- The use of weak passwords should be totally prohibited.

The potential benefits of the above recommendations may lead to reduced cost for the business organization in solving security threats. Secondly, it may help in developing a better security awareness culture for employees due to the integrated approach in dealing with malware related issues. Indeed, malware attackers are becoming more creative in manipulating the susceptibilities in desktop and server operating systems, thus bypassing anti-virus softwares, firewalls and other complex security mechanisms. Consequently, there is a need for a better security awareness framework in order for individuals and concerned business organizations to 'keep up' with the propagation speed of malicious payloads on their networks. Furthermore, the cases in this chapter have shown that attackers will continue to exploit the weakest link in the security chain: humans, as a result of the inadequate security awareness system provided for employees in business environments. The growing polymorphic state of modern day malware makes it extremely hard to control and eliminate their attacks. However, further research may and actually is going to consider the possibilities of implementing cost effective and security awareness systems that can be feasible both for individuals and business organizations.

References

1. CNC Group (2010) http://www.computernetworksit.com.au/blog/the-impact-of-malware-in-a-business-environment/. Accessed 27 Oct 2015
2. Mcafee (2015) Malware threat detection and malware block effectiveness – reviews/McAfee. In: McAfee. http://www.mcafee.com/us/threat-center/malware-threat-detection-effectiveness.aspx. Accessed 27 Oct 2015
3. Grossman J (2007) Cross-site scripting worms & viruses – the impending threat & thee best defense, pp 1–18
4. Micro T (2015) Social media malware on the rise. http://blog.trendmicro.com/social-media-malware-on-the-rise/. Accessed 4 Jun 2015
5. Bu Z, Dirro T, Greve P, Lin Y, Marcus D (2012) McAfee threats report: first quarter 2012. McAfee Lab
6. Faghani MR, Saidi H (2009) Malware propagation in online social networks. In: 4th International conference on malicious and unwanted software, MALWARE, pp 8–14. doi:10.1109/MALWARE.2009.5403023
7. Mohtasebi S, Dehghantanha A (2011) Defusing the hazards of social network services. Int J Digit Inf Wirel Commun 1(2):504–515
8. Almeida F (2012) Web 2. 0 technologies and social networking security fears in enterprises. Int J Adv Comput Sci Appl 3(2):152–156
9. Ikhalia EJ (2013) A new social media security model (SMSM). Int J Emerg Technol Adv Eng 3 (7):3–8
10. Loukas G, Gan D, Vuong T (2013) A review of cyber threats and defence approaches in emergency management. Future Internet 5:205–236. doi:10.3390/fi5020205
11. Hoekstra T, Turner M, Lee B, Tyler C (2013) Advanced malware detection and protection trends. Enterprise Strategy Group

12. FireEye (2013) The advanced cyber attack landscape, pp 1–14
13. Villeneuve BN (2011) Trends in targeted attacks trends in targeted attacks. Trend Micro
14. Landesman M (2013) A brief history of malware; the first 25 years. http://antivirus.about.com/od/whatisavirus/a/A-Brief-History-Of-Malware-The-First-25-Years.htm. Accessed 25 Jul 2015
15. Bain ISC (2012) McAfee threats report shows global expansion of cybercrime/McAfee Press Release. http://www.mcafee.com/uk/about/news/2012/q4/20121114-01.aspx. Accessed 27 Jul 2015
16. Latka N (2014) 25 Facebook facts and statistics you should know in 2014. http://www.jeffbullas.com/2014/07/29/25-facebook-facts-and-statistics-you-should-know-in-2014/. Accessed 25 Jul 2015
17. Panda Security (2011) Global survey on social media risks survey of IT & IT security practitioners sponsored by Websense. Phonemon Inst 0–21
18. Merrill T, Latham K, Santalesa R, Navetta D (2011) Social media: the business benefits may be enormous, but can the risks – reputational, legal, operational – be mitigated? ACE Limited, p 13
19. Morabito V (2014) Trends and challenges in digital business innovation. Springer, New York. ISBN 978-3-319-04307-4
20. Thomas K, Nicol DM (2010) The Koobface botnet and the rise of social malware? In: Proceedings of the 5th IEEE international conference on malicious unwanted software, malware, pp 63–70. doi:10.1109/MALWARE.2010.5665793
21. Yan G, Chen G, Eidenbenz S, Li N (2007) Malware propagation in online social networks: nature, dynamics, and defense implications categories and subject descriptors. In: Proceedings of the 6th ACM symposium on information, computer and communications security, pp 196–206. doi:10.1145/1966913.1966939
22. Anderson RJ (2008) Network attack and defense. In: Anderson RJ (ed) Security engineering: a guide to building dependable distributed systems, 2nd edn. Wiley, New York
23. Fisher M (2013) Syrian hackers claim AP hack that tipped stock market by $136 billion. Is it terrorism? The Washington Post. https://www.washingtonpost.com/blogs/worldviews/wp/2013/04/23/syrian-hackers-claim-ap-hack-that-tipped-stock-market-by-136-billion-is-it-terrorism/. Accessed 25 Jul 2015
24. Daniel Politi (2013) Burger king gets 30 % more followers after twitter hack. http://www.slate.com/blogs/the_slatest/2013/02/18/burger_king_gets_30_more_followers_after_twitter_hack.html. Accessed 13 Nov 2015
25. Baker L, Finkle J (2011) Sony PlayStation suffers massive data breach/Reuters. http://uk.reuters.com/article/2011/04/27/us-sony-stoldendata-idUSTRE73P6WB20110427. Accessed 13 Nov 2015
26. Solutionary (2013) Solutionary SERT Q4 2013 threat intelligence report reveals US is top malware hosting nation, Press Release https://www.solutionary.com/news-events/press-releases/2014/01/sert-threat-intelligence-report-q4-2013/. Accessed 27 Jul 2015
27. Whitney L (2013) Malware getting smarter, says McAfee. http://news.cnet.com/8301-1009_3-57570534-83/malware-getting-smarter-says-mcafee/. Accessed 9 Sept 2014
28. Arduini F, Morabito V (2010) Business continuity and the banking industry. Commun ACM 53:121–125. doi:10.1145/1666420.1666452
29. Bilge L, Dumitras T (2011) Before we knew it an empirical study of zero-day attacks in the real world categories and subject descriptors. In: CCS '12 Proceedings of 2012 ACM conference on computer and communications security, pp 833–844
30. Faghani MR, Matrawy A, Lung CH (2012) A study of Trojan propagation in online social networks. In: Proceedings of the 5th international conference on new technologies, mobility and security (NTMS), pp 6–10. doi:10.1109/NTMS.2012.6208767
31. Yury Namestnikov DM (2012) Kaspersky security bulletin 2012. The overall statistics for 2012, Securelist. https://securelist.com/analysis/kaspersky-security-bulletin/36703/kaspersky-security-bulletin-2012-the-overall-statistics-for-2012/. Accessed 25 Jul 2015

32. Tamir D (2013) Twitter malware: spreading more than just ideas. https://securityintelligence.com/twitter-malware-spreading-more-than-just-ideas/. Accessed 13 Nov 2015
33. Neal RW (2013) Facebook virus: "Zeus" malware steals passwords and drains bank accounts, thrives on social network. http://www.ibtimes.com/facebook-virus-zeus-malware-steals-passwords-drains-bank-accounts-thrives-social-network-1294881. Accessed 27 Jul 2015
34. Millman R (2013) Zeus resurfaces to steal credit card details/ITPRO. http://www.itpro.co.uk/malware/19871/zeus-resurfaces-steal-credit-card-details. Accessed 13 Nov 2015

Part II

Digital Management Trends

NeuroIS

6

Abstract

The chapter explores the opportunities and challenges facing the application of neuro-information systems in solving real-world problems. Recently, there has been some significant interest by organizations to shift from the traditional techniques of data gathering, such as focus groups and interviews towards getting data directly from the human body with the aid of neurophysiological tools, also known as NeuroIS. The aim of this chapter is to elucidate the existing progress made so far towards the development and application of neurophysiological tools. We explore a new innovative business phenomenon—neuro-marketing, reviewing its benefits and adoption challenges. Finally, critical recommendations are highlighted towards increasing the economic benefits of neuro-marketing for business organizations.

6.1 Introduction

Neuroscience focuses on what occurs within the nervous system during the neurological and psychiatric activity by individuals. It is the study of development of the nervous system and how it functions [1]. Neuroscientists seek to understand how the human brain impacts on behavior and cognitive functions [2, 3].

Various methods and tools have been developed from neuroscience to improve the understanding of human cognition, emotion, and behavior within the context of information systems, and to develop neuro-information systems commonly referred to as NeuroIS. NeuroIS is a process of capturing real-time data from the human body with the aid of neurophysiological tools [4]. Neurophysiological tools include psychophysiological and brain imaging tools which have the capabilities of capturing the unconscious processes with direct responses from the human body [1]. Neurophysiological data can provide information that may be inconsistent with traditional data gathering techniques such as self-reporting interviews and questionnaires, due to their less subjective nature [2]. The goal of NeuroIS is to

V. Morabito, *The Future of Digital Business Innovation*,
DOI 10.1007/978-3-319-26874-3_6

contribute to the advancement of new theories that increase the prospects of making precise forecasts of behaviors relating to information technology [1]. The phenomenon, NeuroIS also aims at ensuring that the development of information technology artifacts can affect economic and noneconomic issues; for example, efficiency, gratification, adoption, and well-being [5].

Before now, different methods and strategies have been developed to examine thoughts and feelings by evaluating the neuro-electric brain activity by means of unconventional technological devices in medicine [6]. Neuroscience researchers are beginning to work with business organizations using innovative techniques to evaluate the brain activity of customers' towards generating real-time and accurate data to make better business decisions [6]. These innovative approaches are gradually leading to the design and development of new varieties of user-interfaces, applications and software that allows organizations to know the mind of the customer and therefore modify their marketing practices, products and services to meet customers' expectations. In the next section, we review a few neurophysiological tools and highlight their functions and real-world application.

6.2 Neurophysiological Tools: An Overview

Neurophysiological tools facilitate the measurement of human reactions when engaged in dynamic activities; such as decision-making or reactions to stimuli. Neurophysiological tools involve the use of sensors on the human body to capture the human senses at real time [3]. Eye tracking tools often need subjects to wear special equipment, such as a headgear, which creates an artificial setting. Some popular tools such as the Electroencephalogram (EEG), the Functional Magnetic Resonance Imaging (fMRI) and the Electro dermal Activity (EDA) are discussed in the following sub-section, see also [1].

6.2.1 Electroencephalogram Tools (Brain Imaging Tools)

Electroencephalogram (EEG) measures and records the electrical activity of the brain. It allows scientists to study brain activities in a non-invasively by evaluating voltage differences across the scalp [7]. By inspecting the voltages at the scalp, neuroscientists tend to gain extra understanding of the role of the brain in terms of its functional units. Though there are other techniques to observe the attentiveness of the human brain, Electroencephalogram has numerous distinctive features that are relatively useful in Neuroscience studies. While conducting an EEG session, generating a view of coordinated activity in the brain is possible because EEG is measuring voltages expressed on the scalp and generated by the neural substrate performing work.

Moreover, because raw EEG data are characterized as real valued time series collected at the sensor locations, the influence of digital signal processing is used to provide a real suite of tools throughout analysis. They are often attached in a flexible headset. EEG headsets are then linked, occasionally wirelessly, to a signal receiver permitting both movement and change in position and direction. Non-invasive procedures for recording neural activations comprise of the sensors placed on the surface of the skin for signal attainment instead of using surgically implanted electrodes. This method has been used for many years by medical practitioners and is now gradually shifting into the real world to allow people to control computers with their minds and to better understand their mental processes in organizational settings [1, 7]. Quite a number of brain signals can be recorded and interpreted using EEG with changing significance depending on the area of the brain from which the recordings were made. Precisely, activities in the foremost part of the brain indicate varying views relating to emotion, engagement, attention, and judgment. Often times, business organizations are mostly concerned with such characteristics.

The use of EEG is beginning to experience rising presence in areas of business such as marketing, economics, and more lately Information Systems (IS). They are being utilized to gain more insights into customers' deeper reactions to various stimuli and understand their decision-making processes. Activation patterns in the brain have also been shown to reveal the unfiltered emotional responses of humans [8]. Such brain imaging information combined with more traditional measures from surveys and observational data can provide a better-off context within which researchers and marketers to effectively understand human behavior.

According to [9], EEG are able to support tools such as fMRI in the analyzing marketing communications to a great extent. Dissimilar to neuro-imaging method, EEG could deliver data of a within a short time. As a result, marketers would have enough money for such an instrument to effectively evaluate their TV advertisements, in an analytic and sequential level.

6.2.2 Functional Magnetic Resonance Imaging (Brain Imaging Tools)

Functional Magnetic Resonance Imaging (fMRI) is an approach that involves measuring oxygenated blood volume with the aid of a magnetized analysis that can reveal brain actions [10]. Traditional Magnetic Resonance Imaging (MRI) makes use of a magnet and radio waves to securely and noninvasively produce images of the brain inside the human body. In the early 1990s, researchers sought techniques to use this imaging technology: as a research tool rather than an investigative method. However, with the "f" placed in fMRI, the focus shifts to function. With the aid of an MRI scanner, they monitored the flow of blood to diverse areas of the brain as their research subjects responded to a precise stimulus; a sound, an image, as well as touch. While traditional MRI shows pictures of the internal features of the human body, fMRI creates movies starring the brain [11].

Researchers are using fMRI to provide answers to problems within the field of psychology; questions such as how do people make decisions? What's the best way to treat Parkinson's disease? Why is smoking and drinking so difficult a habit to break? Although psychologists debate that increased blood flow to specific parts of the brain really means something, numerous psychologists are linking fMRI and behavioral data as in their search for answers to these classic questions.

6.2.3 Electro Dermal Activity (Psychophysiological Tools)

Electro dermal activity (EDA) is used to define autonomic modifications in the electrical characteristics of the skin. A widely investigated property is the skin conductance, which can be measured by applying an electrical potential between two points of skin contact and evaluating the resulting current flow between them. EDA is debatably the most valuable guide to observe changes in sympathetic stimulation that are subject to emotional and cognitive conditions. It is the only autonomic psychophysiological variable that is not polluted by parasympathetic activity [12].

The link between cognitive states, stimulation, emotion and attention allows EDA to be utilized as an impartial guide to study emotional states. EDA can also be used to study hidden emotional responses that may occur without conscious awareness or are beyond cognitive intentions such as anticipation, threat, novelty and salience. Studies have also shown that EDA is a valuable pointer of attentional processing, where noticeable stimuli and resource demanding tasks induce improved EDA reactions [11, 12].

6.3 Challenges of Neurophysiological Tools

Some technical challenges are in-built in engaging neurophysiological tools control for real-world tasks. As shown in Fig. 6.1, these challenges are related to the limitations of neurophysiological tools, including slow information transfer rate; high fault rate; autonomy and cognitive load. In what follows details on each challenge are provided.

6.3.1 Slow Information Transfer Rate

The best average data transfer speeds for experienced subjects and well-tuned Neurophysiological systems are relatively slow, about 24 bytes (roughly three characters)/min [1]. This is too slow for natural interactive conversation; new research works in this field should focus on ways of optimizing selection techniques and incorporating prediction mechanisms to speed communication. In addition, the capability of neurophysiological tools to gather real-time data directly from the human body is faced with a difficulty in extracting such large amounts of data, including correcting for movement, preparation for proper recordings, sometimes manual data extraction, and enormous amounts of imaging data (such as fMRI/EEG). The analysis of huge amounts of neurophysiological data can also be an

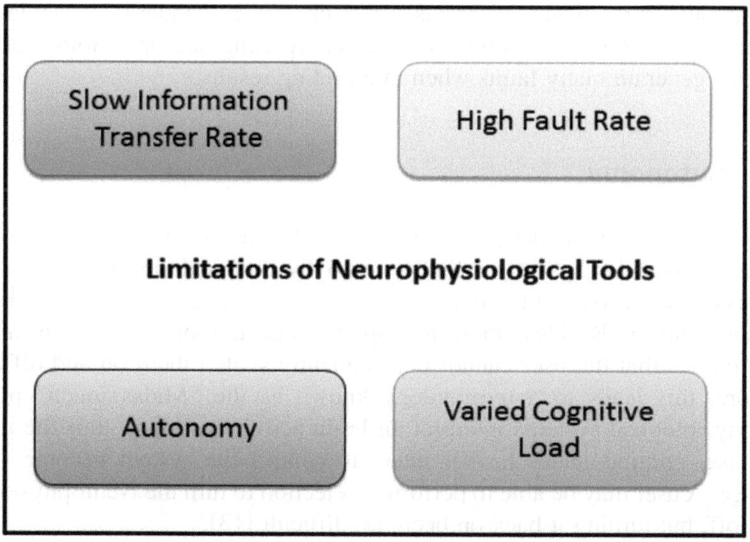

Fig. 6.1 Limitations of neurophysiological tools

overwhelming duty, particularly if there is a need for data pre-processing (such as fMRI data). Though advanced software tools can support data analysis for each tool, the numerical analysis of huge amounts of data from the human body is still a non-trivial assignment. For instance, fMRI data must go through slice timing correction, readjustment, co-registration, segmentation, regularization, and smoothing in preparing for data analysis.

6.3.2 High Fault Rate

One of the substantial problems facing the use of neurophysiological systems is the high likelihood for errors or faults. Brain signals are extremely subject to fluctuations, and this difficulty is worsened in severely incapacitated users by exhaustion, medications as well as medical circumstances such as seizures. Self-reporting errors are also particularly difficult, especially if the subject has little communication channel outside of the neurophysiological system [13].

Furthermore, the results derived through analysis done with Neurophysiological tools may not be as straightforward to understand when compared with traditional sources of data. This is mainly as a result of the mapping of neurophysiological processes to theoretical constructs. For instance, the meaning of many eye tracking processes is still an argued subject, and eye fixations and gaze have been credited to numerous constructs, such as complication, difficulty, interest, and importance.

Likewise, in fMRI studies, a simple expectation of a one-to-one mapping between a brain area and a theoretical construct has made it hard to interpret the meaning of brain activations. Basically, neurophysiological measures can be linked to numerous theoretical constructs. A lack of a standard vocabulary and descriptions may produce complications in interpreting neurophysiological results and hence generate many faults when interpreting results.

6.3.3 Autonomy

Communication systems designed for individuals with severe disabilities needs to be entirely controlled by its user. Sadly, neurophysiological tools require assistance from custodians who need to apply electrodes or signal-receiving devices before a user can connect. Besides, most neurophysiological tools are system-initiated, which implies that the user cannot independently switch them on and off at will. Therefore, this leads to a terminology known as the "Midas touch" problem. Neurophysiological systems interpret all brain activity as input, thus the issue on how a user communicates his/her intent to control the system becomes a huge challenge. A user may be able to perform a selection to turn the Neurophysiological system off, but turning it back on becomes difficult [13].

6.3.4 Varied Cognitive Load

Cognition is described as the practice of acquiring knowledge and reasoning, it is responsible for our understanding of visualizations through absorption and interpretation of an image. Working memory is an essential construct of the cognitive practice, and the burden placed on working memory and cognitive load can be used as a means to evaluate the effectiveness of visualization. Examining the activity of the brain in the course of a cognitive task provides an opportunity to measure the cognitive performance connected with many visualization approaches.

Majority of neurophysiological tools or systems are tested in silent laboratory settings, in which the capacity for users focus on the task at hand with least distractions is high. Conversely, neurophysiological system users have may have to face the real world, which involves more complex situations. This includes the cognitive load of the task being completed, emotional responses, interactions with other people, and perhaps even safety considerations. In both situations, the test results derived would significantly vary which affects its validity and reliability; therefore it is vital for more research works to investigate the effects of cognitive load on the effectiveness of neurophysiological controls in order to decide whether neurophysiological systems could be used for everyday living conditions.

6.4 Business Application of NeuroIS: Neuromarketing

Neuromarketing is the application of cognitive neuroscience theories and techniques to the field of marketing [9]. Neuromarketing can be considered a sub-area of neuroeconomics, as the practice springs from research initially related to economic relevant behaviour. Neuroeconomics emerged from the crossing of boundaries between economics, psychology and neuroscience and its original outset was to investigate a large number of theories of decision-making, bearing irrationality and emotions in mind, in an effort to advance models of choice and decision and to simply better understand people's economic behavior. However, instead of just focusing on decision making processes, neuromarketing is also concerned with evaluating whether a person will respond positively to marketing efforts and potential impact of marketing elements, and can therefore be considered as a radical and much more specific sub-category of neuroeconomics. By understanding how the human brain activates in response to marketing and advertising motivations. The goal of neuromarketing is to build better models to understand consumer behavior and market products.

Combined with traditional marketing research principles neuromarketing can provide better insights that elucidates the decision making process of humans just as the functional brain imaging methods provides real-information on the fundamental brain processes before, during and after the purchasing stages of the consumer (see Fig. 6.2 for a conceptual idea of brain-imaging, adapted from [14]). It deals with relevant marketing challenges with techniques and awareness from brain research. The growing acceptance for using neuro-scientific approaches as a tool for marketing management was due to the inadequate potentials from traditional market research [3, 9].

The traditional techniques used by product designers, salesmen and marketers to gain insight into the thoughts and intentions of their targeted consumers have been focus groups and survey based techniques. With new advances in neuroscience, neurophysiological tools are now helping business owners (especially marketers) to gain an increased understanding of consumers by through the illumination of unconscious thoughts. Neurophysiological tools are assisting marketers with an improved understanding of their targeted consumers by uncovering their unfiltered thoughts and emotional state [4]. The objective for integrating neurophysiological tools into existing practice is to do so with slight invasion to the person.

Neuromarketing has seen two technological dimensions that have sought to examine the human unconscious reasoning: the first dimension concentrated on

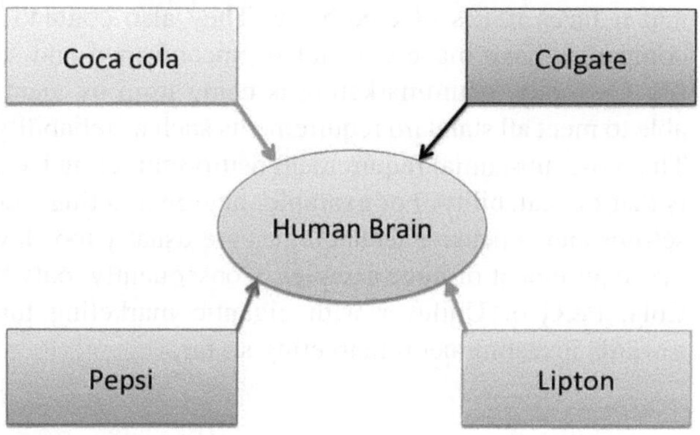

Fig. 6.2 A conceptual idea of brain-imaging adapted from [14]

direct studies analyzing brain activities with the aid of Electroencephalography (EEG) or the more contemporary functional Magnetic Resonance Imaging (fMRI); and the second dimension concentrated on indirect studies analyzing variations in a human's physiological state, such as facial expressions, eye-movement, skin conductance, rate of inhalation, and heart rate using EDA systems [5].

Drawing on neuro-scientific technologies to comprehend the involuntary reasoning and behavior of customers, neuromarketing measures brain and body signals instead and provide useful information alongside traditional self-reporting tools such as surveys, focus groups or interviews [6, 10]. Neuromarketing offers new methods to further advance conventional marketing tools by using innovative forms of end-user interfaces, and softwares [15]. It adds to a more profound understanding of customers' real emotions about their products and services as well as enhanced insights into how to engage with customers on an emotionally.

Most technological developments are not necessarily innovative ideas; there are a number of factors that have such development and trend the growth of this trend. For example, business organizations are engrossed by neuromarketing's prospective to displace old-fashioned market research techniques such as interviews and focus groups which are relatively subjective, costly and time-consuming. Moreover, some organizations are interested in neuromarketing because of its potential to lead to the expansion of new brain-computer interfaces that allows the human brain to communicate directly with outside devices. For instance, beverage manufacturers—Coca-Cola are using neuromarketing in all their quantitative advertisement presentation projects. The integrated neuromarketing involves the recording of participant's facial records while they watch advertisements within a regular survey setting. The technology automatically interprets the emotional and cognitive states of the participants momentarily [16].

6.4.1 The Barriers of Neuromarketing

Some barriers to the development of neuromarketing trend are also encountered. Actually, experts argue that neuromarketing lacks supporting scientific evidence and it faces issues of credibility. They also contend that some neuro-marketing companies have made overstated, unconfirmed and scientifically reckless claims [3]. Currently, neuromarketing is being used by giant companies who have been able to meet all standard requirements such as reliability, scalability and credibility. The most substantial requirement neuro-marketing has not been able to accomplish is that of scalability. For example, neuromarketing studies that trust on laboratory set-ups and expensive technologies are usually too slow and cumbersome to fulfill the requirement of huge samples. Consequently, only big companies such as Coca Cola, P&G or Unilever with gigantic marketing funds have been enthusiastic towards investing neuromarketing so far.

6.4.2 Benefits of Neuromarketing

According to the European Society for Opinion and Market Research (ESOMAR) there has been an upsurge in global market expenditures in 2013 to 29 billion euros. This represents a yearly increase of 0.7 % after inflation. Emerging markets sustained the global market research industry and countered losses and slow-moving performances in 2012 [3] (see also Fig. 6.3).

Furthermore, 70 % of all novel products introduced into the market are taken off the within 2 years; as a result, the burden to boost advertising efficiency remains great [15, 17]. Neuromarketing research offers novel techniques to contribute to these goals as it improves traditional marketing tools by drawing on innovative user-interfaces. In the future, findings originating from neuromarketing could revolutionize the interaction between humans and machines and then lead to the advance of novel brain-computer interfaces that facilitate direct communication between external devices and the human brain [9, 18].

More findings originating from neuromarketing activities have the prospective of adding significant academic value especially in the way researchers collate and analyze their primary research data. New brain-computer interfaces could also ease the living situations of people living with various forms of disability, such as autism patients to better understand social interaction and non-verbal communication.

Neuromarketing may be further incorporated in the fast growing wearable smart electronics market. According to Gartner [19], it will emerge as a 7.5 billion euros industry by 2016. Thus, such neuromarketing applications would create immense value for consumers, mainly when joined with personal preferences, while also providing more-detailed information to retailers for targeted advertisements [3].

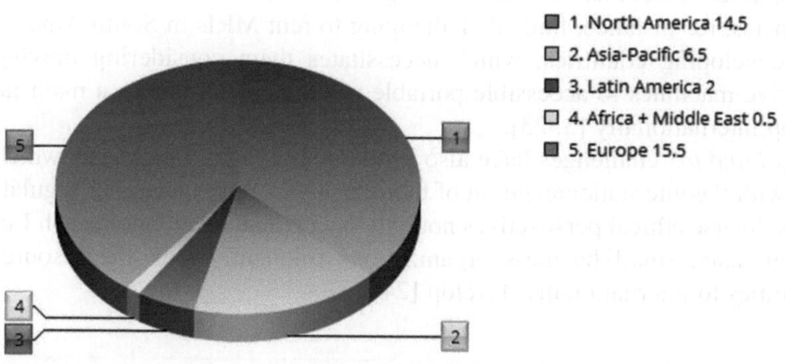

Fig. 6.3 Global market research turnover by continent. *Source*: PwC Analysis; ESOMAR, Global Market Research 2013 adapted from [3]

6.5 Challenges of Adopting Neuromarketing

A primary weakness of neurophysiological tools is the high *cost* needed for its implementation. The cost of psychophysiological tools is currently between $10,000 and $20,000 for a lab to be well equipped. While the use of frequent measures from each subject as well as the precision of objective data require fewer subjects per study [20–22] (for instance, most fMRI experiments only need 10–20 subjects), cost is still an issue that is belter answered by the person incurring the expenses for the studies relative to the predictable insights. *Availability* is another concern, because most neurophysiological tools exist in medical facilities devoted to clinical use. Nevertheless, foremost universities are well equipped with neurophysiological tools. Often times, hospitals and clinics rent their neuroimaging tools for research purposes [1].

Furthermore, market entry barriers are another challenge of adopting neuromarketing. Actually, experts argue that neuromarketing lacks credibility coupled with the controversy that has frequently encircled its activities. For example, some neuromarketing researchers usually promise to "read the customer's" thoughts, while critics dispute that such claims are rash and unsubstantiated [3, 15]. There is also an estimated consensus that the trend is still in its nascent stages and lacks the reliability to evolve as an innovative trend [6, 18]. In their attempt to solve this barrier, neuromarketing organizations currently try to make neuro-marketing more transparent process. For instance, neuromarketing company Synetiq, wishes to publish all data it gathers, while being confidential with its software code [18].

Due to the high interest experienced by neuromarketing organizations, companies such as Neurosense do not encounter bigger challenges in seeking international connections for more business opportunities. However, neuromarketing organizations whose business model depends on the usage of computerized machines are still facing other issues when *internationalizing*. Neurensics, for instance, finds it challenging to rent MRIs in South America or in other developing countries, which necessitates them considering moving from expensive machines to accessible portable or online solutions as a main factor to develop internationally [3, 23].

Legal and tax challenges have also been highlighted as challenges which come along with the internationalization of their business. With dissimilar regulations as well as diverse ethical perspectives not only on a global level, but in each European member state, small business organizations frequently lack the resources and capabilities to internationally develop [24].

6.6 Case Studies

This section discusses four case studies on the application of Neurophysiological tools.

The first case is based on a study conducted by [6]. In this case, the authors attempted to evaluate and study the actions of the brain as well as the sensitive engagement that occurs during an observation of TV commercials with aid of EEG technology. Their objective was to connect variations of data signals built on these neurophysiological actions with cognitive and emotional responses to the presented television advertisement.

Diverse brainy guides were used to summarize the performed measurements at the level of subjects and then later used in statistical analysis. In addition, the authors conducted a gender analysis to investigate and compare cerebral reactions of men and women during the observation of specific two TV commercials falling in several categories. The survey questions of the study were intended to investigate any EEG activity, which differentiated the stages of cognitive and emotional processing connected to the observation of TV advertisements. They also sought to find out if there were particular scenes of the video clips, which were differently perceived by men and women. Their research questions were answered through the application of the EEG techniques.

They recorded the subjects EEG while watching a series of TV advertisements, which were selected from several commercial categories. Furthermore, compared the percentage of spontaneous recall and appreciation of such commercial categories for Men and Women. The related neurophysiological indices measuring cognitive and emotional processing were computed and compared between the two experimental groups and within particular scenes of interest of dissimilar video clips. The findings of the research by [6] show that the levels of memorization of the two TV commercials analyzed were low for both women and men and there were no difference between the two groups.

Point of Attention An advantage of neuromarketing techniques is the direct positive impact it has on the improvement of video-based information. There is a huge likelihood of media production organizations to utilize EEG technology to evaluate the impact of their products.

The second case concern the measurement of anxiety in autism using wearable Sensors and is based on [25]. When autistic children get stressed their tension usually builds up until they have a meltdown, which may lead to being aggressive to others and sometimes inflicting self-injury. Due to the fact that autistic children experience difficulty in expressing their emotions, caregivers may have a challenging time averting meltdowns. These kinds of communication and emotion control difficulties are referred to as Autism Spectrum Disorders (ASD), making interpersonal communications, which are devastating and extremely stressful for children and their families.

In 2009, Affectiva developed its body sensor network technology to detect and record physiological signs of stress and excitement by measuring slight electrical changes in the skin, known as electro-dermal activity (EDA) [25]. The wearable device has the ability to compensate for motion and temperature. Affectiva's central technology is the Q Sensor which is a wearable biometric sensor used by 150 leading universities and organizations which tracks user engagement, excitement, stress and anxiety. The Q Sensor has been developed in two unique models, the Q Sensor Curve and the Q Sensor Pod.

The curve-shaped Q Sensor is intended to be worn on the wrist, which makes it relatively comfortable and modest to wear all day at work, play, or sleep. The pod-shaped Q Sensor can be worn in diverse ways, but the company offers custom bands for wearing the pod in the palm of the hand or on the wrist. The Q Sensor can be worn as a wristband with an actual sensor of about 4 × 4 cm. The device also has a temperature sensor to support the correction of mistakes, for example the device can alert a user simply when he/she enters a hot room rather than having an emotional reaction.

Point of Attention Advances in NeuroIS has the potential of enhancing the manner through which data will be gathered in the nearest future. Although this comes with economic benefits through the sales of wearable technologies, it is important that a more research should critically evaluate the potential health hazards.

Q Sensor software displays skin electro-dermal activity, temperature and motion. A user can view, note and share Q Sensor data, or download the raw data in regular formats. As well, Q Sensor software has loads of built-in utilities plus explanation windows and multiple data views. This particular development has introduced some substantial level of progress in the health sector. Devices such as the Q sector have been designed to take advantage of growing wearable technology market to solve complex issues such as the management of autism. Arguably, this offers business organizations the opportunity to expand on the functionality of such devices towards solving other health related issues. A development of wearable technologies such as these has the capability of creating a healthy market competition amongst practitioners and consequently increases the scalability and reliability of Neuro-psychological tools.

The third case study is based on [15, 26] and describes how Hyundai Motor utilizes the Neuropsychological tool—EEG for their Neuromarketing strategy. Hyundai makes use of EEG-tests while designing design-process of their cars to measure consumers' reactions, when looking at specific parts of a car's exterior design. According to the brand strategy manager at Hyundai Motor the company wants to know what consumers think about a car before the manufacturing process of thousands of cars begins. This simply implies that by applying EEG-tests to the design stage, the technology can possibly reduce the production cost of Hyundai and prevent unnecessary expenditures designing what customers don't need. Through an effective EEG test, apparent poor designs will be identified and hereby prevent Hyundai to develop models that will not impress their potential buyers when they are launched. Hyundai affirms their enthusiasm towards the continued use of EEG-tests and the results hereof to modify innovative models' external design in the future.

Point of Attention Neuromarketing is demonstrating an enormous potential in helping business organizations to save running costs while gaining maximum benefit of their investments. This single effect it has the capability to double the size of the economic growth of any business ready to harness this immense technological opportunity.

The fourth case study is based on [27] which describes how the American snack producer Frito-Lay has made use of neuromarketing on numerous times. By using neuroimaging the company discovered that the bright-colored wrapping they were using for potato chips in 2008 activated the anterior cingulate cortex of the brain, a part linked with guilt feelings. When testing another kind of product wrapping in matte beige colors with potatoes image as well as some other ingredients perceived as healthy, there were no evident activity of the anterior cingulate cortex. Therefore, Frito-Lay swapped out of bright—colored product wrappers and chose the matte design pictured with healthy ingredients [26]. By means of EEG-tests the company also found out that an, when customers were selecting Cheetos over other snacks, they normally considered the orange cheese dust sticking to the fingers after having touched the snack. As a result, Frito-Lay established a campaign of TV-commercials named "The Orange Underground", with stories growing around tricks using the orange colored cheese dust [7].

Point of Attention In carrying out an effective neuromarketing evaluation of a product or a service, it is essential for business organizations to integrate traditional techniques such as focus groups into the process in order to compare the outcome of both results. This comparison can lead to an improved decision making process for any organization eager to use neuromarketing for their product or service innovation. Actually, neuromarketing tools and the traditional data gathering techniques complement each other during the evaluation of advertising campaigns.

The advertisements were assessed through a traditional focus interview and through EEG-tests. According to Frito-Lay Chief Marketing Officer, the EEG-tests showed a much better accuracy than the focus group. The focus group responded negatively to an advertisement in which a woman puts Cheetos in a dryer full of someone else's white clothes, as the group responded that they did not like the trick. Nevertheless, when carrying out EEG-tests where the participants were shown the same advertisement, the brain activity revealed that the participants actually enjoyed the commercial [26]. Interestingly, "The Orange Underground" campaign was received The Grand Ogilvy Award from the Advertising Research

Foundation in 2009 [27]. Hence, the advertisement campaign is a major illustration of how neuromarketing might prove to be beneficial. It was expected by Frito-Lay that participants of the focus group claimed not to like the advertisement campaign because they did not want to appear "unkind" to the other participants, yet, when carrying out the same "interview" of the brain, the participants did indeed like the advertisement [26].

6.7 Summary

To a large extent, the chapter has explored the usefulness of NeuroIS and brain imaging for business and specifically marketing purposes. It is clear that neuroimaging can assist to improve the potentials of research in marketing and thus refining an effective interchange between costs and benefits. This hope is founded on the expectations that people are not able to fully express their preferences when demanded. Neurophysiological methods could be seen as an objective addition to individual, declarative data. When joined, they may allow marketers to depict cognizant and hidden customer feedbacks to persuasive advertising. The chapter also reveals the magnitude of information that can be gained from consumers' brain activities or actions about their correct favorites. Such hidden information could be used to better understand their buying behavior and meet their needs. Although there have been some considerable progress made in this area, the challenges previously discussed shows that neuromarketing is still lingering financial and ethical constraints which affects its global adoption and internationalization. There are certain measures that are worth implementing to face these limitations.

Firstly, policy makers and stakeholders could consider developing tactical initiatives in the field of neuroscience that would progress the business environment for the neuromarketing methods as it enhances the scientific base on which the active enterprises work. Additionally, we have observed that neurophysiological tools initially originated to assist medical practitioners in studying brain activities of humans; therefore, it is important for medical practitioners to work closely with independent business marketers in order to gain deeper scientific knowledge about the human brain. For example, a more profound knowledge about the human brain could help to increase the credibility of neuromarketing and give organizations that would be involved in such study a competitive advantage. Such advantages would be an added boost to encourage neuromarketing organizations to publish more data on their research and methods and thereby tackle the issue of the lack of credibility. Likewise, the policy makers may invest more financial resources to facilitate the set-up of small and medium sized neuromarketing organizations. The cases study of [25] shows that establishing new businesses is usually much harder than undertaking the progression stage that follows. The government may also support infant organizations by decreasing their tax load during the early phases of their neuromarketing business activities.

Better ethical codes can be created and strictly adhered by due to the sensitivity of the data gathered through neuromarketing. An ethical code, which also protects the health hazards that may occur during processes like brain imaging, should also be enforced accordingly. Personal information of experimental subjects may not be kept by the organizations for too long and also experimental subjects less than 18 years of age shall only partake in studies with a legally written consent of their parents.

Finally, the advent of neuroeconomics, where techniques for brain research are applied for commercial purposes, has been a subject for scholars and economic experts for over a decade. As shown in the chapter, a key area of neuro-economics is neuromarketing in which NeuroIS data are used by companies seeking to carry out their marketing campaigns. In previous years, it was relatively challenging to collect objective customer data from conventional research approaches. Now, with the innovative evolution of neuromarketing, "objective" data gathering could be potentially easier.

Although the benefit of neuroscience for research appears to be noticeable, the consequences for marketing management have not been given the required attention in a large extent. Apparently, it seems that only big organizations are making use of neuromarketing due to the huge costs needed for its execution. Small and medium sized organizations are left to rely on traditional research techniques and tools, thus limiting the scope and impact of neuromarketing. Neuromarketing tools and techniques can gain more societal impact if practitioners investigate ways through which every class of businesses can participate innovatively using neuromarketing for cost-effective management of their product/service marketing and sales.

References

1. Dimoka A, Banker R, Benbasat I, Davis F, Dennis A, Gefen D, Gupta A, Ischebeck A, Kenning P, Pavlou P, Müller-Putz G, Riedl R, Vom Brocke J, Weber B (2012) On the use of neurophysiological tools in is research: developing a research agenda for neurois. MIS Q 36:679–702. doi:10.2139/ssrn.1557826
2. Riedl R, Randolph AB, vom Brocke J, Léger P-M, Dimoka A (2010) The potential of neuroscience for human-computer interaction research. SIGHCI 2010 Proceedings. Paper 16
3. Business Innovation Observatory (2014) Neuro-marketing innovations. European Commission
4. Randolph AB, Borders AL, Loe TW (2013) Into the mind of the seller: using neurophysiological tools to understand sales techniques. In: Proceedings of annual Hawaii international conference on systems and sciences, pp 425–429. doi:10.1109/HICSS.2013.283
5. Tudy NES, Dimoka BA (2010) What does the brain tell us about trust and Distrust? Evidence from a functional neuroimaging study. MIS Q 34:1–24
6. Vecchiato G, Maglione AG, Cherubino P, Wasikowska B, Wawrzyniak A, Latuszynska A, Latuszynska M, Nermend K, Graziani I, Leucci MR, Trettel A, Babiloni F (2014) Neurophysiological tools to investigate consumer's gender differences during the observation of TV commercials. Comput Math Methods Med, Article ID 912981:12. doi:10.1155/2014/912981

7. Ohme R, Reykowska D, Wiener D, Choromanska A (2009) Analysis of neurophysiological reactions to advertising stimuli by means of EEG and galvanic skin response measures. J Neurosci Psychol Econ 2:21–31. doi:10.1037/a0015462
8. Kosaka B (2006) Neuropsychological assessment in mild traumatic brain injury: a clinical overview. http://www.bcmj.org/article/neuropsychological-assessment-mild-traumatic-brain-injury-clinical-overview. Accessed 29 Jul 2015
9. Kolar E (2014) Neuromarketing and marketing management: contributions of neuroscience for the traditional marketing mix. In: 3rd IBA Bachelor thesis conference, University of Twente, Enschede, 3 Jul 2014
10. Bullmore ET (2012) Functional magnetic resonance imaging: a new research tool. Am Psycol Assoc Sci Dir 197–201. doi:10.1093/med/9780199696758.003.0025
11. Berman MG, Jonides J, Nee DE (2006) Studying mind and brain with fMRI. Soc Cogn Affect Neurosci 1:158–161. doi:10.1093/scan/nsl019
12. Psychlab (2013) Skin conductance explained. http://www.psychlab.com/SC_explained.html. Accessed 29 Jul 2015
13. Moore MM (2003) Real-world applications for brain – computer interface technology. Rehabilitation 11:162–165
14. Promotrader (2013) Promotrader. http://www.promotrader.es/blog/page/2/?goback=.gmp_2446140.gde_2446140_member_275068755. Accessed 31 Jul 2015
15. Nielsen CG, Fibaek M (2014) Neuromarketing – a brain new world. AU-BSS, Department of Business Communication, Aarhus University
16. Dooley R (2013) Neuromarketing: for coke, it's the real thing – forbes. http://www.forbes.com/sites/rogerdooley/2013/03/07/coke-neuromarketing/. Accessed 17 Nov 2015
17. Bridger D (2015) The 7 main benefits of neuromarketing. http://www.koganpage.com/article/the-7-main-benefits-of-neuromarketing. Accessed 17 Nov 2015
18. Randolph AB, Pierquet S (2015) Bringing advertising closer to mind□: using neurophysiological tools to understand student responses to super bowl commercials. In: 48th Hawaii international conference on systems and sciences. doi:10.1109/HICSS.2015.68
19. Gartner (2012) Gartner reveals top predictions for IT organizations and users for 2013 and beyond. http://www.gartner.com/newsroom/id/2211115. Accessed 17 Nov 2015
20. Dimoka A, Pavlou PA, Davis FD (2011) NeuroIS: the potential of cognitive neuroscience for information systems research. Inf Syst Res 22:687–702. doi:10.1287/isre.1100.0284
21. Riedl R, Banker RD, Benbasat I, Davis FD, Dennis AR, Dimoka A, Gefen D, Gupta A, Ischebeck A, Kenning P, M̈uller-Putz G, Pavlou PA, Straub DW, vom Brocke J, Weber B (2010) On the foundations of NeuroIS: reflections on the Gmunden retreat 2009. Commun Assoc Inf Syst 27:243–264
22. Lee N, Broderick AJ, Chamberlain L (2007) What is "neuromarketing"? A discussion and agenda for future research. Int J Psychophysiol 63:199–204. doi:10.1016/j.ijpsycho.2006.03.007
23. Kivikangas JM, Ekman I, Chanel G, Järvelä S, Cowley B, Henttonen P, Ravaja N (2010) Review on psychophysiological methods in game research. J Gaming Virtual Worlds 3 (3):181–199
24. Braithwaite J, Watson D, Robert J, Mickey R (2013) A guide for analysing electrodermal activity (EDA) & skin conductance responses (SCRs) for psychological experiments. Behavioural Brain Sciences Centre, University of Birmingham, pp 1–42
25. Edwards B (2011) Wearable sensor by affectiva can measure anxiety and is helping autism research. http://www.imedicalapps.com/2011/10/wearable-sensor-by-affectiva-can-measure-anxiety-and-is-helping-autism-research/. Accessed 29 Jul 2015
26. Burkitt L (2009) Neuromarketing. http://www.forbes.com/forbes/2009/1116/marketing-hyundai-neurofocus-brain-waves-battle-for-the-brain.html. Accessed 18 Nov 2015
27. Nobel C (2013) http://www.forbes.com/sites/hbsworkingknowledge/2013/02/01/neuromarketing-tapping-into-the-pleasure-center-of-consumers/. Accessed 18 Nov 2015

and micro changes that assail us on an individual level" (p. 42), explaining that for many employees change implies a loss of the security that goes with a specific job. Other people may fear that they lack the skills and stamina needed for change. Still others may be afraid that good working conditions may be taken away. Some employees may fear that change implies a loss of responsibility and power. Other people may see a proposed change as an attack on their previous performances and react defensively.

As for the above issues, Duck [38] explains change as something deeply personal because it requires people to do something different, to think something different and to feel something different. Duck [38] also adds that it is not simply whether people feel positive or negative about a change but how they handle it. Taking the above issues into account, researchers have therefore identified various employees' responses to organizational changes ranging from strong positive attitudes to strong negative attitudes [39]. As a result, change can be received with excitement and happiness or anger, fear, anxiety, uncertainty and worry, while employees' responses may range from positive intentions to support the change to negative intentions to oppose it.

Change requires the participation of people who must first change themselves for organizational change to succeed. Managers need to develop an understanding of how people respond to change. Organizational change entails the ending of something and the beginning of something else [25, 40, 41]. For example, it might involve the introduction of a new organizational structure, a more automated production process, job transfers, closure of a plant or the mergers of two units. While these changes might be carefully planned and happen on a prearranged date, it might take some time until those involved have adapted to these external events [42]. Because organizations consist ultimately of people, organizational change essentially involves personal change. Bridges [4] introduces a model of transition in which he conceptualizes transition as beginning with an ending and then going on to a new beginning via a neutral phase. Bridge [4] explains each phase as follows:

- ***Ending phase*** involves 'letting go' of the old situation and the identity that went with it. It is impossible for employees to fully engage in a new role or have a new purpose until they have let go of the old role or purposes. Change can only begin when one thing ends and something new starts.
- ***Neutral zone*** is the in-between stage. This phase is a period of disorientation, self-doubt and anxiety, but it can also be a period of growth in which new opportunities are identified. It involves recognition of the need to change and uncertainty about the nature of desirable end states.
- ***Beginning phase*** involves direction to a new situation and the development of a new identity. In this phase as the new situation is identified more clearly and a new identity is internalized, the forces for maintenance and growth achieve a new balance.

This process can be mapped to Kurt Lewin change theory and Lewin's three-step model that is very much an important part of change management strategies for managing planned change in the workplace in the twenty-first century. Although this change management model was developed long ago during 1940s, the concept of '*unfreezing-transition-freezing*' however still remains very relevant today. Lewin's three-step change model can be summarized as follows:

- ***Unfreeze***: The aim of this step is to reduce the forces that are striving to maintain the status quo and undoing the current mind set by showing problems make individuals realize the necessity of change.
- ***Transition***: Developing new ways of doing things, values, behaviours and attitudes through organizational re-structuring process and development techniques.
- ***Freeze***: The final stage of refreezing and the adaptation of ownership of the new 'as is'. This phase is very critical as the organization may revert to former ways of doing things unless the changes are reinforced through freezing.

In summary, the Kurt Lewin model demonstrates that to move an organization from point A to B first managers should create compelling and motivating reasons to change (*unfreeze*). Then necessary changes should be implemented to the way managers wish for things to be (*transition*). Then the aim should be to re-stabilize the operation at a higher level of performance (*freeze*). IT-related organizational changes, which actually are a type of organizational change initiative, have particularly attracted the attention of academics and practitioners for several decades and have been a central concern in the field of information systems [43–46]. The changes that continue to occur as ICTs and technological advancements pervade organizations and become intensely involved in intra- and inter-organizational relations, decision-making processes, operational procedures, as well as employees' work practices are multi-faceted, complex and unpredictable to say the least [27, 47–49].

7.2.1 IT Innovations as Disruptive IT Events

The implementation of new IT systems suggests modifications in organizational processes, tasks and the nature of work [50] and very often it is accompanied by complementary administrative innovations [51]. While non-disruptive IT systems[1] still offer challenges to individuals as system users, the technology itself is not fundamentally new to them [33]. The same, however, cannot be said about disruptive IT events. System users who make sense of the technological innovation and appraise their roles, tasks, and utility to be empowered by the new IT system usually support its adoption, while those who perceive their roles, tasks, and utility as

[1] Non-disruptive IT events are compatible with previous systems or work processes with which the IS users are already familiar [33].

diminished usually resist its adoption [24, 52]. Sherif et al. [51] define a disruptive IT innovation as

> a novel idea or behavior that when introduced in organizational settings, causes dramatic changes in the structure of work processes (p. 340).

Lyytinen and Rose [11] similarly suggest that when the technology is disruptive IS users do not behave in a predictable manner. The result of a study by Lazar et al. [53] also indicates that 43 % of IS users' time is wasted in frustrating experiences resulting from disruptive IT systems. As a result, changes induced by disruptive IT events can be threatening for IS users who are also social actors [54]. This is why it is crucial for researcher, managers and change agents to learn how employees adapt to radical technological advancements in work settings because their needs can be better under stood and addressed.

7.2.2 Types of IT Events

Sometimes, modifications made to an existing IT can be viewed as significant enough to stimulate similar user responses as with the implementation of a new IT system [28]. Taking the above issues into account, it is worth considering a *disruptive IT event* as referring to IT artifacts as a whole including computers as both hardware and software components, IT infrastructures, peripherals as well as the consequences that result from this encounter such as changes in work routines. However, part of a disruptive IT event includes difficulties that users face when working with the new technology and the interruptions it causes. Thus, this section briefly covers this aspect of disruptive IT systems in work settings.

Guinea and Webster [31] explain that during an IT interaction there are three types of *encounters* that can take place, classifying them into the following categories:

1. *a good event* (*discovery*);
2. *an expected event* (*normal*); and
3. *an unexpected technological interruption* (*negative*).

The discovery encounters take place when users find new functions in an IT or a new way of using the IT that makes the completion of their tasks easier or more effective. The second type of encounter occurs when things go smoothly and IT behaves as expected. Finally, the third type of encounter represents a stressful situation and will be appraised by the computer users as threatening. Coraggio [55] describes an *interruption* as a

> externally-generated, randomly occurring, discrete event that breaks continuity of cognitive focus on a primary task (p. 19).

In this definition the term '*externally-generated*' indicates that the nature of the interruption is not controlled by the system user; '*randomly*' occurring means that the user cannot foresee the timing of the interruption; and '*discrete*' implies that the interruption has a finite duration [55].

Within an IT context, negative interruptions include misunderstandings, confusions or troubles with the new IT system [56]. These circumstances occur when there is 'an unexpected failure', 'a disruption', 'a problematic situation' or when there is a significant difference between expectations and reality" [57]. Because of the characteristics of the negative unexpected IT events, they will be perceived as demanding, which represents a specific case of a stressful situation within the coping theory. After over two decades of research on IS use and users' numerous frustrating experiences with IT, we do not know yet much about the complexity of coping processes and particular adaptive strategies by which users deal with IT interruptions [30, 31].

7.3 The Challenges of IT-Induced Changes for System Users

A major challenge facing organizations is that of adapting to major technological advancements that influence daily work routines. Griffith [28] refers to the complexity of human responses to major changes in their immediate environment and explains it this way:

> given the complex systems within which new technologies are implemented, it is even more difficult for implementers of modern technologies to anticipate users' sense-making and its effect (p. 472).

This indicates that while the functioning of new devices or technologies can be predicted, experience tells us that this is not the case with human reactions to these changes [13]. Thus, gaining insight into employees' perspectives concerning technological changes will strengthen the IT use-performance link.

7.3.1 Employees' Emotions

Up until now, many researchers have tried to investigate to various degrees the complex processes involved in individual's emotional responses. Walinga [58] refers to the challenges of change and explains:

> organizational change poses many challenges to the individual [...] Effectively meeting any challenge demands certain physical, emotional and psychological resources in such areas as creativity, problem solving, focus, memory recall, and task performance (p. 7).

Furthermore, Beaudry and Pinsonneault [21] indicate that emotions felt by users early in the implementation of new IT have important effects on subsequent IT use. Similarly, Schraeder et al. [50] examine the relationships between employee reaction to specific technological changes and the job-related attitudes of these employees. Kashefi et al. [19] in the same stream of research investigated the crucial role and impact of one's emotions and cognition towards their receptivity to and mobilization for an IT-related organizational change.

Emotions influence our beliefs and attitudes and they help guide our thinking, decision-making and actions [29, 59]. Beaudry and Pinsonneault [21] indicate that cognitive-based models such as, e.g., technology acceptance model [60, 61] or the unified theory of acceptance and use of technology [60] predict IT use based on perceptions and beliefs about the instrumental nature of technology such as effort and performance expectancy and perceived compatibility. As a result, they are thought not to be able to capture the full range of emotional reactions of users in order to account for their relationship to IT adoption. Emotion-based models of IT use are thus needed to complement cognitive-based approaches since usage of a new IT is complex and multifaceted, and human behavior does not always comply with technical/rational models [62]. However, to date, little attention has been given to understanding how emotions can influence employees' IT adoption and use [21].

7.3.2 Users' Psychological Stress

Stress when experienced in an acute form, is the most unpleasant feeling that a human being can experience. It exists when routine thoughts, feelings and behaviors in the subconscious conflict with new thoughts and feelings in the conscious mind [29]. Moreover, these unconscious forces can have more power over an individual's behavior than consciousness does [40]. In terms of definition, stress can be categorized into three types; the first type is stimulus-based which considers stress as environmental or situational based stimulus, impinging on the person. The second type is response-based, defining stress as an individual's psychological response to environmental and situational forces. The third definition brings together the concepts of the first two definitions in the sense that it defines stress as both the stimulus (source of stress) and the response [63].

In terms of the impact of stress on attitudes to change and organizational commitment, many studies have suggested that organizational change efforts most of the time are very stressful for employees [35, 64]. Several research contributions have also compared these stressful phases and responses to change, with individual responses to shocking changes such as death and grief. Vakola and Nikolaou [63] explain that

> Stress caused by organizational change will result in creating negative attitudes toward change and therefore will become an inhibitor to change (p. 163).

Benamati and Lederer [65] studied the coping mechanisms used by IT managers to reduce the stress associated with rapid changes in IT. Similarly, Tsai et al. [66] investigated how IT professionals perceived and coped with the stress associated with continuously having to update their technical skills. Furthermore, stress is a well-known factor for low motivation and morale [19, 63], decrease in performance and low job satisfaction [67] and finally low quality services and poor internal communication [8].

7.4 User Adaptation to Disruptive IT Events

Organizations usually implement information systems to improve efficiency, reduce errors and enhance productivity, among other goals [1]. However, empirical evidence has revealed that such benefits occur only to the degree that system users of the technology adapt by proactively changing themselves (self), their work routines (task) and even the IT system itself (technology) in order to leverage its strategic capability [22–24, 32, 33, 68]. Notwithstanding the importance of user adaptation to IS and its impact on IS success outcomes has been documented by several studies, various aspects of user adaptation surrounding how, why, when and to what extent adaptation unfolds at the individual level remain unclear [69]. This highlights the need for studying the link.

7.4.1 Coping to IT-Related Organizational Changes

People constantly evaluate various aspects of their environment to see if they are personally or professionally relevant. They are thus dynamically responsive to events affecting them that occur in their surroundings [70], or, according to Folkman and Lazarus's [29] terminology, the '*person-environment*' relationship. These active reactions to stressful events shape the core arguments of the 'psychological stress and coping theory' that has its origin in the domain of psychology [29]. *Coping theory* in essence was developed to explain the dynamics underlying individual's appraisal and reactions to disruptive events in their life. While this theory over the years has been referred to by different names, the most common terminologies include: stress theory, emotion theory, appraisal theory of emotion, coping theory, relational cognitive theory and contextual theory of coping and stress. In Organizational Behavior and Information Systems research, coping theory has been applied to a large array of events from interruptions in organizational context such as organizational downsizing [71] and users' adaptation behaviors to IT events [23].

While the study of coping has produced a huge literature in psychology over the past several decades or so, IT research on users' coping efforts facing disruptive IT events is nevertheless quite limited [31]. This is somewhat surprising because a considerable amount of research in IS has been directed towards negative reactions to technology (e.g. computer anxiety) and the coping theory provides an appropriate framework from which to examine them. Moreover, since the implementation of a new IT system can be seen and understood as a disruptive event in the habits and work systems of users [21, 23], the behaviors of users facing such events can be analyzed using the coping theory.

Coping theory is well suited to study the individual adaptation process caused by a new IT implementation because it shares three key characteristics with existent user adaptation studies [22]. First, adaptation studies typically center on users' reactions to the implementation and use of a new technology (i.e., IT artifacts) as these types of IT-induced changes can potentially involve significant consequences in organizations. Second, both coping theory and user adaptation studies focus on similar components of the individual-environment relationship, which in IS literature is usually referred to as the "context" [72], as we have also seen in previous sections. Each person subjectively evaluates the *encounter* with the environment and the available resources to manage it [29, 73]. Third, both coping theory and user adaptation studies are concerned about the vast array of potential consequences of the adaptation/coping process ranging from solving the problem at hand, increasing one's efficiency, reducing the undesirable effects of the stressor, to restoring emotional stability and maintaining one's sense of well-being.

7.5 IT Ambidexterity and Organizational Agility

In today's business environment, organizational agility is becoming a focal point for competitive success because it reflects a firms' responsiveness to market changes [74, 75]. Businessdictionary.com [18] and Zain [76] define organizational agility as the capability of a company to rapidly change or adapt to dynamic changes in the market. A high degree of organizational agility will help business firms to better react to the emergence of new competitors, the development of new industry-changing technologies, or sudden shifts in overall market conditions.

It has also been acknowledged that information technologies provide a key stage on which contemporary organizations compete through utilizing their digitized processes, knowledge, and design capital [77, 78]. Aligned with this, the strategic management of organizational IT resources has attracted attention as a key enabler of organizational agility [77, 79]. Particularly, with continued advances in IT solutions and services, IT ambidexterity has been recognized as a fundamental capability that can enable organizational agility and firm performance [78, 80]. So, what is *IT ambidexterity* and how is it related to the above-mentioned user IT adaptation behaviors? Organizational learning theorists have so far identified two distinct ways by which business firms influence their resources and capabilities: *exploration* and *exploitation* (see e.g., Levinthal and March [81], March [82]), where:

- ***Exploration*** refers to the efforts to learn and discover how to combine and recombine potential resources in novel ways to create new capabilities and opportunities [83, 84].
- ***Exploitation***, on the other hand, relates to the efficient leverage and refinement of existing resources through known processes [82, 83].

Different researchers have so far highlighted the need for simultaneous pursuit of these two processes, which is referred to as ambidexterity [85, 86]. *Ambidexterity* is argued to be highly desirable for modern companies because they face regular changes in business environments [87, 88]. To be responsive to environmental changes, firms should be able to conduct both exploration and exploitation in a way that these processes complement each other and are balanced, rather than increase the tension between the two [83, 85, 89]. *IT ambidexterity* as a particular case of organizational ambidexterity is defined as a firm's ability to concurrently follow exploration and exploitation in their management of IT resources and practices which could be an antecedent of organizational agility [90, 91].

So how is ambidexterity achieved? Tripsas [87] and Taylor and Helfat [26] suggested that in order to adjust the conflicting alignments required for innovation and efficiency, business firms required to modify their structures over time to align to meet the firm's policy, which represents a *sequential fashion* by shifting structures over time. This approach suggests that sequential ambidexterity may be more useful and beneficial in stable, slower moving environments and for smaller firms that lack the resources to pursue simultaneous ambidexterity [84].

Tushman and O'Reilly [88], in a different view, argued that in the face of rapid change, sequential ambidexterity might be ineffective and thus organizations needed to explore and exploit in a *simultaneous fashion*. They suggested that this could be achieved by, e.g., forming autonomous 'explore' and 'exploit' subunits that were structurally separated but with targeted integration to ensure the use of resources and capabilities. This approach, in essence, is usually considered as *structural ambidexterity* and requires not only separate structural units for exploration and exploitation but also different capabilities, systems, procedures, and cultures—each internally aligned. Both sequential and structural ambidexterity as discussed above attempt to solve the exploration-exploitation tension through structural means. Gibson and Birkinshaw [85] in 2004 proposed that this tension could be resolved at the individual level through what they termed *contextual ambidexterity*:

> Building a set of processes or systems that enable and encourage individuals to make their own judgments about how to divide their time between conflicting demands for alignment and adaptability (p. 210).

In their view, the ability to balance exploration and exploitation tension requires a "supportive organizational context" that

> encourages individuals to make their own judgments as to how to best allocate their time between the conflicting demands for alignment and adaptability (p. 210).

Although each of the modes of ambidexterity were initially proposed as separate ways to deal with the need for exploitation and exploration, in reality a combination of these methods can be used to achieve the desired outcomes [92]. For example, Raisch et al. [83] found that incumbent firms created new business by initially employing structural ambidexterity and switched to integrated designs when the exploratory unit achieved political and economic legitimacy. As above argued, IT

Fig. 7.3 IT ambidexterity

ambidexterity can be considered particular case of organizational ambidexterity. '*IT exploration*' accordingly refers to the experimentation with new IT resources and practices, whereas IT exploitation refers to the utilization of existing and proven IT resources and practices. IT exploration is, in fact, related to the ability of a business firm to dedicate and allocate necessary resources and managerial time to gain an understanding of different IT systems and artifacts. In so doing, organizations should tryout the most promising ones to learn about their functionalities, and select those few technologies that are most likely to have a positive impact on the current and future business operations. *IT exploitation,* in contrast, is related to the ability of a firm to properly manage its current portfolio of IT assets, reuse them in different business activities, invest in complementary technologies to improve their effectiveness, and finally to fuse the technologies with the firm's business processes [91].

From an ambidexterity perspective, while IT exploration is needed to direct attention toward the emerging technologies, methodologies, and skills, IT exploitation is also needed to ensure that organizations are able to fully utilize their current IT resources to reap their full benefits [78, 91, 92]. As a result, firms can better respond to both current and emerging business needs, thus becoming agile. As shown in Fig. 7.3, IT ambidexterity therefore can be defined as a firm's capacity to experiment technologies with promising commercial potential (*IT exploration*) and implement an efficient means of leveraging these technologies (*IT exploitation*), thus properly managing both current and emerging technologies as well as understand their potential value for business [82, 83, 91, 92].

Several studies have described leadership processes as a supporting factor towards an ambidextrous organization. Tushman and O'Reilly [88], for example, state that ambidexterity is facilitated by the top-management team's internal processes. Gibson and Birkinshaw [85], similarly, note the

> important role played by senior executives in making an organization context effective and developing ambidexterity (p. 223).

From a different perspective, Patterson et al. [90] point out the characteristics and behaviors of people in organizations who are at the core of organizational innovation, as consider them as equally important as the role that top management teams play. They argue that whilst the biggest challenge for many organizations may be surviving the dynamic fluctuating economic climate, promoting and

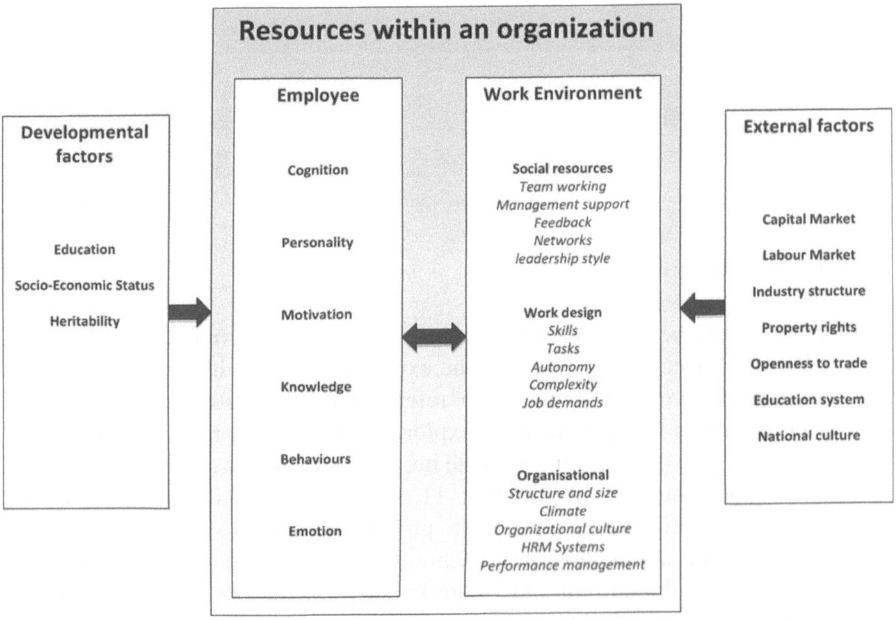

Fig. 7.4 Employee related resources for innovation in organizations, adapted from [90]

encouraging innovative working may contribute to long-term organizational survival (Fig. 7.4).

Managers should realize that this process is very complicated. The CEO and his/her team members have a critical role in this complex process. First, they need to make a thoughtful decision as to how much they are willing to sacrifice in the design of a IS that is capable of managing strategic contradictions effectively. Second, they need to inform both internal and external stakeholders by explicit decisions and actions how and which forms of ambidexterity will be achieved. One way to engineer this complex process more smoothly is by demonstrating small successes to the entire system constituencies. This will engender more confidence that although the journey to ambidextrous organization is difficult and complex, it will reap fruit. As said above and also shown in Fig. 7.4, employees' psychological factors play an important role in this organizational modernization. This suggests the importance of attention to the social side of any organizational change initiatives such as IT-related organizational transformations. Better understanding of user IT adaptation behaviors and the extent to which such psychological processes can be properly managed and addressed by top management can therefore have significance influences on organizational agility and firm performance for reaching an effective IT ambidexterity.

7.6 Case Studies

This section discusses two case studies showing the importance of attention to social side of organizations' digital transformations.

The first case study, based on a research by Kashefi and Abbott [19], is about an organization that underwent three organizational changes over the past three decades in one of the middle-east countries. In the first two organizational changes, the structure was transformed whereas in the last one computerized work systems were introduced. Amongst all the organization's divisions, the Department of Sport's development programme and budget were selected for the purpose of this chapter since it was one of the core departments for computerizing the work system. Prior to the computerization, work processes were completely paper-based and manually driven. The organizational structure was therefore changed twice in order to advance the workflow but the outcome was not as effective as expected. As a result, management suddenly decided to introduce IT systems to the organization in order to automate the workflow.

This raised concerns as management had no clear strategies toward IT implementation and use. Such ambiguous strategies can be referred to as the absence of certain milestones for IT implementation progress; adherence to traditional managerial approaches which were opposed to computerized work systems; and allocating inadequate budgets for effective implementation and employee training. These resulted in very slow uptake of the system by employees. Those undesirable appraisals of the situation affected employees' willingness directly and generated negative emotions concerning their system use. Negative evaluations made employees not to be mentally ready and motivated in order to take concrete actions toward the adoption and use of the new computerized work system.

Point of Attention If users have very little or no computer skills, they may be sensitive to the management's decisions, thus relying heavily on the social supports and available resources to adapt to new ways of doing things. Evaluating an IT event based on the availability of coping resources- and not necessarily based on the quality of the implemented IT system- represents an area of concern for managers.

In the second case study, based on Usseiman [93], we consider IBM's technological transition to mainframe computing between 1949 and 1965. The case is quite a classic, but still providing important insights on the topics considered in this Chapter. IBM's technological transition encompassed *economic incentives*, *organizational structure*, *social context*, and *organizational cognition*, each favored ambidextrous linkages within IBM involving the new core technology and preceding complementary assets such as its sales force and field engineering staff. These four influences also reinforced one another during IBM's transition.

Point of Attention IBM's experience demonstrates how managerial influences can strengthen linking activities during a technological transition. The economic incentives, organization structure, social context, and cognition at IBM did favor ambidextrous linkages within and between units in charge of the new core technology and existing complementary assets.

For example, IBM's sales managers had economic motivations to sell leases for the new electronic computing machines, worked within an organizational structure that emphasized on-going communication with other functional areas involved with the new machines, and operated within a social context and shared organizational cognition that placed a high value on coordination between business functions in supporting the new computing business.

7.7 Summary

This chapter has introduced the reader to research on IT adaptation behaviors, organizational agility and IT ambidexterity happening during organizations' digital transformation. In particular, the chapter has investigated user adaptation to IT-related organizational changes and its connection with IT ambidexterity. Furthermore, it argued that for technological transitions to succeed, the new core technology and complementary assets must function as an interdependent system. This requires organizational linkages between units in charge of the new core technology and old complementary assets, as well as linkages between and within units in charge of complementary assets. Thus, the chapter also pointed out that the top management-employee linkage is vital for a successful organizational change. Leaders opening/encouraging behaviors create a psychologically safe environment, which is necessary for employees' exploration behaviors such as, e.g., learning. On the other hand, leaders closing behaviors direct employees' focus on goal accomplishment, which should facilitate exploitation behaviors.

References

1. Fadel K (2012) The role of appraisal in adapting to information systems. J Organ End User Comput 24:18–40. doi:10.4018/joeuc.2012100102
2. Fadel KJ, Brown SA (2010) Information systems appraisal and coping: the role of user perceptions. Commun Assoc Inf Syst 26:107–126
3. Eriksson C (2004) The effects of change programs on employees' emotions. Pers Rev 33:110–126
4. Bridges W (2009) Managing transitions: making the most of change. Da Capo Lifelong Books, Boston
5. Tams S, Craig K, Murphy R (2011) Coping with interruptions in computer-mediated environments: the role of computer self-efficacy. In: Proceedings of South Association for information systems conference, Atlanta, 25–26 Mar 2011, pp 175–180

6. Claggett J (2010) Understanding primary appraisal in user adoption: an exploratory case study of a telehealth project. In: Proceedings of the South Association for information systems conference, Atlanta, 26–27 March 2010
7. Barki H, Titah R, Boffo C (2007) Information system use-related activity: an expanded behavioral conceptualization of individual-level information system use. Inf Syst Res 18:173–192
8. Vakola M, Tsaousis I, Nikolaou I (2004) The role of emotional intelligence and personality variables on attitudes toward organisational change. J Manage Psychol 19:88–110
9. Swarnalatha C, Prasanna TS (2005) Employee engagement and change management. Int J Bus Manage Invent 2:1–6
10. Rogers E, Shoemaker F (1971) Communication of innovations; a cross-cultural approach. Free Press, New York
11. Lyytinen K, Rose GM (2003) The disruptive nature of information technology innovations: the case of internet computing in systems development organizations. MIS Q 27:557–595
12. Markus M (2004) Technochange management: using IT to drive organizational change. J Inf Technol 19:4–20
13. Bruque S, Moyano J, Eisenberg J (2008) Individual adaptation to IT-induced change: the role of social networks. J Manage Inf Syst 25:177–206. doi:10.2753/MIS0742-1222250305
14. Swanson E (1994) Information systems innovation among organizations. Manage Sci 40:1069–1092
15. Shabanesfahani A, Tabrizi M (2012) Information technology adoption and related policy issues in Malaysia. IOSR J Environ Sci Toxicol Food Technol 2:43–47
16. Hirschheim R, Klein HK (2012) A glorious and not-so-short history of the information systems field. J Assoc Inf Syst 13:188–235
17. Alter S (2008) Defining information systems as work systems: implications for the IS field. Eur J Inf Syst 17:448–469
18. BusinessDictionary.com. http://www.businessdictionary.com/. Accessed 15 Nov 2015
19. Kashefi A, Abbott P (2012) The influences of employees' emotions and cognition on IT adoption: some perspectives from Iran. In: 45th Hawaii international conference on systems and sciences, pp 5152–5161
20. Walsham G (1993) Interpreting information systems in organizations. Wiley, Chichester
21. Beaudry A, Pinsonneault A (2010) The other side of acceptance: studying the direct and indirect effects of emotions on information technology use. MIS Q 34:689–710
22. Beaudry A (2009) Coping with information technology. In: Handbook of research on contemporary theoretical models in information systems, pp 516–528
23. Beaudry A, Pinsonneault A (2005) Understanding user responses to information technology: a coping model of user adaptation. MIS Q 29:493–524
24. Tyre M, Orlikowski W (1994) Windows of opportunity: temporal patterns of technological adaptation in organizations. Organ Sci 5:98–118
25. Liu Y, Perrewé P (2005) Another look at the role of emotion in the organizational change: a process model. Hum Resour Manage Rev 15:263–280
26. Taylor A, Helfat CE (2009) Organizational linkages for surviving technological change: complementary assets, middle management, and ambidexterity. Organ Sci 20:718–739. doi:10.1287/orsc.1090.0429
27. Zorn T (2002) The emotionality of information and communication technology implementation. J Commun Manage 7:160–171. doi:10.1108/13632540310807296
28. Griffith T (1999) Technology features as triggers for sensemaking. Acad Manage Rev 24:472–488
29. Folkman S, Lazarus RS, Dunkel-Schetter C et al (1986) Dynamics of a stressful encounter: cognitive appraisal, coping, and encounter outcomes. J Pers Soc Psychol 50:992–1003. doi:10.1037/0022-3514.50.5.992
30. Fadel KJ (2012) User Adaptation and Infusion of Information Systems. J Comput Inf Syst 52:1–10

31. De Guinea A, Webster J (2011) Are we talking about the task or the computer? An examination of the associated domains of task-specific and computer self-efficacies. Comput Human Behav 27:978–987
32. Elie-dit-cosaque C, Pallud J (2010) User adaptation and IS success□: an empirical investigation among French workers. In: ICIS 2010 Proceedings, p 158
33. Elie-Dit-Cosaque CM, Straub DW (2011) Opening the black box of system usage: user adaptation to disruptive IT. Eur J Inf Syst 20:589–607. doi:10.1057/ejis.2010.23
34. Humphrey A (1986) Gearing up for change. Manage Decis 24:12–15
35. Morrison K (1998) Management theories for educational change. Sage, London
36. Harvey-Jones J (1988) Making it happen: reflections on leadership. Profile Books, London
37. Robbins H, Finley M (1996) Why change doesn't work. Petersons, Princeton
38. Duck J (1993) Managing change: the art of balancing. Harv Bus Rev 71(6):109–118
39. Piderit S (2000) Rethinking resistance and recognizing ambivalence: a multidimensional view of attitudes toward an organizational change. Acad Manage Rev 25:783–794
40. Bovey W, Hede A (2001) Resistance to organisational change: the role of defence mechanisms. J Manage Psychol 16:534–548
41. Weick KE, Quinn RE (1999) Organizational change and development. Annu Rev Psychol 50:361–386. doi:10.1146/annurev.psych.50.1.361
42. Cheng J, Petrovic-Lazarevic S (2005) The flair of resistance to change: an employee-centred perspective. Monash University Faculty of Business and Economics, Working Paper 9/05
43. Markus M, Robey D (1988) Information technology and organizational change: causal structure in theory and research. Manage Sci 34:583–598
44. Orlikowski W, Iacono C (2001) Research commentary: desperately seeking the "IT" in IT research—a call to theorizing the IT artifact. Inf Syst Res 12:121–134
45. Luo J, Fan M, Zhang H (2012) Information technology and organizational capabilities: a longitudinal study of the apparel industry. Decis Support Syst 53:186–194
46. Ramirez R, Melville N, Lawler E (2010) Information technology infrastructure, organizational process redesign, and business value: an empirical analysis. Decis Support Syst 49:417–429
47. Ciborra C (2004) Encountering information systems as a phenomenon. In: Avgerou C, Ciborra C, Land F (eds) The social study of information and communication technology. Oxford University Press, Oxford, pp 17–34
48. Brown J, Duguid P (2000) The social life of information. Harvard Business School Press, Boston
49. Choi JN, Sung SY, Lee K, Cho DS (2011) Balancing cognition and emotion: innovation implementation as a function of cognitive appraisal and emotional reactions toward innovation. J Organ Behav 32:107–124. doi:10.1002/job
50. Schraeder M, Swamidass PM, Morrison R (2006) Employee involvement, attitudes and reactions to technology changes. J Leadersh Organ Stud 12:85–100
51. Sherif K, Zmud R, Browne G (2006) Managing peer-to-peer conflicts in disruptive information technology innovations: the case of software reuse. MIS Q 30:339–356
52. Orlikowski WJ, Gash DC (1994) Technological frames: making sense of information technology in organizations. ACM Trans Inf Syst 12:174–207. doi:10.1145/196734.196745
53. Lazar J, Jones A, Shneiderman B (2006) Workplace user frustration with computers: an exploratory investigation of the causes and severity. Behav Inf Technol 25:239–251. doi:10.1080/01449290500196963
54. Lamb R, Kling R (2003) Reconceptualizing users as social actors in information systems research. MIS Q 27:197–236
55. Coraggio L (1990) Deleterious effects of intermittent interruptions on the task performance of knowledge workers: a laboratory investigation. The University of Arizona
56. Benbunan-Fich R (2001) Using protocol analysis to evaluate the usability of a commercial web site. Inf Manage 39:151–163
57. Louis M, Sutton R (1991) Switching cognitive gears: from habits of mind to active thinking. Hum Relat 44:55–76

58. Walinga J (2008) Toward a theory of change readiness the roles of appraisal, focus, and perceived control. J Appl Behav Sci 44:315–347
59. Gratch J, Marsella S (2004) A domain-independent framework for modeling emotion. Cogn Syst Res 5:269–306
60. Venkatesh V, Morris MG, Davis GB, Davis FD (2003) User acceptance of information technology: toward a unified view. MIS Q 27:425–478
61. Davis F (1989) Perceived usefulness, perceived ease of use, and user acceptance of information technology. MIS Q 13:319–340
62. Markus M (1983) Power, politics, and MIS implementation. Commun ACM 26:430–444
63. Vakola M, Nikolaou I (2005) Attitudes towards organizational change. Employ Relat 27:160–174. doi:10.1108/01425450510572685
64. Elrod PD, Tippett DD (2002) The "death valley" of change. J Organ Chang Manage 15:273–291. doi:10.1108/09534810210429309
65. Benamati J, Lederer A (2001) Coping with rapid changes in IT. Commun ACM 44:83–88
66. Tsai H-Y, Compeau D, Haggerty N (2007) Of races to run and battles to be won: technical skill updating, stress, and coping of IT professionals. Hum Resour Manage 46:395–409. doi:10.1002/hrm
67. Schabracq MJ, Cooper CL (2005) The changing nature of work and stress. J Manage Psychol 15:1–3
68. Vance A, Elie-Dit-Cosaque C, Straub DW (2008) Examining trust in information technology artifacts: the effects of system quality and culture. J Manage Inf Syst 24:73–100. doi:10.2753/MIS0742-1222240403
69. Majchrzak A, Rice RE, Malhotra A et al (2000) Technology adaptation: the case of a computer-supported inter-organizational virtual team. MISQ Q 24:569–600
70. Pearlin LI, Schooler C (1978) The structure of coping. J Health Soc Behav 19:2–21. doi:10.2307/2136539
71. Shaw J, Barrett-Power E (1997) A conceptual framework for assessing organization, work group, and individual effectiveness during and after downsizing. Hum Relat 50:109–127
72. Avgerou C (2001) The significance of context in information systems and organizational change. Inf Syst J 11:43–63
73. Smith CA, Ellsworth PC (1985) Patterns of cognitive appraisal in emotion. J Pers Soc Psychol 48:813–838. doi:10.1037/0022-3514.48.4.813
74. D'Aveni RA, Dagnino GB, Smith KG (2010) The age of temporary advantage. Strateg Manage J 31:1371–1385. doi:10.1002/smj
75. Overby E, Bharadwaj A, Sambamurthy V (2006) Enterprise agility and the enabling role of information technology. Eur J Inf Syst 15:120–131. doi:10.1057/palgrave.ejis.3000600
76. Zain M, Rose RC, Abdullah I, Masrom M (2005) The relationship between information technology acceptance and organizational agility in Malaysia. Inf Manage 42:829–839
77. Sambamurthy V, Bharadwaj A, Grover V (2003) Shaping agility through digital options: reconceptualizing the role of information technology in contemporary firms. MIS Q 27:237–263
78. Sambamurthy V, Wei K-K, Lim KH, Lee D (2007) IT-Enabled organizational agility and firms' sustainable competitive advantage. In: 28th international conference information systems (ICIS 2007), pp 1–19
79. Bharadwaj A (2000) A resource-based perspective on information technology capability and firm performance: an empirical investigation. MIS Q 24:169–196
80. Subramani M (2004) How do suppliers benefit from information technology use in supply chain relationships? MIS Q 28:45–73
81. Levinthal D, March J (1993) The myopia of learning. Strateg Manage J 14:95–112
82. March J (1991) Exploration and exploitation in organizational learning. Organ Sci 2:71–87
83. Raisch S, Birkinshaw J, Probst G, Tushman ML (2009) Organizational ambidexterity: balancing exploitation and exploration for sustained performance. Organ Sci 20:685–695. doi:10.1287/orsc.1090.0428

84. O'Reilly CA, Tushman ML (2013) Organizational ambidexterity: past, present, and future. Acad Manage Perspect 27:324–338
85. Gibson C, Birkinshaw J (2004) The antecedents, consequences, and mediating role of organizational ambidexterity. Acad Manage J 47:209–226
86. Im G, Rai A (2008) Knowledge sharing ambidexterity in long-term interorganizational relationships. Manage Sci 54:1281–1296
87. Tripsas M (2013) Exploring the interaction between organizational identity and organizational design in technological transitions. Working Paper
88. Tushman ML, O'Reilly CA (1996) Ambidextrous organizations: managing evolutionary and revolutionary change. Calif Manage Rev 38:8–30. doi:10.1080/09652540903536982
89. Raisch S, Birkinshaw J (2008) Organizational ambidexterity: antecedents, outcomes, and moderators. J Manage 34:375–409. doi:10.1177/0149206308316058
90. Patterson F, Kerrin M, Gatto-Roissard G (2009) Characteristics and behaviours of innovative people in organisations. NESTA Policy Research Unit
91. Lee OK, Sambamurthy V, Lim KH, Wei KK (2015) How does IT ambidexterity impact organizational agility? Inf Syst Res 26:398–417
92. Andriopoulos C, Lewis M (2009) Exploitation-exploration tensions and organizational ambidexterity: managing paradoxes of innovation. Organ Sci 20:696–717
93. Usseiman SW (1993) IBM and its imitators: organizational capabilities and the emergence of the international computer industry. Bus Econ Hist 22:2

Digital Business Strategy and IT Alignment 8

Abstract

Over the past decades, the role of Information Technology (IT) has transitioned from being just an administrative tool to one that aids organizational activities in a strategic way, thereby supporting the realization of business strategy. Technological innovations are on the rise, as IT is becoming more integrated with goods, processes and services. Consequently, most businesses seek ways to benefit from and also adapt to these technologies. In view of the current global information economy, it is becoming increasingly important for organizations to have digital business strategies. Actually, Big Data are being generated from millions of sensors, automobiles, smart energy meters, and also machines that have the ability to create, sense and communicate data. Big Data potentially hold information that can change the decision making strategy and also improve the performance of an organization. In this context, the alignment of IT strategy and Business strategy has given birth to the term "Digital Business Strategy" (DBS). There are various schools of thought on the value of DBS and are justifiable. However, it is noteworthy that the inability for an organization to realize value from an IT investment may be as a result of the poor fusion between their IT strategy and business strategy. This chapter explores the concept of Digital Business Strategy, while raising questions that will enable organizational survival in the face of incessant technological advancement.

8.1 Introduction

Word processing like typing and printing were seen to be the basic functions of Information Technology (IT) in past times and was believed to be the only role IT could play within an organization [1]. Today, technology has evolved not only the way people reason but also how business is conducted causing a shift from an analog era to one that is digital by a union between services, processes and products [2].

V. Morabito, *The Future of Digital Business Innovation*,
DOI 10.1007/978-3-319-26874-3_8

Smart business owners have seen the need to adapt to the rapidly changing business environment, by evaluating their current business and IT strategies while exploring ways to combine both strategies to form new ones that could potentially place the organization ahead of its competition. Owing to these same advancements in innovation, large volumes of data are being generated in high velocity and variety that totally changes the way data was perceived. It is termed Big Data and within it lies vast amounts of information that could help decision makers make better decisions [3]. It is therefore, very important for an Organization to have a clear understanding of their *Digital Business Strategy* and develop one.

8.2 IT and Business Strategy

Strategy has very close links with several other management approaches (total quality management, benchmarking, time-based competition, outsourcing, partnering, reengineering, change management), all of which help improve on productivity, quality, and speed however its distinction should not be undermined. The profound edge that strategy has over all other management practices is that it considers the organization's unique competitive positioning rather than adopting a generic set of rules which other organizations can very easily replicate. The challenge many businesses face in present times is replacing strategy with implementing management tools [4]. Strategy is about deliberately choosing to do different sets of activities to deliver a unique mix of value. Its essence is in performing different activities from rival companies [4]. It is almost about redefining business parameters from individual organizational capability to obtain the greatest possible output from the littlest effort. This is very different from organization efficiency. Strategy comes down to what sets a company apart as a business [4].

A clear example of company which decided to set themselves apart in the market is IKEA, it made its business strategy very clearly cut out. It differs from the typical by designing its business processes to meet a previously unserved class of people [5]. It serves customers who are willing to trade off service for cost. It does so by producing ready to assemble low cost modular furniture in contrast to the traditional made to order process. It also eliminates the need for sales agents and decorators by setting up its shows in a complete home setting manner hence customers can by themselves imagine the outlook of their home by walking round themselves [4]. It must be emphasized that strategy is the uniqueness an organization offers not just in its products but also in its activities. It begins with an organization assessing its position in the market and then using its unique abilities to address an unserved market need [4].

It is worth noting that Information System (IS) Strategy is another term that is used in place of "Information Technology Strategy" [6, 7]. However, when it comes to the understanding there are different schools of thought regarding the concept of IT Strategy. According to Teubner [7] IT Strategy is perceived as:

- the outlined contributions of IT within an Organization,
- planned course of action designed by the IT department for the entire Organization,
- an instrument for the realization of a company's business strategy and
- a plan containing a list of activities for information processing that would be implemented in an Organization.

Organizations take certain precautions when developing an IT strategy, these precautions are normally structured in form of questions which when answered will lead to a better understanding of what the IT strategy would potentially address within the organization. For example:

- *What is our inclination towards IT investments?*
- *What is the function of IT for our business?*
- *What is the use of IT?*
- *How do we manage IT?*
- *How do we distribute the tasks and which resources are required?*
- *How can IT be used to support a given business?*
- *How can we leverage on our IT infrastructure to gain and also sustain a competitive advantage in the market?*
- *What are the constituents of the IT ecosystem?*
- *What will be the best methodology that could be used in developing the IT Strategy?*

All of these questions allow an organization to wear different hats as regards position adopted (*organization-centric*, *department centric*, *business-centric*, *competitive success-oriented*, *build-out oriented* etc.), thus steering the organization in the direction of aligning both IT strategy and the business strategy [7].

Henderson and Venkatraman [1] put forward a *Strategic Alignment Framework.* They argue that the framework is instrumental to directing future advancements in innovation. Furthermore, using four domains: business strategy, IT strategy, organizational infrastructure and processes and IT infrastructure and processes the model proposes the integration between the IT and business domains. The model uses terms like *strategic integration* for the external components and this comes as result of the interaction between business strategy and IT strategy. Within this lies the potential for IT not only to re-model but also aid the achievement of an organizational business strategy. The second type of integration proposed by Strategic Alignment Model focuses on the internal domain with the interactions between IT infrastructure and processes and organizational infrastructure and processes. This is key because it helps to strike a balance within the internal domain by exploring the potential of IT functions within in accomplishing the organization's requirements [1]. Invariably, as seen above, people began not only to identify the gap but more importantly the need for the handshake between IT and business Strategy.

8.3 Digital Business Strategy

Organizations are in business to make profit; and this causes decision makers to adopt new technologies and leverage on innovations to stay ahead of their competitors. However, there is a clear distinction that has been seen in the past with the way organizations handled IT strategy and Business Strategy [1]. Today innovation coming from the digitalization of business [8, 9] has caused an evolution in business by the fusion of IT and Business Strategy to give birth to the term '*Digital Business Strategy*' [10]. Therefore, Digital Business Strategy (DBS) is the alignment between IT Strategy and Business Strategy [2, 10–12].

With Digital Business Strategy comes strategic alignment and this alignment cannot just be achieved instantaneously, rather it involves careful implementation and infinite number of adjustments until the desired strategy is achieved. Digital Business Strategy is unique when compared with other strategies because it accommodates all the functional strategies as well as the process strategies [10]. Consequently Bharadwaj et al. [10] suggest four themes that give more insight into the concept of Digital Business Strategy: *scale*, *scope*, *speed* and various *roots of business value creation* in digital business strategy (see Fig. 8.1). The diversity of DBS makes it unique because it can be applied in almost any kind of industry or business. For example Oestreicher-singer and Zalmanson [12] put forward that contrary to the belief that having loads of contents for customers' consumption stimulates purchase, it was observed that customers' willingness to pay for a product or service online becomes highly increased due to an increased level of participation within an online community. What this means is that based on the empirical study they carried out on online communities they discovered that customers were more attracted to make purchases on websites when the owners found a way to engage them within their online community, and this was in itself a DBS [12]. With the current level of innovation it is of great advantage for companies to merge social computing with service delivery for business growth. Social computing is more than just uploading photos or videos or sharing of such contents amongst users but rather it forms a very significant part of Digital Business Strategy [12].

The following sections take a closer look at the four key themes of Digital Business Strategy: Scope, Scale, Speed and Sources of value creation and capture.

8.3.1 Scope of Digital Business Strategy

As shown in Fig. 8.1, the scope a business strategy could be also seen as the definition of a "boundary", which encompasses all activities relating to its business processes or product development. Furthermore, this boundary must wholly be under the organization's direct influence. Current literature have also shown that organizational scope can have a profound influence on a firm's performance [13–15]. In effect, it is necessary to understand the scope of DBS as well as how it can be effectively characterized. In understanding the scope of DBS, it is important to

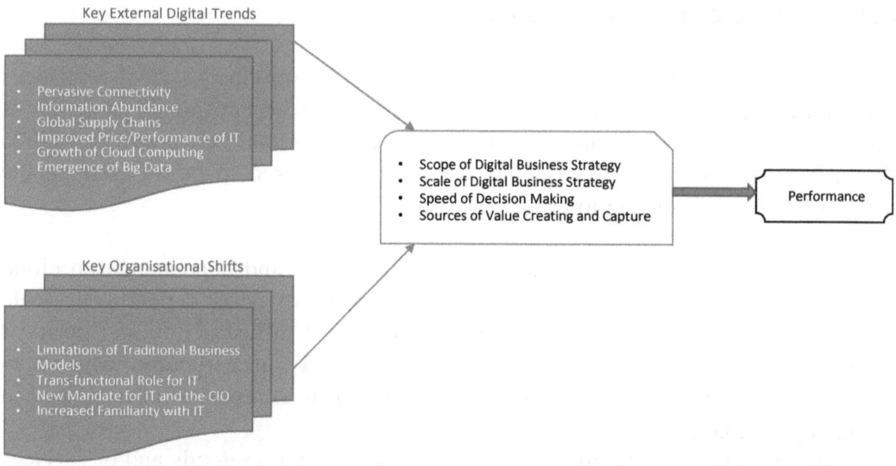

Fig. 8.1 Drivers of the four key themes of digital business strategy. Adapted from [10]

recognize that DBS extends beyond traditional business functions. It should be noted that it may encompass basic business processes such as marketing, procurement, logistics, operations as well as IT enhanced processes (order management, customer service, ERP). Hence, DBS can be said to be inherently trans-functional.

DBS largely encompasses information exchange through digital platforms both from within and without the organization. This allows for a close looped interconnection of several strategies and processes through the aid of inter-firm IT capabilities [16]. Digital business strategy is broader, more prominent, more embedded, and more encompassing than other functional strategies. Consequently, while IT strategy may be positioned as a functional-level strategy (under the province of the chief information officer), digital business strategy should not be positioned below business strategy but treated as business strategy itself for the digital era [10]. DBS also includes the design and development of products and services and their ability to interoperate with other complementary platforms as well as its deployment by taking advantage of digital resources. As for these issues, consider for example the cloud computing and web services offering by Amazon. As pointed out by [10], this innovation has significantly expanded the Amazon's strategy beyond that of a typical online retailer. Furthermore, firms usually operate within business ecosystems such that a firm's DBS cannot be designed without taking into account business ecosystem, alliances, partnerships, and competitors. As for these issues, examples of successful DBS include well known companies such as Apple, which redefined the entertainment as well as the mobile ecosystem [10].

8.3.2 Scale of Digital Business Strategy

Scale proffers the benefits of reduced unit cost of products, which enhances profitability. Hence when thinking of scale it should be considered in terms of physical factors of production, supply chains, or geographic coverage as well as digital terms. The scale of DBS has been conceptualized to be different in the following ways, according to [10]:

- ***Rapid Digital Scaling***: The increase in availability and dependence on cloud computing services provides firms with a strategic dynamic capability to scale up/down their infrastructure. The fusion of digital infrastructure and business strategy enhances the rapid scaling ability of IT infrastructure, which can become a strategic dynamic capability for the firm to reposition themselves in the digital marketplace.
- ***Network Effects***: Network effects occur when the value goods and/or services increases because (i) more consumers start to engage in the purchase or use of these products/services (e.g., e-mail, social media, and buy–sell exchanges) or (ii) more products and services become digitally linked. As business strategy increasingly becomes digital, the effect of multisided business models becomes apparent to firms in a wide variety of industries and markets.
- ***Information Abundance***: It is common knowledge now that the combination of several digital platforms with broadband networks, cloud computing, and billions of smart end-user devices all cumulate into an abundance of data, information, and knowledge. This abundance in information is further intensified by the diffusion of drivers such as, e.g., the "Internet of Things" [3, 17], which not only includes the interconnectivity of things, but also a radically increasing digital network of data and people. This actually requires organizations to be able to develop their capabilities to harness the accumulating heterogeneous data, information, and knowledge that are continually being generated.
- ***Alliances and Partnerships***: With the increase of digital intensity and business strategy, alliances and partnerships become inevitable. This happens through the sharing of digital assets with other partner firms within their existing business ecosystem, which could span across different traditional industry boundaries. This kind of partnerships can be see already amongst travel and hospitality companies that now share reservation systems, loyalty programs etc. (e.g., SkyTeam, Star Alliance, One World, Carlson Hotels).

8.3.3 Speed of Digital Business Strategy

Time is generally accepted to be a focal driver of competitive advantage for firms, this role is even more profound in digital business. Pervasive connectivity compels firms to consider time (speed) in very important manner. It is suggested that speed can be examined in about four dimensions, according to [10].

- ***Product Launching Speed***: This speed become very apparent with firms that are in the purely digital market spheres e.g. Facebook, Amazon etc. This companies rely heavy on improvements and update made in the IT industry and hence have to set product delivery with this in mind. Therefore, when a traditional company introduces digital strategy into its business, it is compelled to adjust its product launching timing to accommodate digital product speed.
- ***Decision Making Speed***: The speed of information transfers both within and without of firms has significant increased. This has also inevitably impacted on the decision making process of most firms. With the advent of social media platforms, companies now have to attend to customers request in real time. Firms like Procter and Gamble (P&G) or Cisco have invested huge sums to equip their management with information acquisition and sharing capabilities both within the firm and across multifunctional partner firms.
- ***Supply Chain Orchestration Speed***: The availability of ERP software that allows the whole supply chain to be visible from one end to the other has impacted greatly on the development supply chain strategies. This development coupled with outsourcing of non core organizational competencies has helped companies like SONY and Apple to compact the time between new product development/announcement to product availability to the about five time faster than the industry average while also reducing their inventory.
- ***Network Formation and Adaptation Speed***: Network development is growing very rapidly virtually every firm and industry [18] The ability to design, develop and manage new networks that compliment organizational capabilities is a huge driver of DBS.

8.3.4 Value Creation and Capture

The concept of value creation and capture in traditional business models have been reasonably studied and there are several theories in strategic management as well as industry practices that help firms to leverage on their physical, tangible resources. The Digital business strategy perspective however brings a new dimension that redefines the concept of value creation and capture [10]. Digital business now avails new opportunities to create value for information. Although, information based business have been in existence, they now have to redevelop their thinking about issues like advertising and subscription. Furthermore, digital business brings into focus the need for a multisided revenue generation [10]. We now see companies offering certain products for free to enhance the revenue generation in other complimentary areas for example Netflix offers one month free subscription as a way of getting customers hooked to their TV shows and movie packages [19]. We now also see firms creating value through coordinated business model networks, where a good example is the synergy between app developers, mobile device manufacturers and telecoms operators. Samsung fits into this category with their play store, which houses millions of apps developed by numerous developers and run on the android technology. The mobile phone developer built their device to be able to run such apps while the telecommunication operators also leverage on both the technology and the applications. Lastly we see that value can be created through the control of digital industry architecture. This is one of the strategic advantages of Apple as a company. They not only earn income from sales of their product but also receive a share of the revenue from their mobile carriers.

Thus, organizations may plan to re-engineer their internal processes in order to create a DBS; however, another motivating factor that could influence the creation of a Digital Business Strategy is the reaction to the competitive digital business environment [11]. Mithas et al. [11] explain that the digital strategic posture of an organization is measured as the variation in status between the organization's current activity in a specific IT engagement relative to the average acquired within the competitive environment. Top management is instrumental to both the development and implementation of a Digital Business Strategy. It starts with the management team articulating the importance of having a DBS for the organization and then effectively driving the development by communicating to the entire organization. To succeed in this, the existing company's IT infrastructure will be aligned with the company's business strategy along with its digital assets [20].

8.4 Getting Digitally Engaged

For any Organization to be successful in their DBS, it is essential that they first discover and learn how to effectively use IT to improve their business by using IT as a key instrument in optimizing operations around the delivery of their goods and services [21]. A few good points to consider when developing a Digital Business Strategy have been articulated by Mithas and Lucas [21], arguing that:

- An organization will need to strategies in terms of positioning itself ahead of its competition using information Technology, especially focusing on cost variations or taking part of the market share.
- Organization can cause a shake within the market that could potentially be of benefit by simply leveraging on IT by focusing on and exploring suppliers, customers and rivals.
- Processes, information and software are all integral parts of a Digital Business Strategy; it is therefore vital to strike a balance when developing a DBS (see also [10]).

Over the years technological innovations have not only improved but has also lead to rapid developments and break-through. To this end looking back in time, a clear distinction can be seen between the digital era now and from what it was in the past. For instance, the digital environment is highly volatile because of the evolving technologies caused by rapid innovation and technological advancements, which have made it increasing difficult to capture static analysis (Big Data). The Strategy for Analysis compensates for this by adapting to the fast pace thereby changing frequently. Another point that stands out in this new technological era, is the innovation of micro-applications that interconnects numerous platforms. Consequently IT has the potential to be disruptive or positively settling as such managers will need to be careful while developing and adopting a DBS [22, 23]. Duality of IT, as argued by Mithas et al. [23], could yield a positive innovation or can be disruptive. IT has the capability to re-shape the market and also create new opportunities all at the same time: thus,, it exposes an organization to competitors, reduces cost, but also the speed to IT creates ambivalence for business strategists.

Organizations need to be well informed before developing their Digital Business Strategy. Nylén and Holmström [24], for example, have proposed a framework that offers some guidance to get digitally engaged. The framework as reflected in Fig. 8.2 was developed covering the following areas: User experience, skills, value proposition, digital evolution scanning and improvisation.

Nylén and Holmström [24] argue that Organizations need to have an overall view of digital innovation when attempting to adapt to the increasingly changing innovative landscape. Analyzing from Fig. 8.2:

- *The User experience* is key, because a positive impression is left in the minds of the users will encourage them not only to reuse the service or product but also suggest it to friends and family (*word-of-mouth* marketing). The user experience goes beyond the user friendliness of products and services, but encompasses usability, aesthetics and engagement.
- *Value Proposition*: this is another critical thing to evaluate, because it is important to ascertain '*how value will be created for the users*'.
- *Digital evolution scanning*: it has been said that knowledge is power and those who tap into it always come out smiling. Organizations need to know the current state of the art and future trends, e.g., in ICTs and innovation management, otherwise how can they plan for it if they don't even know it exist. One can only get ahead of the competition, if you stay constantly informed using platforms like social media, mobile solutions, Big Data etc.
- *Skills*: one can have the fastest car, but still get to destinations late, and this is due to the fact that the driver of the car is also very important in the whole picture. It is therefore essential for organizations to have a strategy in-place for continuous learning to ensure that all required skill sets are available when needed.
- *Improvisation*: to be one step ahead, means that the organization will need to be prepared adapt and improvise when necessary, staff will need to step up to the challenge of doing new things that might be different from their normal routine.

When an organization implements a DBS, it consequently triggers the generation of more data in both structured and un-structured forms. This data could be utilized to gain competitive advantage and it usually comes in high velocity, variety and volume (Big Data).

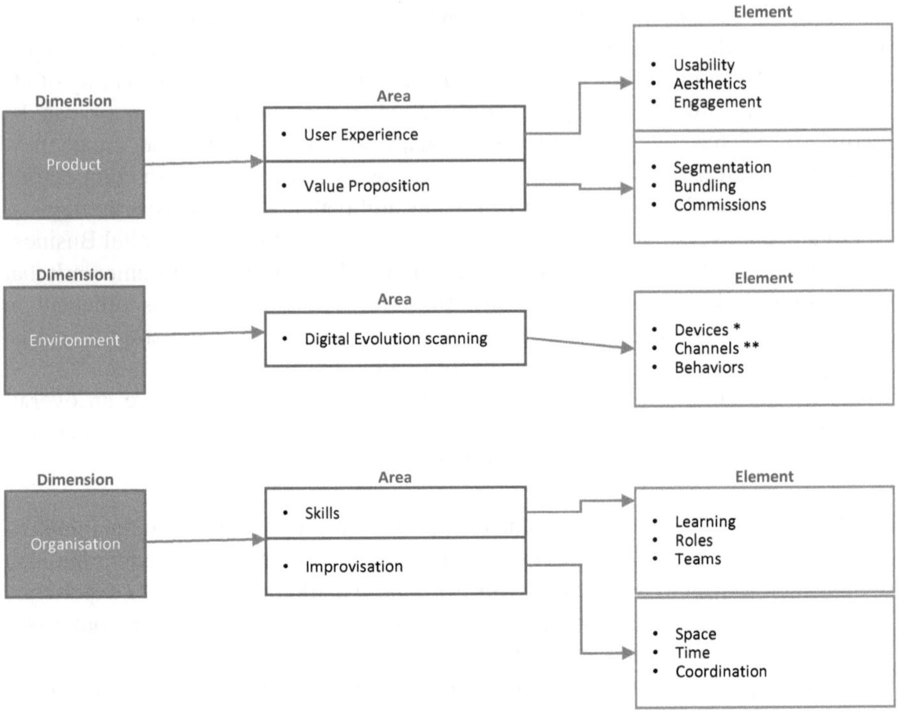

Fig. 8.2 Framework for developing a DBS adapted from [24]. *Hardware such as memory, processors, chips, PCs, smartphones, tablets, etc. **Web services and platforms such as social media and app stores

8.5 Think Data Think Bigger

In a previous book on Big Data and analytics [3], we explored the Big Data domain extensively highlighting the role it plays in gaining dynamic competitive advantage. In this section, the arguments will be developed further in the context of digital alignment.

On Google Trends, when the key word "Big Data" is searched, it can be observed that the term has become even more popular in recent times and awareness started to build up right from the year 2004 (see Figs. 8.3 and 8.4a, b).

Big Data is fast becoming a hot topic, as more organizations and Governments get interested in this new area. Figure 8.4a, b show the spread across different regions of the world based on Google trends search done on the search term "Big Data". Big Data are believed to hold valuable information that can help strategic decision making within organizations. It is a game changer, which makes it very attractive for organizations to pick on. However the complexity of Big Data makes it different from conventional data. It is usually classified with its high volume,

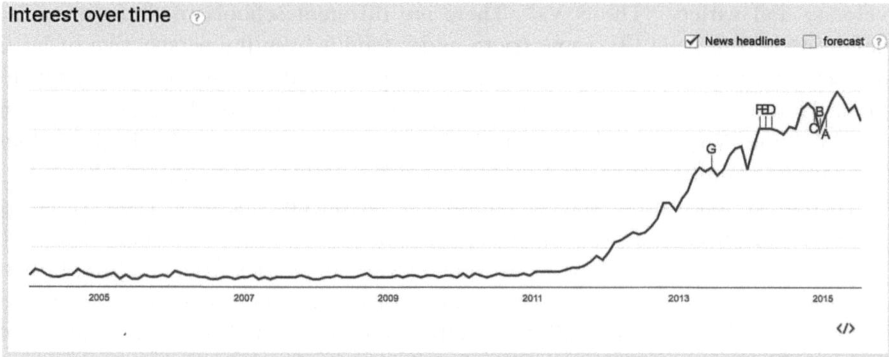

Fig. 8.3 Big data trend adapted from Google trends [25]. *Legend* (Sources of Information): *G*—Sydney Morning Herald, *F*—ZDNet, *E*—Business week, *C*—The Australian, *B*—Business Standard, *D*—Information Week, *A*—Forbes

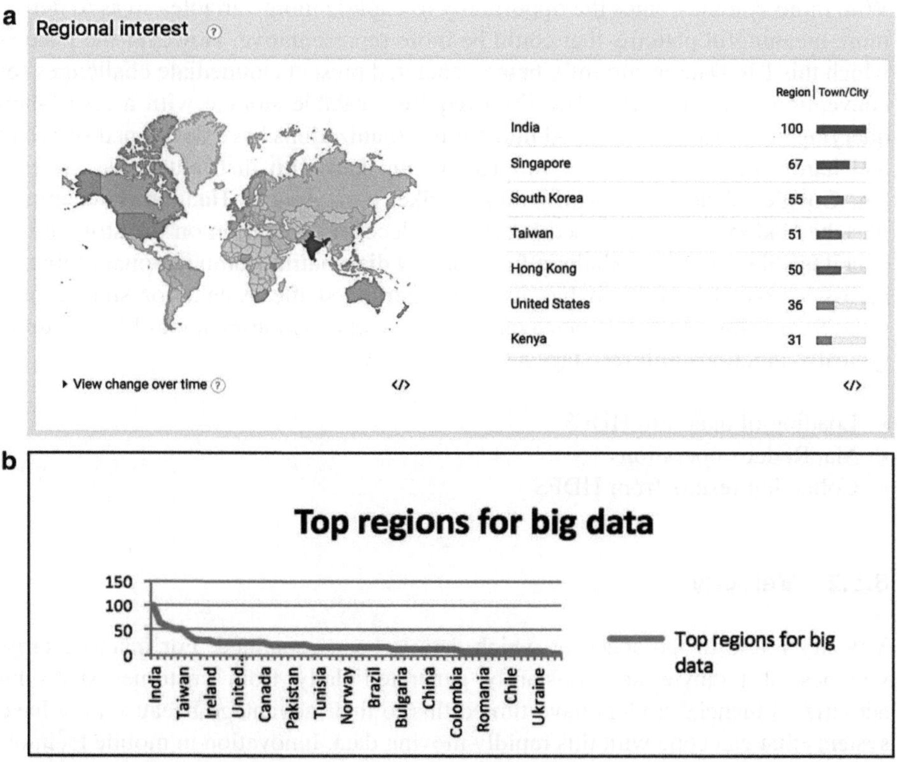

Fig. 8.4 (**a**) Top region spread on Map adapted from Google trends [25]. (**b**) Top region spread adapted from Google trends [25]. Y-axis represents the value of the Google Trends Search related to the specific country

velocity and variety "The 3 Vs". There are different schools of thought on the definition of Big Data [3], some try to understand it from the perspective of large datasets that can not be acquired, perceived, processed and managed by conventional IT tools within a given time frame; some even classify Big Data with four Vs—Volume, Variety, Velocity and Value; Some others have added a few other "Vs" to the definition such as: Validity, Veracity, Value and Visibility [26, 27].

Owing to innovation and technological advancements, Big Data is being generated in different forms and from different media such as: Social networks, sensors from traffic flow, logs from webs servers, imageries from satellite, broadcast audio streams, podcasts, GPS, financial data e.g. stock market data, sensors from automobiles etc. They all have certain similarities and, yet, the three Vs of Volume, Velocity and Variety easily classify these.

8.5.1 Volume

With more volume comes the opportunity to explore more variables so as to derive more meaningful patterns that could be more representative. However the pace at which this Big Data is currently being generated presents immediate challenges for conventional IT structures. Big Data requires scalable storage with a distributed querying approach [28]. A good number of organizations have developed software and hardware that handle the storage of big data with distributed file systems e.g. Google, Yahoo, etc. with solutions like, e.g., Apache Hadoop, Greenplum. Apache Hadoop is mostly used because it places no condition on the structure of data it is able to process. Hadoop functions by distributing computational problems across a several servers. It has its own distributed file system for storing data (HDFS) and this makes the data available to several computing nodes [28]. Hadoop typically functions in three stages:

- Loading of data into HDFS
- MapReduce operations
- Collecting results from HDFS

8.5.2 Velocity

Velocity refers to the speed at which data is been generated. For instance large volumes of terabyte are constantly generated daily from customer shopping activities. Financial traders have turned this to their advantage because they have systems that can cope with this rapidly moving data. Innovation in mobile technology and also the internet being a network of networks has made it much easier for products and services to be consumed at a high pace, thereby generating data rapidly. For example millions of tweets are being generated daily at very high speeds and volumes. However, it is imperative that interested parties extract the information they seek from such data and utilize it quickly before new sets of data are generated with new variables. Another example is the use of smart mobile phones by customers, which allows the generation of geo-located imagery and audio data [28].

8.5.3 Variety

Data can come in different forms, some times structured, most times unstructured or semi-structured. However, it has been observed that data hardly comes in a perfectly ordered form that can be processed immediately: e.g., tweets are unstructured when stored, thus requiring cleaning before they can be processed and analyzed. Even data on the web, usually require cleaning with different browsers sending different data and users sending incomplete information, it could even be caused by varying software versions. One major use of Big Data is to collect unstructured data and convert it to a structured form so that meaningful importation can be acquired from it and utilized [28].

It is a drawback not to know how to efficiently plan in anticipation to accomplish a "Big Data" task, to this end Philip Chen [29] proposes a set of principles to guide the development of a Big Data Strategy:

- ***Good architectures and frameworks***: The complex nature of Big Data makes it mandatory to have the ideal architecture in place to cater for the volume, velocity and variety of data, using a distributed and parallel processing architecture makes it possible to handle Big Data.
- ***Variety of analytical methods***: Big Data collected will sometimes require a number of different analytical methods. This comes as a result of the nature of Big Data and its characteristics. Another reason that may necessitate the application of different analytical methods is the kind of problems that the data is meant to address. For example, people or crowd "sentiments" will require sentiment analysis.
- ***No blanket fix***: Applications and tools are designed as solutions for specific problems, which imply that they will have limitations and strengths. It is therefore necessary to use the most appropriate tool for the specific task.
- ***Bring the analysis to data***: Carrying out analysis of data at the data sites is suggested to be a more effective method of compensating for the large volumes of Big Data. This is a more efficient, cost effective and practical approach because of the large volume of Big Data, allowing the data to be the driver rather than the machines or analytical human.
- **Processing must be distributable for in-memory computation**: In-memory analytics handles the manipulation of data in the RAM this helps the processing time especially because Big Data comes at a high velocity, large volumes and variety.

- ***Coordination between processing and data units***: This involves effective management of the distributed system. It helps to improve the efficiency of the Big Data system e.g. Latency in real-time analytics.

8.6 Case Studies

In this section we discuss fact-sheets of case studies, which illustrate at a glance how the topics discussed in previous Section have been addressed in practice, emphasizing point of attention and insights for managers. The first case is based on Mithas and Lucas [21] and presents insights from the DBS at Netflix.

Netflix is a typical example of an organization that succeeded with their Digital Business Strategy. Their DBS was what gave them the game changing strategy against competitors like Blockbuster. Netflix's initial plan was to leverage on IT infrastructure to develop more effective way of distributing DVDs via the post mail. Then the strategy slowly evolve to a system by which customers will download videos to PCs over the internet, while also forming alliances with relevant bodies in media to achieve downloading from TV directly while connected to the internet [20].

Netflix earned its place as a new-economy company with its ingenious Digital Business Model. It merged IT with its business strategy—adapted diverse business models and fused them with new digital innovations—by leveraging on the Internet. This gave Netflix the required boost not only to out-smart a major rivals (Blockbuster) but also to overtake them [30].

As for the video rental market, Blockbuster stood out and endorsed its dominance in this market, pushing out other smaller rental stores. The company steadily built its brand and optimized its operations with an efficient distribution network, which made it a worthy contender in the industry. Blockbuster business model was successful as they evolved from VHS tapes into DVDs and probably would have even evolved again to the Blu-Ray discs if not for Netflix's game changing business model.

Netflix saw the weaknesses in Blockbusters business model and used it to its advantage by making goods and services available to customers in a more convenient way, thus increasing the chances of return customers "simple logic". Actually, Blockbuster had stores in major US towns countrywide which was their own attempt at making it convenient for their customers. However using the mailbox as a more convenient medium for renting to customers made it a difficult model for them to compete with. Here it is worth mentioning the "Landlord" business model, which emphasizes the convenience factor as important [30]. In the Landlord business model, the landlord owns the asset and sets out to make profit by charging customers/clients for temporal use of the asset. The Landlord business model has three variations namely: virtual, physical and intellectual property (IP). For instance, Ad-space on Google is an example of virtual Landlord, Hertz car rental company is a typical example of a physical landlord and SBB's licensing its trademark clock face design to their client Apple is an example of the Intellectual property landlord [31].

Another weakness that Netflix capitalized on and also exposed was the portions of revenue Blockbuster was making from late fees. From the customer's viewpoint, the late fees were too high because most times they come up much more than the cost of rental. This is one of the drawbacks of the Landlord business Model, which requires the enforcement of penalty fees. One of the earlier marketing punch lines for Netflix was that they offered unlimited rentals with no charge for late fees.

It is always important for organizations to discover hidden opportunities within their line of business. Netflix capitalized on the weaknesses of the old video rental business model, but was quick at adapting and leveraging on innovation and technological advancements as they evolved from mailing VHS tapes to mailing discs, which were much smaller and weighed far less thereby coming much less. Netflix was one of the pioneering companies to develop an online engine for recommendations which gave customers the ability to find TV shows and movies based on past rental history. The company was very innovative and also created the concept for *movie queues* which enables the creation of movie wish lists by customers, thus enabling a stronger interaction between the customers and the company [30].

Point of Attention Through its digital business model, Netflix carved a niche for itself as a leading company in the entertainment industry. It merged its IT strategy with its business strategy by leveraging on the Internet.

Netflix combined known business model sand at the same time took strategic decisions to overcome the limitations of the models. They combined the physical landlord model with all you can eat model and subscription. They offered customers monthly DVD rental at a flat fee and with no late return date penalty. Customers were happy to pay the monthly subscriptions and this gave Netflix a steady cash flow to grow the business. Blockbuster tried to cut off its own late fee penalty and started to offer its own package for 'all you can eat DVD subscription' but it came too late.

The second case is based on Mirow [32] and presents insights from the DBS at Amazon.

Amazon broke into the book retail industry at the time when Barnes and Noble (B&N) the Largest retailer representing about 11 % of the total book sales in the Unites States operated it stores as superstores which covered about 6000 m^2 and stocking up to 175,000 titles [32]. B&N operated a centralized logistics and distribution center, and made savings through direct purchases from publishers thereby avoiding wholesalers. The centralized stocking system improved its efficiency in delivery, by avoiding delivery delays from publishers. B&N then implemented a management system, which enabled real time access to information among its stores, wholesalers and distribution center giving them access to a database holding about 2.5 M titles. However customers had no access to the database [32].

Amazon was able to redefine book retailing industry using a Digital Business Strategy leveraging on the Internet. Actually, Amazon identified several challenges the traditional book retailing industry had. For example the limitation of physical store space affected availability of title selection. Likewise, traditional book retailers were burdened with the cost and responsibility of investing in inventory, qualified staff and real estate for each retail location. Yet, utilizing the internet provided retailers with a great advantage that enabled them capitalize on the centralized inventory management system and minimal occupancy costs [32].

Point of Attention Amazon, beside being a retailer itself, it also operates as a gateway for other retailers offering a robust marketplace for new and used goods owing to its Digital Business Strategy.

Amazon is known as one of the largest Internet retailers with a global reach. However, asides being a retailer itself, it also operates as a gateway for other retailers offering a robust marketplace for new and used goods [33]. Actually, Amazon's line of business is centered around online retail, Internet services and Kindle ecosystem:

- *Online Retail*: In this line of business, Amazon functions as a traditional retailer by selling products but at a low cost. The company claims to have the largest selection of products available to customers globally. The company initially started out as a bookseller online but has diversified into music, movies, electronics and household goods. One of its strategies as a retailer is not to stock up on everything it sells, rather it operates as a channel for other retailers to sell their products while they get a fraction off each transaction. Amazon tapped into the market of selling used products using its seller marketplace platform [33].
- *Internet Services*: Amazon's Internet service business is practically fused with its retail and kindles line of business (LOB). For example, Amazon offers customers services such as Amazon prime, which is a 2-day free shipping on purchases made off Amazon's retail business. Another popular service offered is the Amazon Web Service (AWS). For the AWS, the company leases out its own server space to customers (individuals or companies) and manages it on their behalf [33]. Consequently, Amazon has become a reference point as a cloud service provider.
- *Kindle Ecosystem*: Amazon has grown its business to a point that it now manufactures tablets. The tablets were initially designed as an electronic book reader to support and also boost its online book selling business, however the newer models now function as a complete tablet and media device [33].

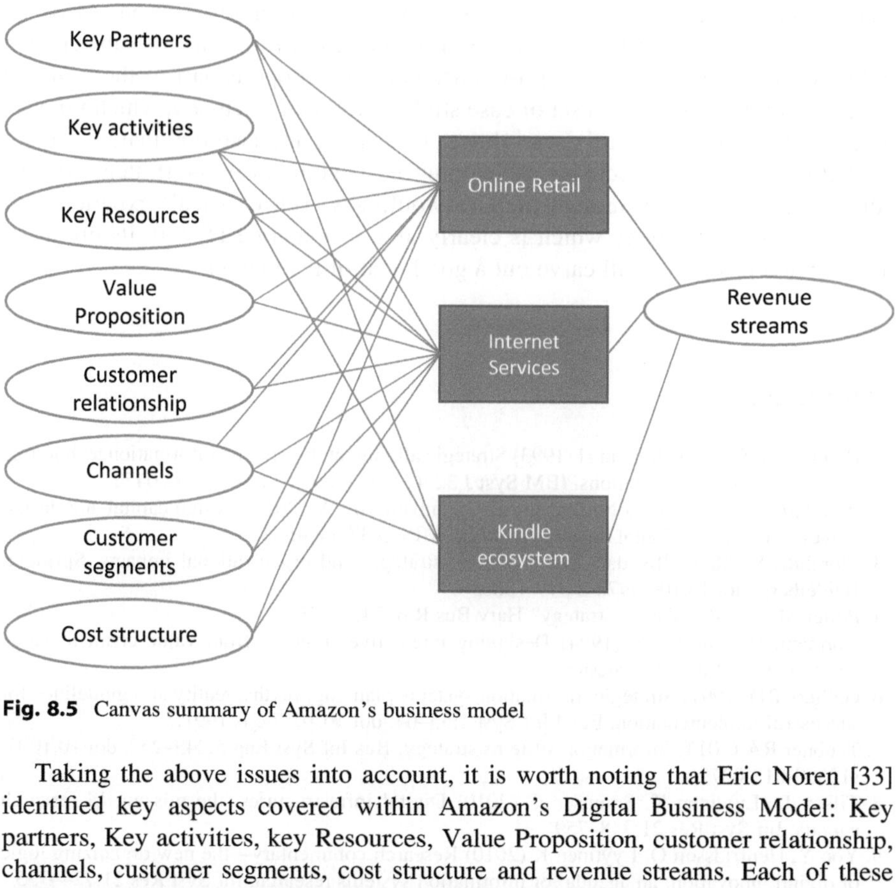

Fig. 8.5 Canvas summary of Amazon's business model

Taking the above issues into account, it is worth noting that Eric Noren [33] identified key aspects covered within Amazon's Digital Business Model: Key partners, Key activities, key Resources, Value Proposition, customer relationship, channels, customer segments, cost structure and revenue streams. Each of these things were carefully thought through, identified and became a canvass for seamlessly integrating IT with Business Strategy. Figure 8.5 shows a canvas which summarizes the Amazon business model.

8.7 Summary

In this chapter, we have introduced the concept of Digital Business Strategy (DBS), while looking at how it all fits. We have discussed the concept of strategy, then explored the concept of IT strategy and Business Strategy. Understanding four themes of Digital business Strategy—Scope, scale, speed and sources of value creation has thrown more light into the DBS domain.

It is clear that for a company today is critical to have a Digital Business Strategy because of the fast rate of technological advancements and innovations that affect the global market.

In this chapter, we have also identified a framework that provides guidance to developing a Digital Business Strategy. It covered areas such as: user experience, value proposition, digital evolution scanning, skills and improvisation. Also, the chapter also identified Big Data as one of the current state-of the art subjects that industry and academia are trying to understand and adopt as part of their Digital Business Strategy. Finally, a set of case studies has been discussed, which reflects, on the one hand, how Netflix was able to out smart, and also dominate its major rival Blockbuster by effectively developing its Digital Business Strategy; on the other hand, has shown through the (we would say, yet, classical) experience of Amazon, how a company which is clearly able to integrate IT with its products, services and processes will carve out a good deal of the market.

References

1. Henderson JC, Venkatraman H (1993) Strategic alignment: leveraging information technology for transforming organizations. IBM Syst J 32:472–484. doi:10.1147/sj.382.0472
2. Woodard CJ, Ramasubbu N, Tschang FT, Sambamurthy V (2013) Design capital and design moves: the logic of digital business strategy. MIS Q 37:537–564
3. Morabito V (2015) Big data and analytics: strategic and organizational impacts. Springer, Heidelberg. doi:10.1007/978-3-319-10665-6
4. Porter ME (1996) What is strategy? Harv Bus Rev 74:61–78
5. Normann R, Ramìrez R (1994) Designing interactive strategy: from value chain to value constellation. Wiley, Chichester
6. Galliers RD (1991) Strategic information systems planning: myths, reality and guidelines for successful implementation. Eur J Inf Syst 1:55–64. doi:10.1057/ejis.1991.7
7. Teubner RA (2013) Information systems strategy. Bus Inf Syst Eng 5:243–257. doi:10.1007/s12599-013-0279-z
8. Tilson D, Lyytinen K, Sørensen C (2010) Digital infrastructures: the missing IS research agenda. Inf Syst Res 21:748–759
9. Yoo Y, Henfridsson O, Lyytinen K (2010) Research commentary—the new organizing logic of digital innovation: an agenda for information systems research. Inf Syst Res 21:724–735
10. Bharadwaj A, El Sawy OA, Pavlou PA, Venkatraman N (2013) Digital business strategy: toward a next generation of insights. MIS Q 37:471–482
11. Mithas S, Tafti A, Mitchell W (2013) How firms competitive environment and digital strategy posture influence digital business strategy. MIS Q 37:511–536. doi:10.1257/jel.50.4.1051
12. Oestreicher-singer G, Zalmanson L (2013) Content or community? A digital business strategy for content providers in the social age. MIS Q 37:591–616
13. Berger PG, Ofek E (1995) Diversification's effect on firm value. J Financ Econ 37:39–65. doi:10.1016/0304-405X(94)00798-6
14. Wade M, Hulland J (2004) Review: the resource-based view and information systems research: review, extension, and suggestions for future research. MIS Q 51:107–142
15. Lang LHP, Stulz RM (1994) Tobin's q, diversification and firm performance. J Polit Econ 102:1248–1280
16. Rai A, Pavlou PA, Im G, Du S (2012) Interfirm IT capability profiles and communications for cocreating relational value: evidence from the logistics industry. MIS Q 36(1):233–262
17. OECD (2012) Machine-to-machine communications: connecting billions of devices. OECD Digital Economic Paper. doi:10.1787/5k9gsh2gp043-en
18. Easley D, Kleinberg J (2010) Networks, crowds, and markets: reasoning about a highly connected world. Cambridge University Press. http://www.cs.cornell.edu/home/kleinber/networks-book/. Accessed 14 Jul 2015
19. Netflix (2015) NETFLIX. www.netflix.com. Accessed 24 Aug 2015

20. Hirt M, Willmott P (2014) Strategic principles for competing in the digital age. McKinsey Q 2014:1–13
21. Mithas S, Lucas HC (2010) What is your digital business strategy? IT Prof 12:2. doi:10.1109/MITP.2010.154
22. Grover V, Kohli R (2013) Revealing your hand caveats in implementing digital business strategy. MIS Q 37:655–663
23. Mithas S, Agarwal R, Courtney H (2012) Digital business strategies and the duality of IT. IT Prof 14(5):2–4
24. Nylen D, Holmström J (2015) Digital innovation strategy: a framework for diagnosing and improving digital product and service innovation. Bus Horiz 58:57–67. doi:10.1016/j.bushor.2014.09.001
25. Google (2014) Google trends. https://www.google.com/trends/explore#q=bigdata. Accessed 14 Jul 2015
26. Chen M, Mao S, Liu Y (2014) Big data: a survey. Mob Netw Appl 19:171–209
27. Elliott T (2013) 7 definitions of big data you should know about. Business Analytics. http://timoelliott.com/blog/2013/07/7-definitions-of-big-data-you-should-know-about.html. Accessed 13 Jul 2015
28. Dumbill E (2012) What is big data? In: O'Reilly. https://beta.oreilly.com/ideas/what-is-big-data. Accessed 13 Jul 2015
29. Philip Chen CL, Zhang CY (2014) Data-intensive applications, challenges, techniques and technologies: a survey on big data. Inf Sci (NY) 275:314–347. doi:10.1016/j.ins.2014.01.015
30. Noren E (2013) Analysis of the Netflix business model. Digital Business Model. http://www.digitalbusinessmodelguru.com/2013/01/analysis-of-netflix-business-model.html. Accessed 14 Jul 2015
31. Noren E (2013) 15 Business models: a complete list. Digital Business Model. How Co. Make Money Online. http://www.digitalbusinessmodelguru.com/2012/12/15-business-models-complete-list.html. Accessed 6 Nov 2015
32. Mirow M (2005) Strategies to achieve market leadership: the example of Amazon, pp 65–67
33. Noren E (2013) Analysis of the Amazon business model: retailer, service provider, and hardware innovator. Digital Business Model. How Co. Make Money Online. http://www.digitalbusinessmodelguru.com/2013/07/analysis-of-amazon-business-model.html. Accessed 24 Aug 2015

Part III

Digital Innovation Practices

Innovation Practices

9

Abstract

This chapter focuses on examples of digital innovation in practice, providing fact-sheets of eight interesting ideas in the field of digital innovation worldwide in 2015. The rationale to select those ideas was twofold. First, whenever possible it was attempted to cover innovation on the areas this book discusses, trying to bring more examples of what it has been explained in previous chapters. Second, most of the selected ideas were based on innovative research projects that have become start-ups and/or spin-offs and have reached the market. Each innovation is described by an introduction highlighting the main characteristics of the application or software, and providing information about who develop it, as well as the main company competitiveness indicators for time-to-market, with some indicators of user value in terms of perception, such as the user Experience and the so called "Wow" effect.

9.1 Introduction

The ideas selected and presented in this chapter originate in effective research projects launched first by excellence centers as well as companies all over the World, that have been developed and brought to the market, and are now up and running. The first case study is in the field of machine learning and artificial intelligence and is about Skytree, a company that developed software that has the capability to learn from large amounts of fast growing data to help enterprises discover hidden trends within data, and to act upon these insights by continuously accumulating the intelligence acquired. In a similar area but more towards the visualization of data is the second case study: DataHero, a company that rapidly became one of the leaders in providing self-service cloud based data analysis and visualization tools, giving an example of what is described in Chap. 4. Similar to this example is our third case: Ripjar, a finalist of the Fin Tech innovative lab start-

V. Morabito, *The Future of Digital Business Innovation*,
DOI 10.1007/978-3-319-26874-3_9

ups; and a company with a combination of products that can be used to carve out meaningful information from the vast number of external data sources.

Oculus is the fourth innovation case, an American virtual reality company for 3D gaming and now acquired by Facebook. In a similar domain but with applications to healthcare is Ginger.io, the fifth innovation case that uses smart phones to collect data to aid mental health patients that may need help. The next innovation case is again in the health care sector, more specifically in Biometrics, namely iMotions. iMotions helps users in conducting state-of-the-art human behavior research in many areas including Psychology, Neuroscience, Education, Health, and Business. The platform enables researchers to simply execute multi modal human behavior research with multiple technologies in a single easy to use software platform.

The last two cases are in the area of data security—Abatis—and Dataloop. Abatis a tech spinout company from Royal Holloway University of London that brings a wealth of law enforcement and private security experience to the market. Dataloop is a cloud monitoring application that aids businesses to stay "up and running" using a sophisticated monitoring technology. The technology alerts clients in real time to events happening on their servers/applications behind the scenes.

9.2 Skytree

Skytree is a start-up company that is specialized in utilizing machine learning algorithms to develop software that have the capability to learn from large amounts of fast growing data (Big Data). More importantly, Skytree's applications not only help enterprises discover the hidden trends within data, but also to act upon these insights by continuously accumulating intelligence acquired by learning from the endlessly generated information [1]. Skytree provides its customers with fast and easy to use Big Data analytics tools that overcome the complexities associated with the implementation of machine learning algorithms to get insights from the data [2]. Instead of performing data mining tasks on limited samples of the Big Data, Skytree helps data scientists to easily investigate the possible associations within the whole data set. As a result, those businesses would have the capability to forecast future market demands and make recommendations to address the emergent of new markets and customers.

9.2.1 Developer

Skytree is located in San Jose, California and founded in 2012 with the aim of bridging the gap between the theoretical concepts of Artificial Intelligence (AI) and the actual implementations of AI's techniques in different business sectors. Skytree's founders represent the optimal example of combining the theory and the practice that helps in establishing the connection between research and industry. This example is embodied by the first co-founder, who is a machine learning professor at Georgia Institute of Technology, and the second one, who is a

Table 9.1 Skytree competitiveness indicators for time-to-market

Solution	Skytree solution
Founded	2012
No. of products	1
Clients	Enterprises
Partners	Different levels of partnership
Market dimension	Growing interest
Competitors	Few
Enabling infrastructure	Ready

professional with 25 years of experience in large organizations such as Sun Microsystems. They were motivated to provide a platform that could be used in different cases to harness the abilities of machine learning in Big Data contexts, such as marketing, fraud detection and prevention, credit scoring, and customer satisfaction [3].

Table 9.1 provides a representation for competitiveness drivers on a time-to-market basis. The information in the table demonstrates an advanced development of the technologies behind Skytree and a growing demand of the market based on the value that can be acquired from Big Data.

9.2.2 Applications

Skytree offers its machine learning enhanced data science solution on premise or as a cloud deployment. Its software, Skytree Infinity, helps organizations mine Big Data, but tens of thousands of times faster than the regular methods. One prominent example of Skytree implementation in industry is the Telecommunications business sector, where the collected data from the variety of resources and shapes such as call records, customer service logs, and geospatial and weather data place a significant challenge for service providers to analyze and to acquire valuable insights.

However, by adopting the combination of Skytree's machine learning tool running on Hortonworks's Hadoop distribution, service providers in such a vital sector can achieve several benefits related to telecommunications network service analysis, improved customer experience, better marketing and enhanced security measures. More specifically, those enterprises would be able to better predict network's disruptions and plan preventive maintenance, forecast traffic trends to decrease congestions, and improve customers' experience to reduce their churn, and plan and implement more efficient marketing campaigns [4]. Table 9.2 lists a set of measures used to evaluate the *User Value* of Skytree's machine learning solution. Considering the complexity associated with understanding and applying machine learning algorithms in a real industrial application, Skytree's Infinity provides relatively easy to use scalable environment to uncover important insights from Big Data, which reflects positive users' experience.

Table 9.2 User value indicators for Skytree

Fast learning	Medium
User interface	Positive
User experience	Positive
Process impact	Low
User feedback	Positive
"Wow" effect	Medium

9.3 DataHero

Despite the fact that DataHero is considered as a start-up business, it became one of the leaders in providing self-service cloud based data analysis and visualization to its customers. Thanks to its user-friendly and intuitive design tools, DataHero's products and services enable non-analysts users to perform complex data analytics and visualization tasks that were previously only achievable by data analysis specialists. With DataHero, it is as simple as connecting to cloud service, uploading the files that need to be analyzed, and drag and drop to create the required visualization chart [5]. As a result, enterprises are able to utilize DataHero's flexible, fast and simple dashboards and predictive analytics tools in order to have informed decisions about the future. Moreover, team members can share the generated visualizations among them in order to have enhanced collaboration. Additionally, DataHero provides unique smart engines that can recommend the best types of presentation charts depending on the hidden patterns in the data, thus, it would be easier for users to interpret the uncovered information [6].

9.3.1 Developer

With a desire to build tools that can cope with the complex analysis tasks associated with nowadays constantly changing markets and emerging demands, DataHero was established in 2011 and is managed by a group of knowledgeable entrepreneurs who have many years of experience in industry. DataHero's founders' vision is to offer its customers a data analysis and visualization environment that can bring real value to them while avoiding the complexities related to the infrastructure required for such advanced data analysis systems. This approach is inspired by DataHero's main driver, which is producing products that consider the end-user as the main focus during the development, marketing and support of its software and services [7].

From Table 9.3, it can be noticed that the continuous growing interest in data analysis and visualization systems accompanied with the simplicity of utilizing DataHero's cloud services by the customers, the time-to-market competitiveness measures look very high.

Table 9.3 DataHero competitiveness indicators for time-to-market

Solution	DataHero solutions
Founded	2011
No. of products	2
Clients	Enterprises
Partners	Different levels of partnership
Market dimension	High growing interest
Competitors	Some
Enabling infrastructure	Ready (Cloud SaaS)

Table 9.4 User value indicators for DataHero

Fast learning	Yes
User interface	Very good
User experience	Very good
Process impact	Medium to high
User feedback	Positive
"Wow" effect	High

9.3.2 Applications

The varieties of business domains that can make use of DataHero's solutions include marketing agencies, e-commerce enterprises, and educational institutions as well as sales and financial departments within organizations. Customers from these industries can easily access and utilize DataHero's cloud based solutions from any platform, desktop, laptop or mobile devices. These data visualization interfaces include advanced business intelligence dashboards and data visualization tools that help businesses streamline their processes and have common ground for work sharing and collaboration. As a result, the entire team would be able to participate in the decision making process.

For example, utilizing DataHero's solutions at ReneSola, which is a green energy producer, enabled its marketing department to optimize their strategic forecasting in order to improve their customer service. Another example for DataHero's success is how its solutions allowed NerdWallet, which is a free tool that people can use to search and find financial services that best suit their needs such as credit card and bank accounts, to have a real-time analysis and visualization of users' interactions with NerdWallet's website. Consequently, they were able to improve their website and services they offer to their customers [8]. In Table 9.4, the measures that replicate the *User Value* of DataHero's cloud based service reflect a very positive users' experience. This positive feedback is based on the ROI of utilizing DataHero's solutions as well as its user-friendly interfaces.

9.4 Ripjar

Ripjar's platform was selected as one of the 2015 FinTech finalist innovative lab start-ups in London [9]. The company is known to provide real-time social media monitoring and data analysis, leveraging on propriety natural language processing, visualizations and deep learning algorithms [9]. With Ripjar's platforms companies can carve out meaningful information from the vast number of external data sources. The Ripjar Explorer avails user with the ability to navigate through large or small amount of big data at unprecedented speed. Users can identify and investigate hot topics and how it relates to their organization. Users can look up for answers to questions such as: What are the sentiments behind critical topics? Which segments are discussing subjects that can influence your brand positively or negatively? What is the best way to engage with those individuals? What are the locations for the different segments? [10].

9.4.1 Developer

A team of engineers who previously worked with the Government of UK birthed Ripjar. The team members comprises of Tom Griffin as CEO, Jeremy Annis CTO, Jeremy Laycock Director Engineering, Rob Biggs Director Data Science, Leigh Jones Engineering, James Ivings Engineering, Safie Chaudhry Digital Consultant, Rob Jennings Digital Consultant, Dave Chapman Engineering, Joe Whitfield-seed Engineering, Simon Smith Data science and John Messenger Engineering [10].

Table 9.5 depicts the representation of the drivers of competitiveness on a time-to-market basis and also a growing demand of the market.

9.4.2 Applications

The core functionality for the Ripjar platform includes:

- **Stream Setup**. The solution allows for several streams to be configured in a single project, which equips the user with the capability of comparing data between topics or brands.

Table 9.5 Ripjar competitiveness indicators for time-to-market

Solution	Ripjar
Founded	2012
No. of products	2
Clients	Enterprises
Partners	Different levels of partnership
Market dimension	Growing
Competitors few	Few
Enabling infrastructure	Ready

Table 9.6 User value indicators for Ripjar

Fast learning	Yes
User interface	Positive
User experience	Positive
Process impact	Medium
User feedback	Positive
"Wow" effect	Medium

- **Retrospective Analysis**. All data acquired on the Ripjar platform can be analysed retrospectively, users have the ability to slice and dice data through several dimensions. Data can also be unraveled through metadata which was available fro source as well as metadata created during processing. All-of-this put together allows for the understanding of trends and identification of select data for further analysis or even comprehensive real-time analysis.
- **Real-time Analysis**. Using a series of dashboards, data or subsets of data can be analyzed in real real-time.
- **Alerts**. Users have the ability to configure warnings/alerts. For example, warnings can be configured for some predefined limits. The alert can be in form of an email, SMS or visual cues on the application.

Table 9.6 depicts the measure of *User value* of Ripjar platform based on positive feedback, ROI as well as user friendliness of the interfaces of their solutions.

9.5 Oculus

Oculus VR is an American virtual reality (VR) technology company founded by Palmer Luckey and Brendan Iribe. The company offers Oculus Rift, a virtual reality headset for 3D gaming; and DK2 that is a development kit for the Oculus Rift that allows developers to build games and experiences for the consumer Oculus Rift [11]. To write the words "A Brief History Of Oculus" is a bit strange for this company as the company's very existence has been quite brief. From the launch of their KickStarter campaign to their massive acquisition, just 601 days had passed [11]. In March 2014, Facebook agreed to acquire Oculus VR for US$2 billion in cash and Facebook stock.

9.5.1 Developers

You never know who you may meet while surfing on the Internet. Lurking around another forum, Palmer found himself chatting with John Carmack—the John Carmack co-founder of id Software; the lead programmer of Doom, Wolfenstein 3D, and Quake. As luck had it, Carmack had been playing with the idea of whipping up some VR goggles of his own, modifying a headset he had on hand. Palmer mentioned the prototypes he'd built. Nevertheless, giving one of his VR prototypes

Table 9.7 Oculus competitiveness indicators for time-to-market

Solution	Oculus
Founded	2012
No. of products	5
Clients	Enterprises/public
Partners	Facebook (parent company)
Market dimension	High growing interest
Competitors	Some
Enabling infrastructure	Ready

Table 9.8 User value indicators for Oculus

Fast learning	Yes
User interface	Positive
User experience	Positive
Process impact	Medium
User feedback	Positive
"Wow" effect	High

to Carmack was the best decision Luckey could have made. A few months later, Carmack was at E3 demonstrating one of Luckey's prototypes. Within weeks, just past halfway to his journalism degree, Palmer dropped out of college to start a company. In June of 2012, Palmer formed OculusVR [11] (see Table 9.7 for Oculus competitiveness Indicators for time-to-market).

9.5.2 Applications

Pulmer Luckey describes his target market as:

> Oculus is a developer of virtual reality hardware for the enthusiast market. Other companies focus on research institutions, military contracts, and large companies as customers, but our mission is to put high performance, low cost, open-sourced virtual reality in the hands of home brewers, experimenters, and gamers [12].

Luckey is much more interested in gaming, and said he believed that the gaming industry was going to become more important as time goes on—it would become the foundation of the VR industry since so much VR technology fundamentally depends on gaming engines [13].

Table 9.8 depicts the measure of *User value* of Oculus platform based on positive feedback, ROI as well as user friendliness of the interfaces and user experience of their solutions.

9.6 Ginger.io

This is a company that has carved out a niche for it self within the Big Data and Health care domain. Ginger.io strategy is primarily engaging the use of smartphones to make improvements to mental health care. Using customized Apps, sensor data are collected through the smart phones and then automatically transferred and used to identify individuals who may need help [14]. Data collected enables service providers deliver the right service to the right person in a timely manner, thereby making health care administered in a more effective way [14]. With one mind-set of the huge benefits that big data potential holds in healthcare, Ginger.io built the company to empower, physicians, researchers and healthcare providers in other to improve patient care. Ginger.io's solution leverages on cutting-edge predictive models developed by MIT scientists and engineers. They seek to constantly unlock patterns in massive amounts of health data generated daily [14].

9.6.1 Developer

Ginger.io team is made up of experts in software engineering, data science, interaction design, medicine and clinical research. Anmol Madan (Ph.D.), is the co-founder and CEO and Data scientist and Karan Singh Co-founder/Sales and Marketing. The rest of the team includes an advisory board who push on innovation and the clinical advisory board who push on clinical matters. The advisory board includes: Alex Sandy Pentland (Ph.D.), Frank Mosss (Ph.D.), Bill Warner and Vicki Sato (Ph.D.). The Clinical advisory board comprises of Ian Gotlib (Ph.D.), Colin Depp (Ph.D.), Stephen Schueller (Ph.D.) [14]. Table 9.9 depicts the representation of the drivers of competitiveness on a time-to-market basis and also a growing demand of the market.

Table 9.9 Ginger.io competitiveness indicators for time-to-market

Solution	Ginger.io
Founded	2011
No. of products	1
Clients	Individuals and health care providers
Partners	Cincinnati children, data design diabetes, Novant health, C3N, HealtheHeart UCSF, Sanofi, Kaiser permanent
Market dimension	Growing
Competitors few	Few
Enabling infrastructure	Ready

Table 9.10 User value indicators for Ginger.io

Fast learning	Yes
User interface	Positive
User experience	Positive
Process impact	High
User feedback	Positive
"Wow" effect	High

9.6.2 Applications

Ginger.io focuses on the behavioral analytics for population health. The company operates by partnering with leading health care organizations to push for better health outcomes by leveraging on passive mobile data and behavioral analytics. The solution was designed to be user friendly and has the ability to initiate an alarm when a patient is at risk [15]. It also ensures timely intervention from health care providers to patients by monitoring and highlighting different behavior patterns.

A smartphone application is downloaded and installed in the patients mobile, which is then used to collect passive data such as movement and communication patterns or patient reports. The next phase is the behavioral analysis, which involves: aggregating, encrypting and anonymizing patient data before analyzing it to gain insights for care providers. The results are presented using dashboard. The dashboard monitors the results, flags patients at risk, thereby empowering the care providers with timely information that can help save a life [15].

Table 9.10 depicts the measure of *User value* of Ginger.io solution based on positive feedback, ROI as well as user friendliness of the interfaces of their solutions.

9.7 iMotions

iMotions Biometric Research Platform is a comprehensive, easy to use and scalable biometric research platform [16]. iMotions helps researchers in conducting state-of-the-art human behavior research in the areas of Psychology, Neuroscience, Education, Health, Business and Human Computer Interaction. The platform enables researchers to simply execute multi modal human behavior research with multiple technologies in a single easy to use software platform. iMotions has a sophisticated stimuli presentation and prebuilt integrations making it very easy to use. The integrated sensor of iMotions gives insights and data otherwise extremely difficult attain. It combines different technologies to get non-conscious responses from participants and takes research to a higher level (see Table 9.11 for iMotions competitiveness Indicators for time-to-market).

iMotions is integrated out-of-the-box with the leading products in each category. iMotions is always scanning the market to integrate the latest devices and then replace out dated hardware with new hardware without losing data. iMotions allows researchers to increase both throughput of research projects and findings. iMotions

Table 9.11 iMotions competitiveness indicators for time-to-market

Solution	iMotions
Founded	2015
No. of products	1
Clients	Universities
Partners	Different levels of partnership
Market dimension	Growing
Competitors few	Few
Enabling infrastructure	Ready

platform has an open input and output Application Programming Interface (API), that allows users to import data from a third party sensor into the platform, process it and forward it back to the sensor, which allows the execution of powerful feedback loops [17]. Moreover, it assists the user in managing their enterprise lab or university lab with iMotions suite. Enterprise functionality for respondent management, study sharing, quality control management and much more ensure an efficient and lab environment [18]. Some of the features of iMotions Biometric Research Platform are:

1. Present images, videos, websites, screen recordings, real world products, scene recordings, and surveys.
2. Full flexibility with any study setup with randomizations, block designs, test plans, group rotations and more.
3. EEG data, stimuli and API data streams are real time synchronized in iMotions. No more manual synchronization of data sets.
4. Export all collected EEG data in sync with stimuli and other sensors in .txt format for easily import into MatLab and other programs.
5. Built in decontamination procedures to reduce artifacts and ensure data quality. Apply only to ABM B-Alert EEG systems.
6. Mark important happenings during data collection or in replay mode to facilitate the analysis.

9.7.1 Developer

iMotions is a high tech software development company specialized in eye tracking and biometric solutions [19]. The company is headquartered in Copenhagen, Denmark with USA office at MIT in Cambridge, Massachusetts, United States. The iMotions software integrates best-in-class biosensors and synchronizes eye tracking, facial expression analysis and Surveys in one unified software platform (formerly known as Attention Tool, but since 2015 they are known as part of the iMotions software platform) [16]. The platform which is targeted at Market, Academic, Usability and Gaming research is used worldwide by leading universities such as Harvard, Yale and Stanford as well as corporations such as P&G, S&P and Nestlé [17].

9.7.2 Applications

iMotions offers exceptional solutions for a wide range of research areas [16]. Some of the real world applications of Host Integrity Technology include:

- **Print Ad testing**. Test customers' emotional and rational responses to print advertising. It can be used to define copy and communication improvements and identifies the best campaign options to launch to market.
  - Eye tracking—attention to brands, products and key messages
  - GSR—emotional arousal during the ad
  - EEG—rational and emotional responses to key items
  - Surveys—customer narratives
- **TV Ad/Movie Trailer testing**. Testing customers' emotional and rational responses to TV ad advertising. It finds peaks and channels to improve the overall emotional engagement of the trailer/TV Ad.
  - Eye tracking—attention to brands, products and key messages
  - GSR—emotional arousal during the TV ad
  - EEG—cognitive and emotional responses to key moments
  - Facial Coding—emotional expressions during the TV ad
  - Surveys—customer narratives
- **Packaging and Product testing**. It can be used to quantify attention, messaging and branding by measuring the emotional and rational reactions of customers. iMotions seeks to find the best packaging option to stand out against other competitive market products.
  - Eye Tracking—attention to key messaging (hierarchy of communication)
  - GSR—novelty of product/design interest
  - EEG—cognitive workload to design elements
  - Surveys—customer narratives
- **In Store/Shopper Testing**. Test consumers' responses in real or virtual store environments to evaluate shelves, packaging systems, merchandising, and the overall shopping experience.
  - Eye tracking glasses—store navigation and product attention
  - GSR—in-store arousal and mood
  - EEG—product desire and in-store cognition
  - Surveys—consumer narratives

Table 9.12 depicts the measure of *User value* of iMotions solution based on positive feedback as well as experience of their solutions.

Table 9.12 User value indicators for iMotions

Fast learning	Yes
User interface	Medium
User experience	Positive
Process impact	Medium
User feedback	Positive
"Wow" effect	High

9.8 Abatis

Abatis innovative automated security technology—Host Integrity Technology, uses an exceptional approach to preventing identified and unidentified malware such as viruses, worms, root-kits, Trojan-horses and key-loggers. It intercepts and mediates file write access to the computer's permanent storage e.g. local hard disk, network shares and removable storage devices such as USB stick and external disk. It is designed to help enforce system and file integrity without complex management overheads [20].

Abatis Security utilizes a customized methodology to security worries, and develops a program that best fits the needs of an organization. Unlike other companies, they provide unmatched management communication for each business associate using their services. As a guarantee to all of their partners, all issues and concerns can be dealt with by a direct owner of Abatis Security. This means that users can have access to an owner, and not an account manager.

Abatis Host Integrity Technology also offers a significantly reduced maintenance cost. In addition, with a small footprint of 100 KB, it guards various infrastructures from servers, workstations and laptops, process control systems and SCADA systems, running new or legacy Windows and Linux operating systems (Note: ***Supervisory Control And Data Acquisition*** is a system operating with coded signals over communication channels so as to provide control of remote equipment) [21]. Some of the features of Abatis Integrity Technology include:

- Legacy Preservation (Buys Time)
- SCADA systems—proven credible technical defence
- Saves Money (90 % lower maintenance and cleanup cost and 7 % lower electricity consumption £35/$60 per server per annum)
- Zero performance degradation—can be performance enhancing
- Tiny footprint—works everywhere
- APT Hunter-Killer when used with CMC
- Risk-free roll-out using LEARN mode (works with other security products in a defence-in-depth approach)

9.8.1 Developer

Abatis is a UK based company established and partially owned by security professionals at Royal Holloway University of London. For the past 5 years Abatis has supplied governments, financial and major corporations around the world with security solutions that have withstood the test of time against all forms of attack [22]. Most recently in 2015 Abatis won an award for the Most Innovative Product of the Year 2015 at the Cyber Security Awards 2015 [22].

Abatis Security brings a wealth of law enforcement and private security experience to the market. Abatis has the flexibility to adapt as necessary to meet these

Table 9.13 Abatis company competitiveness indicators for time-to-market

Solution	Abatis
Founded	2005
No. of products	1
Clients	Enterprises
Partners	Royal Holloway University
Market dimension	Growing
Competitors few	Many
Enabling infrastructure	Ready

tests as they come. Abatis' philosophy is to deliver world-class security services, while maintaining a small company feel (Table 9.13).

The core values of the organization comprise of integrity, commitment and dedication. Therefore, clients are valued and the company strives to demonstrate this each and every day Abatis (UK) have unrivalled security experience in public and private sectors of information security. The innovative security systems development company Abatis, are consistently challenging themselves towards providing a service that far exceeds the expectations of clients.

9.8.2 Applications

Host Integrity Technology (HIT) is a proven defense against identified and unidentified malware—reducing the cost of cleaning up infected systems and avoiding the damage or loss associated with the productivity in production environments. It has been tested by Lockheed Martin (UK) and established to save over 7 % of the energy costs of a data center while offering better security to out-of-date forms of protection [23]. HIT is effective at preventing all attempts to write malware to the permanent storage of the device regardless of system privilege. It protects novel and legacy operating systems as old as windows NT4 and also extends life of legacy equipment to preserve current investment in it. It saves energy, satisfies carbon creativities and be seen as an eco-friendly security organization. Some other real world applications of Host Integrity Technology include:

- No Signature File or Whitelist Updates
- Proactive not Reactive
- Defeat Zero Day Malware
- Small, not Bloat-ware—<100 KB
- Deterministic
- Extremely Fast in Operation
- Safe to use in SCADA, Real-Time, IOT and Safety-Critical Environments
- Block Rootkits, Trojans, APTs
- Block Alternate Data Stream (ADS) attacks
- Work in embedded, virtualized and real environments

Table 9.14 User value indicators for Abatis

Fast learning	Yes
User interface	Positive
User experience	Positive
Process impact	High
User feedback	Positive
"Wow" effect	Low

Table 9.14 depicts the measure of *User value* of Abatis solution based on positive feedback, user interface and experience of their solutions as well as process impact.

9.9 Dataloop

Dataloop is one of the start-ups that has grown very rapidly since its launch 2 years ago and have reach a sound customer base including British Gas, Moz.com and BBC Worldwide. The aim of Dataloop is to help businesses "stay up and running" using their exclusive cloud monitoring technology, that alerts in real-time clients to concerns happening on their servers and applications behind the scenes.

In a nutshell, Dataloop's monitoring software is designed to eliminate the aggravation of adapting open-source monitoring tools, acutely observe online services, and alert companies to broken features and downtime in real time. The ability of setting-up monitoring across multiple (literary thousands) of servers very quickly, together with a demand for monitoring that is growing, this business' innovative offering has attracted large corporations that want their online services protected [24, 25]. At its current growth rate, Dataloop seems to be on the way to be a leading player in the monitoring space and they believe it has the potential to unscramble an increasingly complex problem for online businesses.

9.9.1 Developers

Dataloop was founded in 2013 founded by David Gildeh, Steven Acreman and Colin Hemmings; the co-founder of Samba Stream software company acquired by Alfresco. The team behind Dataloop.IO have over 12 years of development and operations experience running large-scale cloud services at large corporations. The idea came after the experience of having to go through the stress of installing monitoring infrastructures over and over again. They search the market for services that offered the flexibility of open source tools without the daunting task of setting up and configuring every time the environment changed, and found a gap in the market [26] (Table 9.15).

Table 9.15 Dataloop competitiveness indicators for time-to-market

Solution	Dataloop
Founded	2013
No. of products	1
Clients	Enterprises/cloud
Partners	N/A
Market dimension	High growing interest
Competitors	Some
Enabling infrastructure	Ready

Table 9.16 User value indicators for Dataloop

Fast learning	Yes
User interface	Positive
User experience	Positive
Process impact	High
User feedback	Positive
"Wow" effect	Medium

9.9.2 Applications

Dataloop has solved the scaling issues and built a platform so that Ops and Devs can live happily within a single tool. The next steps are to solve the fundamental problem of setup, adoption and engagement. To reduce the burden of setup on monitoring staff and to get everyone engaged with the real time data being produced by the systems in order to improve the quality of your online service. To this end Dataloop helps you to distribute the setting up of the monitoring into teams, devolving in this way responsibility down to each product team but letting central Ops/Platforms/Systems/WebOps/DevOps/teams having oversight and control.

What most organizations have been asking for in a roundabout way is for a Github style account model. Users should be able to move freely between projects, or even organizations, and they should be able to contribute to the setup of monitoring for whatever they have been given access too. While also potentially being able to see but not change other areas. For the central platforms team they want to be members of the 'owners' group so they can dip in and provide some oversight and even pass down the costs of monitoring to their teams in larger organizations.

Table 9.16 depicts the measure of *User value* of Dataloop solution based on positive feedback, user interface and experience of their solutions as well as process impact.

9.10 Summary

This chapter has offered examples of eight interesting digital innovation in practice available worldwide in 2015. The main rationale of this selection was to search for those innovations that have already had some impact in their domains and that are somehow related to the topics studied in this book. The selection process also considered the following parameters for selection: the impact on current processes and the steepness of the learning curve; the perceived value of the specific user, based on ease of use, pleasure and the so called "Wow" effect.

The evaluation of the innovation presented in this chapter comes from the observation of the technology readiness, the existence of a market demand, and the stage of development of the competitors, if any. To this end, the innovation practices considered covered three main areas. The first three cases, Skytree, DataHero and Ripjar are innovations in the area of data analysis and visualization. Skytree developed software that has the capability to learn from large amounts of fast growing data to help enterprises discover hidden trends within data. DataHero, is becoming one of the leaders in providing self-service cloud based data analysis and visualization tools, and Ripjar offers a combination of products that can be used to carve out meaningful information from the vast number of external data sources.

The second area is concerned with innovations in virtual reality and neuroscience, two areas that represents the state-of-the-art in technological start-ups. Three cases were presented in this domain: Oculus, Ginger.io and iMotions. Oculus is an American virtual reality company for 3D gaming and now acquired by Facebook. Ginger.oi is a startup that uses smart phones to collect data to aid mental health patients, and iMotions helps users in conducting state-of-the-art human behavior re-search in many areas including Psychology, Education, Health, and marketing to mention a few.

The third and last area is concerned with security. Two case studies were presented: Abatis—and Dataloop. Abatis is a tech spinout company from Royal Holloway University of London that brings a wealth of law enforcement and private security experience to the market. Dataloop is a cloud monitoring application that aids businesses to stay "up and running" using a sophisticated monitoring technology.

Taking these all cases into account suggest that the potential evolution trends are going to focus on applications that will generate data (*Internet of Things*), analyze data (*Big Data and Data Mining Analytics*) and protect data (*Information security*).

References

1. MAPR (2014) Bring machine learning to life in the enterprise with MapR and Skytree. https://www.mapr.com/resources/skytree-and-mapr-bring-machine-learning-life-enterprise. Accessed 16 Nov 2015
2. Bloor R (2014) Skytree – machine learning for the data scientist. http://pages.skytree.net/report-bloor-group-report-on-skytree-server.html. Accessed 16 Nov 2015

3. Enterprenurial Insights (2014) Interview with Martin Hack (founder of Skytree) http://www.entrepreneurial-insights.com/interview-martin-hack-founder-skytree/. Accessed 29 Jul 2015
4. HortonWorks (2014) Improve customer service and satisfaction with big data and machine learning. https://hortonworks.com/wpcontent/uploads/2013/09/HWX_Skytree_Telecom_Brief.pdf. Accessed 16 Nov 2015
5. Freekampus (2014) Data visualization for everyone – the beginner' s guide to analyzing your data like a pro. http://freekampus.com/items/976. Accessed 16 Nov 2015
6. DataHero (2015) DataHero – true self-service – how it works. https://datahero.com/what-is-datahero/how-it-works/. Accessed 16 Nov 2015
7. DataHero (2015) DataHero – our story. https://datahero.com/our-story/. Accessed 16 Nov 2015
8. DataHero (2015) DataHero. https://datahero.com. Accessed 16 Nov 2015
9. Techworld (2015) Finalists selected for 2015 FinTech innovation lab startup competition. http://www.techworld.com/news/startups/seven-finalists-selected-2015-fintech-innovation-lab-startup-competition-3592800/. Accessed 8 Aug 2015
10. Ripjar (2015) Ripjar. Unlock your data. http://ripjar.com/2015/07/ripjar-serves-up-andys-social-media-analysis/. Accessed 31 Aug 2015
11. Techcrunch (2014) A brief history of oculus. http://techcrunch.com/2014/03/26/a-brief-his tory-of-oculus/. Accessed 16 Nov 2015
12. Lang B (2102) Early oculus rift specifications and official site, confirms $500 target. http://www.roadtovr.com/early-oculus-rift-specifications-and-official-site-confirms-500-target/. Accessed 18 Nov 2015
13. Bohn D (2015) The oculus crescent bay is a two-screen VR headset. http://www.theverge.com/2015/3/13/8212205/oculus-crescent-bay-two-screen-vr-headset-palmer-luckey. Accessed 16 Nov 2015
14. Ginger.io (2015) Big data, better health: smarter care starts with your smartphone. Ginger.io. https://ginger.io. Accessed 11 Aug 2015
15. Ginger.io (2014) Behavioral analytics for your population's health. https://ginger.io/static/docs/Ginger.io%20Overview%20for%20Providers.pdf. Accessed 16 Nov 2015
16. IMotions (2015) http://imotions.com/. Accessed 16 Nov 2015
17. Shimmersensing (2015) iMotions integrates attention tool with Shimmer's wireless GSR sensor. http://www.shimmersensing.com/news/imotions-integrates-attention-tool-with-shimmers-wireless-gsr-sensor. Accessed 16 Nov 2015
18. S-oliver-associates (2015) iMotions biometric research platform. http://www.s-oliver-associates.com/imotions-biometric-research-platform. Accessed 16 Nov 2015
19. Eyetechds (2015) iMotions now supporting EyeTech VT3 eye tracker. http://www.eyetechds.com/. Accessed 16 Nov 2015
20. IAAC (2012) Mobiles, BYOD, zero day malware & APTs. www.iaac.org.uk/media/1159/iaacposter2012abatis.pdf. Accessed 16 Nov 2015
21. Abatis (2015) Abatis host integrity technology. Accessed 16 Nov 2015
22. Davies K (2015) Abatis host integrity technology – a disruptive new malware defence/ Infosecurity Europe Blog. Infosecurity Europe. http://blogs.infosecurityeurope.com/abatis-host-integrity-technology-a-disruptive-new-malware-defence/. Accessed 16 Nov 2015
23. Abatis (2015) Most innovative product of the year at cyber security awards. Information security buzz. http://www.informationsecuritybuzz.com/news/most-innovative-product-of-the-year-at-cyber-security-awards/. Accessed on 16 Nov 2015
24. Dunsby M (2015) People's champion finalist: Dataloop. Startups. http://startups.co.uk/startups-awards/peoples-champion-finalist-dataloop/. Accessed 11 Nov 2015
25. Hamilton D (2014) IT Monitoring Solution Dataloop.IO Granted $800 k in Early Seed Funding. Thewhir. http://www.thewhir.com/web-hosting-news/next-gen-monitoring-solu tion-dataloop-io-granted-800k-early-seed-funding. Accessed 11 Nov 2015
26. Dataloop (2015) https://www.dataloop.io/about. Accessed 16 Nov 2015

Conclusion 10

Abstract
The book has discussed and presented challenges, benefits, and experiences for the future of Digital Business Innovation. In this chapter, conclusive remarks are provided as a result of the issues discussed and analyzed in the volume.

10.1 Digital Business Innovation: A Toolbox for a Future Agenda

This book has aimed at discussing and presenting the main challenges and trends for the future of Digital Business Innovation to a composite audience of practitioners and scholars. To this end, the book has developed the argument along three main axes in order to cover the *technological* (digital systems trends in the Part I), *managerial* trends (digital management trends in the Part II), as well as *practical facets* (digital innovation practices in the Part III) for businesses willing to have a toolbox for understanding the future of digital business innovation.

As for the digital systems trends we have considered the business challenges of machine intelligence (Chap. 1) as a key factor for making sense of the large amount of data currently available and probably increasing in the future, due also to the diffusion of wearable technologies discussed in Chap. 2. Then, a specific attention has been then dedicated to digital currencies and distributed ledgers (Chap. 3), potentially changing payment habits and perhaps disrupting various industries besides the finance and banking ones. Furthermore, these trends make central the issues of accessibility and the business oriented "packaging" of information through data visualization techniques and technologies (Chap. 4); also the above digital systems trends in the future will ask organizations, and in particular the CIOs, to extend the current focus on digital security (Chap. 5) and understand the diverse challenges impacting on digital services/products offering and delivery.

Yet, the digital systems trends analyzed in the Part I of the book have been related to new or renewed topics of interest and strategic as well as managerial

V. Morabito, *The Future of Digital Business Innovation*,
DOI 10.1007/978-3-319-26874-3_10

perspectives coming, for example, from the use of neuroscience for marketing and improving the business value of digital driven products and services through a new breed of Neuro-Information Systems (Chap. 6). Furthermore, the book has discussed the role of IT ambidexterity in managing digital transformation (Chap. 7), and how IT strategy and alignment are reconfigured by digital business (Chap. 8).

Finally, taking the above trends into account, it is worth arguing that the future of digital business innovation necessitates IT leaders able to couple (i) the right knowledge of benefits and weaknesses of the above mentioned digital systems trends, to (ii) the ability to implement digital management solutions for new products and services. As for these issues, this book has also provided "templates" for putting in practice digital business innovation. Accordingly, as in [1, 2] a set of characteristics have been identified for introducing managers to what we consider "eight short stories" about interesting global experiences of digital business innovation applications. As for this selection, it is worth mentioning that also in this case as in [1, 2], the choice has considered innovations that are actually applied and "in use"; thus, a pragmatic approach has been adopted, balancing between the so called "Wow" effect (i.e. the perceived novelty and interest in the idea), feasibility, and actual user adoption. Consequently, not only digital innovations potentially inedited if not disruptive, but also "ready-to-use" ones, have been selected and analyzed.

In conclusion, taking all the above issues into account, we hope the book has provided a toolbox for managerial actions for understanding trends challenges and opportunities suitable to support both IT and non-IT executives in the design of the next strategic agenda for the digital business innovation of their organizations.

References

1. Morabito V (2014) Trends and challenges in digital business innovation. Springer, Heidelberg ISBN 978-3-319-04307-4/2/1
2. Morabito V (2015) Big data and analytics. Springer, Heidelberg

Index

V. Morabito, *The Future of Digital Business Innovation*,
DOI 10.1007/978-3-319-26874-3

MIX
Papier aus verantwortungsvollen Quellen
Paper from responsible sources
FSC® C105338
FSC
www.fsc.org

If you have any concerns about our products,
you can contact us on
ProductSafety@springernature.com

In case Publisher is established outside the EU,
the EU authorized representative is:
Springer Nature Customer Service Center GmbH
Europaplatz 3, 69115 Heidelberg, Germany

Printed by Libri Plureos GmbH
in Hamburg, Germany